Maria F
Nicole K

CITYSCAPES

Mayia F
Nicole K

CITYSCAPES

Cultural Readings in the Material and Symbolic City

Ben Highmore

palgrave
macmillan

First published 2005 by
PALGRAVE MACMILLAN
Houndmills, Basingstoke, Hampshire RG21 6XS and
175 Fifth Avenue, New York, N. Y. 10010
Companies and representatives throughout the world

PALGRAVE MACMILLAN is the global academic imprint of the Palgrave
Macmillan division of St. Martin's Press, LLC and of Palgrave Macmillan Ltd.
Macmillan® is a registered trademark in the United States, United Kingdom
and other countries. Palgrave is a registered trademark in the European
Union and other countries.

ISBN-13: 978–0–333–92934–6 hardback
ISBN-10: 0–333–92934–9   hardback
ISBN-13: 978–0–333–92935–3 paperback
ISBN-10: 0–333–92935–7   paperback

This book is printed on paper suitable for recycling and
made from fully managed and sustained forest sources.

A catalogue record for this book is available
from the British Library.

A catalog record for this book is available
from the Library of Congress.
Library of Congress Catalog Card Number :2005431179

10   9   8   7   6   5   4   3   2
14 13 12 11 10 09 08 07 06

Printed in China

For Molly and Zebedee

Contents

List of Figures

Preface and Acknowledgements

The city, according to Michel de Certeau, is that 'most immoderate of human texts' (de Certeau 1984: 92). Responses to this immoderate text, in the shape of academic books or aesthetic objects, have often sought a form of moderation, a way of managing the superabundance of the city. No doubt this is itself a sign of the strategies we generate to cope with the city. This book 'manages' the city in a less manageable way: it tries to keep the immoderation of the city near the forefront of the study. Perhaps another sign of immoderation, though, is the plethora of books that continue to take the city as its theme. The current proliferation of books about the modern city, its literary and artistic productions, its life-worlds, its planned and unplanned environments, seems to grow exponentially. Such ceaseless production could well be taken as a sign of the attractions that the creative and destructive energies of the city exert. But it also poses a question: why another book on the city, why *this* book?

Cityscapes: Cultural Readings in the Material and Symbolic City doesn't attempt to offer a thorough account of the city. It is piecemeal and relatively ad hoc in its range of examples. Vast expanses of the urban world fall outside its sway. But then the intention hasn't been to suggest that exhaustiveness is a particularly worthwhile response to the city. Indeed this book is designed to question some of the fundamental operations of cultural inquiry, in particular the rush to explain and summarize. Instead of privileging explanation and legibility, this book wants to prevaricate and procrastinate, to abstain from assessment and interpretation – if only for a while. It wants to argue for the critical and analytic value of description; description that isn't immediately translatable into assessment, valuation and judgement. The politics of this are obviously problematic, but then so are the politics of assessment, solution and urban planning.

Instead of taking positions in relation to urban issues ('globalization', for instance), I have chosen instead to concentrate on questions of how cultural studies can attend to the city and suggest that rhythm and circulation provide a productive form of attention. It is not that I see social and political urban issues as unimportant (far from it), just that I also see the need for more inventive and exploratory *preliminary* investigations into how cities have been experienced, how the city has a hold on the imagination and what some of the coordinates of this 'lived imaginary' are. Methodology,

then, is a central concern, and my priority has been to fashion methodological approaches that are appropriate to these questions. Methodology
is often associated with the social sciences, with either their abstract gener-
alizations or their insistence on fashioning rigorous and testable 'methods'
for collecting and collating data. Here, though, I want to make a claim for
another orientation for methodology. Methodology here is practice; the
'practice of doing' urban cultural studies, reading various textual objects
and getting them to reflect and refract the cultural material out of which
they are made. This methodology is not directed at a world of facts and
testable data; it is a methodology that has to adjust to the peculiar and
particular forms of the cultural objects being investigated. It is not a toolkit
that can be pulled off the shelf and put to work.

In his essay 'Semiology and Urbanism' from 1967, Roland Barthes starts
by listing the disciplinary requirements for someone wanting to 'sketch a
semiotics of the city': they 'must be at once a semiologist (a specialist in
signs), a geographer, an historian, an urbanist, an architect, and probably a
psychoanalyst' (Barthes [1967] 1988: 191). This unfeasibly wide range of
disciplinary knowledges posits the city as an object of multidisciplinary
studies or perhaps, better still, an object that is fundamentally anti-
disciplinary. Anyone studying the city would be hard pressed to claim
expertise in all these areas, and Barthes himself makes a virtue of his
amateur status. The list that Barthes makes is interesting, not to say
provocative: why, for instance, 'a psychoanalyst'? History and geography
are immediately understandable, and insist on the need to recognize the
city both as a spatial and temporal practice. Architecture suggests a
concern with the physical materiality of the city, just as semiology insists
on the signifying materiality of the urban. Perhaps, then, psychoanalysis,
for Barthes, is there to foreground group dynamics, urban pathologies or
traumas and desires involved in city life? Perhaps it just suggestively
insists on the need to recognize the city as an entity that is experienced, and
experienced emotionally.

If Barthes begins his essay by burdening the nascent urban semiologist
with a vast quantity of learning, by the end he has shifted the emphasis;
now the requirements are not disciplinary knowledge, but a certain canny
inventiveness, and a facility for description:

> If we seek to undertake a semiology of the city, the best approach, in my
> opinion, as indeed for any semantic enterprise, will be a certain ingenu-
> ity on the reader's part. It will require many of us to attempt to decipher
> the city where we are, beginning, if necessary, with a personal report. . . .
> the most important thing is not so much to multiply investigations or
> functional studies of the city as to multiply the readings of the city, of
> which, unfortunately, till now, only the writers have given us some
> examples.
>
>   (Barthes [1967] 1988: 201)

Barthes ends up privileging the methodological and theoretical accomplishments of novelists and poets (Victor Hugo and Raymond Queneau, for instance) over historians, urban planners, geographers and the like. Such a manoeuvre is itself methodological: it means treating cultural texts not as texts *requiring* analysis but as *analytic* texts; it also means that while the urban context requires interdisciplinary knowledge, such knowledge has to be utilized by a creative and ingenious attitude. While this book doesn't share Barthes' ambition of mapping out a structural linguistics of the city, it does share his methodological incentives: namely the refusal to find 'theory and method' only in the academy; the serious consideration of literary and artistic work as sophisticated ethnographic material; and the desire to multiply accounts of the city (which is also to recognize the impossibility of any particular account, including this one, as being adequate).

This book is structured around two methodology chapters that open and close the book: sandwiched between these are a series of micro-studies of urban culture. These micro-studies work centrifugally; they take a text, a cultural form or a genre and endeavour to connect these objects to a larger social and cultural urban world. In various different ways they all take mobility and movement as their central thematic orientation, and seek to generate accounts of urban culture that are sensitive to the various rhythms that animate urban life.

Foregrounding movement, mobility and rhythm is a way of continually reminding yourself that the city is a dynamic and living object that orchestrates a variety of competing rhythms. It is also a way of creating a vivid bridge between the physical world and the signifying, textual world (both roads and novels can be pacey, for instance).

Cityscapes can be read in a number of ways. If your preference is for practical demonstrations of methodology (implicit rather than explicit), you might want to start with Chapter Two and read to Chapter Six, and then read the two methodology chapters. If, however, you want to get to grips with the methodological coordinates prior to delving into concrete case studies, you might want to begin by reading both Chapter One and Chapter Seven before you read the middle chapters. Alternatively you might want to follow the structure as it is laid out here (this, of course, is my preference), and begin with some methodological matters, but hold back on the discussion of rhythmanalysis until it crops up in the final chapter, after you have seen it at work in the preceding chapters. The choice is yours.

This book is dedicated to Molly and Zebedee. Molly's random reading of bits of city script and Zebedee's deep love of diggers, bulldozers, cranes, trucks and building sites constantly reminded me that if the city is a text, it is a fairly provisional one, and one that often looks more like a demolition site than a decipherable message. Molly and Zebedee weren't simply bystanders in the production of this book; they were theoretical and methodological accomplices! Wendy Bonner has had to live through this book from start to finish and must have wondered at times if it was ever going to end. The fact that it has is an accomplishment that is as much hers as mine.

It was Catherine Gray at Palgrave Macmillan who first encouraged this project and Catherine has been a constantly supportive and patient editor. The students at the University of the West of England who took my 'urban cultures' course enthusiastically responded to some of my more unformed ideas. As an audience actively trying to put into practice (and assessed practice at that) ideas that I was awkwardly pointing towards, they were my first and most challenging readers. The Arts and Humanities Research Board awarded me a research leave grant, which, along with support from the University of the West of England, allowed me to take a year's research leave to work on this book. I am grateful to both institutions for this much-needed help.

Stuart Elden generously let me read, in manuscript, his book on Lefebvre, and his and Gerald Moore's translation of Lefebvre's rhythm-analysis writings (both books were in preparation for publication as I was writing this). Jeff Stahl and Anthony Kinik provided a truly inspiring forum for thinking about urban culture at their Night and the City conference, at McGill University, Montreal. Melanie Brown's Movement and Urban Geography 1875–1935 panel at the Midwest Modern Language Association conference in Kansas City provided me with the first opportunity to try out rhythmanalysis. The following have all provided support in various shapes and form: Dana Arnold, Timothy Bewes, Zeynep Çelik, Stephen Connor, Barry Curtis, Shobha Das, Michael Gardiner, Michelle Henning, Steven 'Stig' Manley, Scott McCracken, John Marriott, Frank Mort, Steve Poole, Liz Ray, Simon Sadler, Greg Seigworth and Martin Thomas. My colleagues in the School of Cultural Studies at the University of the West of England, Bristol have provided inspiration and friendship. I want to thank them all for being such great comrades! While all of them have made researching in a teaching-intensive university pleasurable, a few deserve further commendation. Josie Dolan, Seth Giddings and Richard Hornsey took the time to read the full manuscript of this book and comment on it. It is a much better book for their critical input. I'd like to thank Maggie Lythgoe for her excellent copyediting. A few pages have been taken from my essay '*Street Life in London*: Towards a Rhythmanalysis of London in the Late Nineteenth Century' which was published in *new formations* (47) in 2002.

Chapter One
Introduction – Methodology I: Culture, Cities and Legibility

Metaphor City

Carol Reed's 1949 film *The Third Man* takes place amongst the ruins of post-war Vienna. The city's nineteenth-century baroque grandeur is still evident, but it has faded and crumbled. The streets are dark and dank and the shadows of solitary figures loom large over the façades of buildings. Here corruption orchestrates the city and watered-down penicillin circulates for the profit of black marketeers and the destruction of those already suffering; dereliction consumes the city both physically and morally. Occupied and divided, Vienna plays host to an emergent Cold War struggle for domination. Split into five zones, it is policed by Russian (Soviet), French, British and American forces, with an 'international zone' governed by all four occupying armies. In the streets German is spoken, but the language of power speaks many languages.

The Third Man is the story of a penniless pulp novelist, Holly Martins, an American, who comes to Vienna on the invitation of an old school friend, Harry Lime. On arriving in Vienna, Martins discovers that Lime has been killed, run down by a car. The story that unfolds (which need not concern us too much here) is of Martins falling in love with Lime's Czechoslovakian girlfriend Anna Schmidt, Martins trying to uncover what happened to Lime and Martins' realization that his school friend is a racketeer selling the lethal penicillin. Harry Lime, it transpires, is not dead and, in a revelatory moment, Martins sees Lime temporarily illuminated in the deep shadows of a bricked-up doorway. The film concludes with Harry Lime's death, shot by Martins in the sewer, and Anna Schmidt, walking unhesitatingly past Martins after Lime's funeral.

'It is the images of desolation which we remember best from *The Third Man*', writes Peter Wollen, 'the ruins, the Big Wheel and the sewers' (Wollen 1999: 17). Sewers, ruins and a fairground wheel make up the crucial ingredients of the metaphoricity of this pictured city; the metaphor

1

city of *The Third Man*. Ruins are everywhere, obliterating the usual Viennese landmarks (the Ringstrasse, for instance, or the zigzag roof of the Stephans-Dom). Vienna's sewers are the conduits through which Lime is able to move about the city unseen; they also turn out to be the site of his ill-fated attempt to escape from the international military police (Plate 1.1). The big wheel is the setting of perhaps the film's most famous scene (Plate 1.2). It is situated in the Prater, an amusement park in a working-class district of the city. Riding the Ferris wheel, Martins confronts Lime with the knowledge of his erstwhile friend's racketeering, and asks if he has ever seen any of his victims. Lime's reply depends for its effect on their being at the top of the wheel's rotation:

> Don't be melodramatic. Look down there. Would you really feel any pity if one of those dots stopped moving for ever? If I said you can have twenty thousand pounds for every dot that stops, would you really, old man, tell me to keep my money – or would you calculate how many dots you could afford to spare?

(Greene 1988: 97)

Plate 1.1 In the sewers, *The Third Man*, Carol Reed, 1949

Plate 1.2 The Ferris wheel (the Reisenrad) *The Third Man*, Carol Reed, 1949

The figure of Harry Lime (played by Orson Welles) exists in the shadows of ruins, his amoral perspective premised on his distance from the daily culture of the street; literally and metaphorically he stands out from the crowd. His navigation of the city is premised, appropriately enough, on his familiarity with the sewers. And it is this that connects *The Third Man* not simply with the Vienna of the late 1940s but with a whole history of the metaphoricity of urban culture.

The 'view from above' (from the top of a Ferris wheel or tower) has been associated with the planner's perspective, privileging the demands of a generalized urbanism over the lives and needs of the city's inhabitants. This is the perspective of military geographers, city surveyors, planners; those the social philosopher Henri Lefebvre called 'technocratic subdividers and social engineers' (Lefebvre [1974] 1991: 38). From here it is easy to turn people into numbers, to imagine decisive solutions for complexly experienced problems. The sewer also conjures up a constant preoccupation; underground space, circulation and waste. Sewers not only signal the feats of nineteenth-century engineering, but an understanding of the city as something like a body, requiring lungs (parks, for instance), good circulation (roads, pavements, traffic lights and so on) and efficient expulsion of waste (drains and sewers). For the social historian Richard Sennett, this city-body metaphor is bound up with the establishment of various ideologies of trade ('free' trade where money and commodities ceaselessly circulate) and subjectivity (the individualism of mobile monads). It figures the urban environment as a containable and controllable space (Sennett 1994).

Traditionally the understanding of cities as bodylike has tended to align itself with the city as seen from above. To envisage the urban as composed of arteries and veins requires a perspective removed from the densely populated streets of the city. And it is a small step from claiming that the health of a city depends on efficient circulatory systems, to suggesting forms of aggressive surgery (slum clearance, new arterial roads and so on) when these systems appear blocked or broken. But the density of such urban figurations as the city-body, or the elevated and disembodied view from above are not limited to the imaginings of those who plan and govern cities. Sewers and subway systems, as well as aerial perspectives, function as material elements in any number of representations of modern urbanism. Watching *The Third Man*, it is hard not to connect Lime's scuttling about in Vienna's sewer with a vast number of filmic representations of subways and sewers, of escape and capture. Dark and dripping, the underground of the city becomes densely metaphoric.

The disembodied voice that starts *The Third Man* states: 'I never knew the old Vienna before the war, with its Strauss music, its glamour and easy charm' (Greene 1988: 12). But if the Vienna of Strauss has been lost, the Vienna of Freud may not be far away. Freud writes that dreams

> stand in much the same relation to the childhood memories from which they are derived as do some of the Baroque palaces of Rome to the ancient ruins whose pavements and columns have provided the material for the more recent structures.
>
> (Freud [1900] 1976: 633)

A city (usually Rome), built on the ruins of its past, with history accumulating but not quite adding up, is a constant analogy for the unconscious in Freud. (For Freud, it also continually falls short of fully articulating the conception of psychic space that he is trying to describe.) Ruins, monuments and urban architecture point to an environment where the past continually impinges on the present. Ruins signal the trauma of history, as the past remains in the present as a reminder of violence and destruction. Ruins, because they are fragments of the past, physical debris cluttering up the present, make the actuality of urban culture vividly evident; here the past haunts the present. And just as psychoanalysis is dedicated to uncovering the power of the past as it acts on the lives of the present, so a study of urban culture must look to history to understand the power of an urban imaginary. Cities as bodies, the disembodied perspective, and the metaphorics of underground spaces exist like debris in the present. In this sense all cities are haunted; they are the ghostly accumulations of past lives, past cities.

It is here in this metaphor city that we must begin and it is here that we must make an initial claim: to privilege the metaphorics of the city is not to leave the real city behind. It is not to privilege a fictional Vienna over a real Vienna, but to insist that our real experiences of cities are 'caught' in networks of dense metaphorical meanings. Or, perhaps more optimistically, it is to insist that experiences are syncopated or punctuated by an accumulation of images and signs. It is the tangle of physicality and symbolism, the sedimentation of various histories, the mingling of imaginings and experience that constitute the urban. It is this messy actuality (which might be understood as the experience of an urban social imaginary) that must be the point of departure. I want to claim that the *real* of the urban is that density of meaning which suggests not a coded poetics but a thickly allusive and illusive reality. Metaphors in this sense are not stand-ins for something else; they are the reality of this lived density. To claim that the city is metaphorical is not then to claim that it is overlaid with poetic codes (the city as body, for instance) that can be unpicked to reveal a truth free of cultural tampering. The city as 'jungle', 'labyrinth', 'body', 'network', 'unconscious', 'crime scene', 'phantasmagoria' and so on are not just literary devices, they constitute part of the material out of which we experience the urban. And they have a history. The actual thickness of experience (so to speak) is dependent on the fact that we inhabit what the sociologist C. Wright Mills calls 'second-hand worlds': worlds 'determined by meanings ... received from others' (Mills [1959] 1963: 405). It is the 'second-handness' of the world that is indicated by the term 'culture': not just some distant realm of complex representations (produced in the dream factories of Hollywood, for instance) but the actuality of experiences shaped by, and propped up on, a world laced with meanings. The actuality of the city is its lived metaphoricity.

To watch Holly Martins stumbling among the ruins of Vienna, or a fearful Harry Lime trying to escape capture in the city's sewers, is to recognize both the opacity and the resonance of urban culture. It is a recognition that the city exists not simply in the physical environment of the urban but also in its material imaginary. To witness Anna Schmidt's struggle with the authorities over her nationality (her passport is forged, her 'national origin' means she officially belongs to the Soviet authorities) is to be thrust into a world where 'imaginary' and textual meanings have profound material consequences.

Two problems animate this book and determine much of what follows. They might already be visible. The first can be best thought of as a *question of legibility*; the second concerns the *intractability of the actual and the imaginary*. This book argues that the figuration of the urban (its existence as a network of metaphors, metonyms, symbols and the like) not only accounts for a variety of representations of city life, but is also a crucial aspect of the material experience of the urban – its actuality. Actual urban experiences, of course, are never reducible to this figural dimension, yet the *work* of urban culture is the proliferation of these complex figures to the point where it makes no sense to talk about urban experience as being free from the figural. But, as I have been suggesting, to treat texts as coinciding with experience in this way doesn't mean that such figuration can simply be undone, decoded, and underlying meanings revealed. To pursue urban culture as 'lived figuration' is to attend to it as peculiarly condensed material. In this sense poetics is not the ornamental 'froth' perched on a more fundamental reality; it is rather the experience of ambiguity, of thickly compressed meanings, that can't be untangled and arranged into neat legible patterns.

In many ways, then, it could be suggested that to refuse to separate 'fictions' and 'reality' and insist that we live our lives in the wake of our own and others' imagination causes a problem about legibility. After all, isn't the separation of 'fiction' and 'actuality' one of the first tasks of making legible? Similarly, to promote urban culture and urban experience as accumulations that don't add up (for instance the city as body metaphor is both extensive and ambiguous) is not to assume that the outcome of urban cultural study is the deciphering of the city. Indeed it may be that the point of such investigation is precisely the *making vivid* of cultural ciphers. In this introduction, I want to explain these problems, why they matter and why they motivate a discussion of urban culture. I also want to begin to outline the orientation and themes that I will be pursuing in this book, as a way of responding to the challenge posed by these problems.

The Question of Legibility

Any project is liable to be questioned about its motivation, and what its aims and objectives are, and the study of urban cultures can't exempt itself from this. In the nineteenth century to study the urban was to attempt to make the city legible. What nineteenth-century social explorers perceived in the rapidly expanding and modernizing city was an unreadable environment, peopled by diverse social groups, generating new and unregulated social and sexual identities and producing unforeseen experiences and practices. Such an explosion of heterogeneity, of diversity, produced an anxiety amongst those who saw it as their duty to regulate and plan metropolitan culture. In many respects the study of urban culture walked hand in hand with forces setting out to modernize and regulate the city. To make urban culture intelligible and legible meant policing it: encouraging particular metropolitan attitudes and outlawing others; bringing assumed 'rogue' elements under control; and planning a regulated form of modernization.

At the start of the twenty-first century such attitudes have been the object of several decades of criticism. This urban 'paternalism', often ruthless in its effects, can be exposed as motivated by explicit vested interests – those of profit and religious disciplining, for example. Its moral mission to save the 'mass' from the social poisons that are seen to propagate in the metropolis can be recognized as grounded in a highly ideological understanding of social classes, sexual desires and 'racial' characteristics. Yet the desire to plan the city, regulate it and control it is as much a feature of present-day urbanism as it was in the middle of the nineteenth century. And while present-day urban planners might well have prioritized 'social diversity' in their mission statements, such an image of diversity is usually highly regulated and continues to necessitate the control and outlawing of perceived rogue elements. So while in some cities the local council might encourage specifically gay-oriented businesses and designate specific areas of the city as 'gay zones', those who seek more casual and less commodified pleasures in the city's parks at night might find that social inclusion still doesn't extend to them. Similarly, 'diversity' still finds it impossible to include those who don't have the financial means or interests to take part in property exchange or renting arrangements. In an environment where every square foot of land is owned and controlled, and where 'common ground' doesn't seem to mean common ownership, the juxtaposition of empty buildings and homeless people should make clear the limitations of terms like 'diversity'.

Given the history of urban legibility and the continued will to legibility of urban planners and other social and cultural managers, we might want to ask about the motivation for a cultural studies' approach to the urban. Does cultural studies' attention to the urban constitute a continuation in the attempt to render the city legible? And if so, isn't it open to the same kind of criticism that I have been briefly rehearsing here, namely that its motivation is to regulate and order the heterogeneity of the social? But if, on the other hand, cultural studies wants to distance itself from such a project, aren't we entitled to ask what its goal is? After all it might be implicit in the very idea of *studying* the urban, that intelligibility and legibility are an expected outcome.

I want to think of the study of urban cultures slightly differently. Instead of setting out to make the urban legible (and necessarily erasing the exceptional and the wayward), the study of urban cultures could declare its object to be the social anxiety caused by the city's perceived illegibility (indeed some of the best writing on urban culture does exactly that). Here then the project's motivation is not to render the city legible, but to render its illegibility legible (so to speak) or make legible the effects and affects of illegibility. But alongside this I'd like to think of the study of urban cultures as doing something else. For if it is the heterogeneity (and waywardness) of the city that is the cause of anxiety for some, for others it is precisely the social promiscuity of the urban that makes the city a source of possibility and hope. Urban cultural studies then might want to side with the wayward and diverse against the forces of legibility (this is the vision of urban cultural studies that I want to give some space to here). This would mean that urban cultural studies would have some obligation to recover heterogeneity, to rescue 'illegibility' at the point where it was about to be subsumed by the forces of order (be they academic or governmental).

I should note, however, that this doesn't translate into a pragmatic politics of the city (nor is it meant to); it leaves unasked political questions about the necessity of some forms of control (for instance in relation to crime). Nor do I mean to romanticize the role of the social outcast or 'rogue' element, or glorify such social positioning. You might want to see such an approach as partly a prevarication in the endless rush to offer new solutions to social situations. This isn't to suggest that the study of urban culture isn't political (far from it) but it is to suggest that studying urban culture is not the same as studying to become an urban planner.

To study urban cultures doesn't necessarily require that you shine *light* into areas of darkness. As the film *The Third Man* seems to suggest, meaning often lives in the shadows. To make such a film part of an archive for urban culture doesn't require that we simply explain what it means and show how it works. A more productive approach (to my way of thinking at least) would be to start by connecting it to other cultural material, to get it to resonate within a more general urban culture. This is to pursue such material centrifugally; to work outwards, from the close and detailed attention of specific texts and experiences (like *The Third Man*), to other texts, other articulations. This approach wouldn't require unquestioned allegiance to legibility. Its aim would be more descriptive than analytic, and it would place value on the ability to register the complex density of the urban. This is what I take to be the productivity of foregrounding culture as the perspective *from which* to attend to the urban. Culture, for this book at least, is the materially real world of meanings. Wherever you locate it – in libraries, on the street, in cinemas and so on – culture is forceful, sometimes vengeful, always animating and promiscuous, not safely tucked away in discrete enclaves.

Movement and Rhythmanalysis

The thematic focus of this book is going to be movement; more particularly forms of circulation and urban rhythms. I should point out, though, that I am not using this theme as an ideological springboard for an assessment of the very real divisiveness that differences of access and mobility generate in cities. Such assessments, while they might be implied in what follows, are the byproduct of a more explicit concentration on movement as a theme for producing forceful descriptions of urban culture. Movement and the rhythmicity of the urban are chosen as themes for a number of reasons.

Firstly, but by no means primarily, the urban is such an unmanageable cultural terrain that, without some form of thematic orientation, discussions of the urban will simply end up courting the worst kind of academic inconsequentiality – the ultra-fragmentation of the cultural field. Secondly, and more importantly, movement and rhythmicity are chosen because they have the ability to overcome some of the problems I have been discussing: they problematize any fixed division of labour between attending to the physical and the signifying. If cities have rhythms, so do all accounts of cities: movement is as essential to film, for instance, as it is to the actuality of the street. Thirdly, and following on from this, a concentration on movement and rhythm insist on figuring the city as a dynamic and living entity, thus curtailing the tendency towards fixed interpretative accounts of historical materials. Foregrounding movement is one of the ways I'm trying to inoculate myself against ignoring the forceful descriptive powers of cultural material. The final chapter to this book offers a more thorough account of rhythmanalysis as a methodological orientation towards urban culture, but since the rest of the book is attempting to *do* a form of rhythm-analysis, it is worth outlining some of the ideas involved.

Rhythmanalysis is not a fully fledged theory or systematic and structured method, which may well turn out to be one of its most attractive and productive features. At a minimum, though, it can be seen as an invitation to consider the speeding-up and slowing-down of social life. It might also require a predilection for complex orchestrations of time and space, a desire to pick out the different beats and pulses of urban experience and find ways of registering their syncopated arrangements. Rhythm is useful not simply in its foregrounding of the dynamics of urban life: rhythm might well be considered as the third term in a number of dualisms, a third term that supplies the active ingredient for thinking through a dialectical relationship. So rhythm overcomes the separation of time and space – rhythm is on the side of *spacing*, on the side of the durational aspects of place and the spatial arrangements of tempo. Rhythmic terms such as 'circulation' overcome the sort of fixity that comes from studying production and consumption in isolation from each other: circulation is the articulation of their relationship. Rhythm isn't simply speed; it is the measure of dynamic relationships and it insists on the plural rhythmicity of the city.

Rhythmanalysis is about the relationships between different forms of movement and spatial arrangements, between durations and moments. It will be interested in direction as well as pace. Urban rhythmanalysis will be concerned with the rhythms of traffic and transport systems, but also communication networks: it will want to be able to describe crowds and individuals, as well as the movements of goods, energy supplies, liquids and waste. It will be interested in the slowest rhythms: the gradual changes in the social geology of the city, the epochal histories of migrations, the almost invariable rhythm of the seasons. And crucially it will be interested in these rhythms as articulated in texts.

While the most elaborated theoretical discussion of rhythmanalysis is to be found in the posthumously published writing of the French Marxist philosopher Henri Lefebvre, it is not my intention to simply try to be true to Lefebvre. One of the elements that Lefebvre doesn't consider is how a form of rhythmanalysis might be possible that isn't simply dedicated to the analytic description of the urban present. Lefebvre doesn't consider the possibility of writing historically about the rhythmicity of the city, whereas here the articulation of rhythmicity through historical materials (even recent ones) is of central concern. One way of exploring rhythmanalysis in more historical ways is to recognize that rhythmanalysis isn't simply going to be a practice owned by sociological or humanistic scholars. It is a practice that is central to the cultural practices that have shaped the twentieth century.

One of the places where we can find rhythmanalysis is in the varied practices that go by the name of modernism. Modernism, in some of its most characteristic forms, is a kind of rhythmanalysis: it is often addicted to the thickness of description, and hooked on the kind of intricate pulsings to be found at the movies or in the street. Rhythmanalysis is what many kinds of cultural works do by dint of their orientation to the flows and movements of urban life. For example, Robert Musil's epic and unfinished novel *The Man Without Qualities* begins with a rhythmanalytic description of a street scene in early twentieth-century Vienna:

> Motor-cars came shooting out of deep, narrow streets into the shallows of bright squares. Dark patches of pedestrian bustle formed into cloudy streams. Where stronger lines of speed transacted their loose-woven hurrying, they clotted up – only to trickle on all the faster then and after a few ripples regain their regular pulse-beat. Hundreds of sounds were intertwined into a coil of wiry noise, with single barbs projecting, sharp edges running along it and submerging again, and clear notes splintering off – flying and scattering.
>
> (Musil [1930] 1995: 3)

This busy street scene presents a cacophony of noises and moving objects that are described in terms of competing force fields of energy. The description pictures the city as a frenetic space of activities. This capturing of the city as a frantic *mélange* of movement is tempered somewhat a few paragraphs later:

> Like all big cities, it consisted of irregularity, change, sliding forward, not keeping in step, collisions of things and affairs, and fathomless points of silence in between, of paved ways and wilderness, of one great rhythmic throb and the perpetual discord and dislocation of all opposing rhythms, and as a whole resembled a seething, bubbling fluid in a vessel consisting of the solid material of buildings, laws, regulations, and historical traditions.
>
> (Musil [1930] 1995: 4)

Musil's Vienna is made up of plural rhythms: the rhythmic throb of the inhabitants and the sedentary pace of its heritage (its laws and traditions, for instance). And between frenetic activity and the stasis of law is, presumably, an entire range of pace. To suggest that Musil, a novelist, is also a theorist of rhythmanalysis should suggest the broad range of accounts that might count as rhythmanalysis; it certainly should guard against the notion that cultural theory is limited to 'theorists'. But even here the emphasis is clearly on the frenzy of movement rather than the stasis represented by the solidity of the buildings. Tradition is merely the container of a sort of chronic restlessness.

It is this insistence on urban modernity as a constant quickening of pace that links many forms of modernism with significant social theorists of the twentieth century. For Georg Simmel, in his well-known essay 'The Metropolis and Mental Life', the psychological foundations for metropolitan individuality are to be found 'with every crossing of the street, with the tempo and multiplicity of economic, occupational and social life' (Simmel [1903] 1971: 325). Modernity thus provides an insistent and ferocious rhythm, a rapid tempo of circulation that the metropolitan type must either adapt to (by adopting a blasé attitude) or suffer from (neurasthenia, agoraphobia and other dis-eases of modernity) (see Vidler 2000). For Simmel the rhythm of the modern metropolis moves at a helter-skelter pace that is most apparent in the increasing quantity and speed of traffic, the extensiveness of financial exchange and the spectacular displays of the commodity. For Walter Benjamin, clearly writing in the wake of Simmel, urban modernity is similarly characterized by increases of nervous energy caused by the shocks that emanate from a sensory bombardment by both physical (traffic, factory work) and textual (advertising, newspapers) material (Benjamin [1939] 1983: 131–4). Benjamin's modernity is one in which technological developments have penetrated everyday life in the guise of innovations such as matches, telephones, cameras and so on. His is an understanding of urban modernity that is perhaps best characterized by what the writer Wolfgang Schivelbusch (1986, 1995) refers to as the 'industrialization' of experience. But Benjamin's perspective is also one that usefully foregrounds some of the slower aspects of modernity and reminds us that acceleration is not a universal condition of modernization.

It is the late work of Henri Lefebvre that will be the main touchstone for the rhythmanalysis that I want to acknowledge in this book. For Lefebvre, rhythmanalysis is an orientation towards the *multiple* rhythms of modernity: the various speeds of circulation; the different spacings of movement; and the varied directions of flows. Its ultimate potential (like most of Lefebvre's writing) is to achieve a complex orchestration of the totality, one that doesn't subsume variety and contradiction in its wake. The project of rhythmanalysis is endlessly ambitious: the view from his apartment window allows Lefebvre to consider not just the rhythms of pedestrians and traffic, but also the rhythms of street entertainers, the rhythms of the body, the rhythms of plants, the cyclical rhythms of the seasons and night and day, the rhythms of international finance, laws and so on. As Lefebvre (1996: 228) puts it, rhythmanalysis concerns itself with everything 'from particles to galaxies'. And if he insists on an economic determinism for urban rhythms, he is also sure that such forces are always articulated in elaborate and illusive ways: 'the essential and determinant factor is money. But money does not make itself obvious as such' (Lefebvre 1996: 225). All the senses are called upon to provide an analysis of the urban with the aim of 'the least possible separation of the scientific from the poetic' (Lefebvre 1996: 228).

Rhythmanalysis is then a number of things; it is a refusal to privilege either the scientific or the poetic but to insist on both; it insists that slower rhythms always exist side by side with faster ones. In this it becomes a useful antidote to modernism's overprivileging of the acceleration of urban culture. It is of course true that cars move more quickly now than they did a 100 years ago, but it is also true that nowadays you are more likely to spend large amounts of time stuck in a traffic jam. In its orientation towards plural rhythms and their orchestration, rhythmanalysis is a useful counter to overzealous declarations that slower forms of urban life have simply disappeared. In Lefebvre's work, rhythmanalysis is an attempt to attend to the experiential side of urban life and it recruits all the senses for doing this. We, however, will be limited in the range of sensory materials that we can bring into account, because, unlike Lefebvre, I will be observing observations (observations that take the form of written and visual text) rather than putting my head out of a Paris window and smelling and hearing the hubbub below.

Cities and Modernity

Much of this book is concerned with the nature of modernity as it impacts on the lives of urban dwellers and shapes and generates the symbolic and material city, so it is worth writing a few words here about modernity. Modernity, as I understand it, is the experience of being caught up in, and at times overtaken by, dramatic changes. Although related to an idea of being modern, reaching for the unattainable dream of total modernization, modernity is a more precarious affair, a *friction* produced when a desire for the new makes contact with local and traditional conditions. Thus, modernity is not the smoothed-out worldscape of so much science fiction but the ad hoc montage of the old rubbing shoulders with the new. And it is this rubbing, which is both a rubbing along and a rubbing against, where modernity is to be found.

Crucially, though, what counts as new, what is experienced as new, is not always the latest gizmo, but more often the foreign, the exotic. The history of modern urban life, though, has been structured by racism and xenophobia in constitutive ways. For example, the modernity of Indian cities is often positioned as the *result* of colonial rule, as if India could only subsist as pre-modern until Western colonial forces arrived with their dual imperatives of industrial control and the promotion of Christianity. Another version of this tale, told from a different angle, might well suggest that, conversely, imperial centres like London fashioned their modernity on the back of colonial wealth and labour. London's modernity, therefore, was dependent on India's. The crucial point to remember here is that urban modernity is international but asymmetrically international. Crucially, from an analytic point of view, it makes little sense to talk about 'modernity' as an order of measurement, whereby one city is assessed as having more modernity than another. More productively, modernity should be seen as an experiential realm that can be described in terms of its intensities, which might be similar and different to the intensities found in other urban centres.

So, while the internationalism of urban modernity is structured by an uneven and unequal patterning that reflects a global distribution of power, any assumption that modernity is an urban condition, which during the nineteenth century (the century that is classically seen as witnessing the birth of modernity) was limited to the 'West', needs to be countered. One way of doing this is by pointing to the nations that included themselves in international exhibitions in the nineteenth century. International exhibitions are a useful index of modern desires as they acted as a competitive field for nations to demonstrate the results of their own particular forms of modernization. The first exhibition, named the Great Exhibition of the Industry of all Nations, was housed in the Crystal Palace in London's Hyde Park in 1851, and was a showcase for displaying the spectacle of modernized production. Accepting the invitation to participate in such an exhibition, especially in the heart of imperial London, was to declare yourself a modern nation, often with your own imperial ambitions, certainly with a sense of a modernizing programme, as well as a sense of past achievements. Those that accepted the invitation to display in 1851 were:

> Austria, Belgium, Brazil, Bremen, Chile, China, Denmark, Egypt, France, Germany (the States of the Zollervein), Greece, Hamburg, Hanover, Holland, Lubeck, Mexico, Mecklenburg-Strelitz, New Grananda, Oldenburg, Persia, Peru, Portugal, Rome, Russia, Sardinia, Schleswig-Holstein, Society Islands, Spain, Sweden, Switzerland, Tunis, Turkey, Tuscany and the United States of America.
>
> (Greenhalgh 1988: 12)

Here the international range of nations and states articulates a whole panoply of different modernities, modernities which alongside their differences are connected by a common desire to, for instance, display their modern wares in an international context.

As well as evidencing forms of racism and xenophobia, urban modernity has also articulated a corresponding cross-cultural pollination, often as a central characteristic of the culture of the modern. In many ways, to be modern, to experience modernity, was something that no nation could do alone. Internationalism, and the varied responses to it (which includes racism as well as creative cosmopolitanism), has been a driving force for modernity. Certainly it has be a driving force for the production of cultural practices attempting to be modern and register the experience of modernity.

In Paris in the mid-nineteenth century, for instance, artists attempting to fashion a visual practice that was modern, urban, cosmopolitan and aesthetically progressive looked to Japan. In the 1860s and 70s, via Japanese displays in international exhibitions and the agency of Parisian galleries, Japanese prints became available and were avidly collected by the modernist cognoscenti. Artists such as Edouard Manet, Claude Monet, Edgar Degas, Vincent van Gogh, Henri de Toulouse-Lautrec and others explicitly used and retooled the perspectival protocols and practices of rendering that they had seen demonstrated in the woodcuts of Japanese artists like Andō Hiroshige and Katsushika Hokusai (see Wichmann 1981; Sullivan 1997). Hokusai's book of woodblock prints, *Manga*, became an essential ingredient for the so-called French impressionists. Artists such as Toulouse-Lautrec used Japanese ways of rendering (*japonisme*) to register vividly something of the intensity of Parisian urban modernity.

But if Western visual art practice evidences a considerable debt to Japan (so much so that it would be hard to imagine Western visual modernism developing in the way it did without it), the debt within Western modernist architecture is even more profound. The architects who laid out the blueprints to the modern city, architects who fashioned the modular, blocklike structures that fill our cities, did so by looking at Japanese building and adopting and adapting their aesthetic strategies. Frank Lloyd Wright, Le Corbusier, Ludwig Mies van der Rohe, Philip Johnson and most other modernist architects of the twentieth century deployed an architectural language that would be impossible were it not for the examples of Japanese practices.

Yet this story of cross-cultural pollination remains incomplete if we only look at what is happening in Western metropolitan centres. Just as French intellectuals are enthusiastically embracing *japonisme*, artists and intellectuals in Tokyo are busy devouring the lessons to be learnt from the French salon:

> The enthusiasm for Western art in Japan reached a climax in the late 1870s – precisely at the moment, in fact, when the fashion for japonaiserie was at its height in Paris. Regular exhibitions of oil painting and sculpture were being held in Tōkyō and Kyōto, at which Western-style artists could be sure of selling everything they showed.
>
> (Sullivan 1997: 124)

In the later decades of the nineteenth century and throughout the twentieth, Japanese artists absorbed Western styles of picturing (particularly perspectival naturalism and detailed realism). But this pictorial technology didn't result in the production of 'Western' imagery, but in a continuation of Japanese art adapting new regimes of visual language to specific cultural ends. In the case of Tokyo, as in the case of Paris, what makes the response to modernity specific is the way that outside cultural practices are adapted and refashioned in particular, local contexts.

The complexity of modernity as a cross-cultural experience under local conditions is exemplified by the practices of Chinese artists and writers working in the early decades of the twentieth century in Shanghai, China. Shanghai itself was a complex amalgam of competing forces existing under conditions of semi-colonialism. From 1843–1943 Shanghai was a treaty port divided into various territories: a French concession, an international settlement (which was a joint British and American concession), an informal Japanese zone, as well as 'official' Chinese zones (although Chinese citizens lived across all these distinct city quarters). We get a sense of the structural racism at work in Shanghai when looking at the prohibitions placed on the public gardens in the international settlement. The following regulations were implemented from 1916 until 1927 (when Chiang Kai-shek took control of Shanghai):

> The second regulation stipulated that 'dogs and bicycles are not admitted,' which was followed by the third: 'Chinese are not admitted' except 'in the case of native servants accompanying their white employers.' The fourth and fifth regulations, respectively, excluded Indians (except for those in dignified attire) and Japanese (except those wearing Western clothing).
>
> (Ou-fan Lee 1999: 91)

This is a complex piece of racism and racialism separating 'races' by class differentiation: Japanese are permissible when westernized; Indians when they evidence high social rank; but Chinese only as servants.

Nevertheless, Western culture (as imported literature and as cultural spaces within the different quarters of Shanghai) was hugely important for Chinese writers wanting to register their particular modernity. Again this points to a complexity of cross-cultural negotiations: for example, one of the most popular cafés for the writer Zhang Ruogu's literary salon was the Balkan Milk Store, a café in the French concession, run by Russians (Ou-fan Lee 1999: 86). Such spaces of complex cosmopolitanism were where young Chinese modernists could discuss newly acquired works by Western modernists such as James Joyce. But, as Leo Ou-fan Lee suggests, even this absorption of Western literature is never geographically simple: 'most of the seminal terms and concepts from Western literature came from Japanese translations which were adopted or retranslated into Chinese'

(1999: 105). Nor should we see this interest in the West as a desire to become Western:

> It was the Chinese writers' fervent espousal of a Western or occidental exoticism that had turned Western culture itself into an other in the process of constructing their own modern imaginary. This process of appropriation was crucial to their own quest for modernity – a quest conducted with full confidence in their own identity as Chinese nationalists; in fact, in their minds, modernity itself was in the service of nationalism.
>
> (Ou-fan Lee 1999: 102)

For Ou-fan Lee, it is this sense of nationalism, coupled with the complex cosmopolitanism practised in Shanghai, that results in the particularity of a Chinese modernism emerging in Shanghai in the 1920s and 30s.

Such examples are useful reminders that modernity, even though it is propelled by the forces of global capitalism and is the result of cross-cultural connections, is always experienced within particular localities. While the majority of this book will be situated in Western metropolitan centres, I hope that something of the international connectivity of modernity is always present. Perhaps more importantly, though, I would hope that the term 'urban modernity' is always used to point to local and particular conditions, rather than carrying the arrogance of the West's ability to imagine its particularity as the general condition which others never quite attain. For this book, the metropolitan centres of Paris and London, but also Algiers, are always peculiar and their peculiarity is most vividly evidenced as the more general conditions of modernization are negotiated.

To be concerned with urban modernity then is to be concerned with the particularity of the general, with the complex connectivity of city life and with the often contradictory density of experience. It is because I am interested in what this feels like, the experience of urban modernity, that this book is grounded in a study of culture.

Situating Culture in the City

It was anthropology that first used the term 'culture' to point to the entirety of meaningful or signifying elements within social life. Thus, in his book *Primitive Culture*, Tylor could say that culture includes 'knowledge, belief, art, morals, law, custom, and any other capabilities and habits acquired by man as a member of society' (Tylor 1871: 1). Since then, of course, the idea of 'culture' hasn't settled into a stable meaning, but has been a continual site of conflict. Today, arguments about the limits of culture, from a small canon of 'great works', through a more expansive array of 'popular culture', to Tylor's all-inclusive definition, are routinely rehearsed in response to the latest art polemic, or in discussion of the illegitimacy (or not) of projects like cultural studies. Leaving aside for the moment such local and repetitive debates, it might seem that Tylor's inclusiveness has much to offer the study of urban culture. In its very ambitiousness it might be able to point to the expansiveness of what can be meant by the term 'urban'. If, as I have been suggesting, the urban is experienced as a lived imaginary (or imaginaries), then belief, art, knowledge and so on will be the very material of this experience.

In so far as Tylor's inclusiveness points to a vast array of items, it might be seen to eschew questions of value. Tylor's list not only doesn't limit what culture is, it doesn't give us any indication that one element of a culture might be more or less important than any other. An anthropological understanding like Tylor's might simply begin by multiplying the sites of culture. For the anthropologist Clifford Geertz (similarly working with a radically inclusive understanding of the term 'culture'), both 'rocks' and 'dreams' exist as 'things of this world' (Geertz 1973: 10). 'Rocks' and 'dreams' stand at either end of a continuum that is so all-encompassing that the ability to attend to culture (exhaustively or, in Tylor's words, as 'a complex whole') is seriously undermined by the extensiveness of the field. By suggesting that the social world would include fantasy (dreams) as well as physicality (rocks) and that fantasy is a social fact, anthropological attention would need to be impossibly extensive (what couldn't be included in its purview?). Here the question of value might need to be raised simply as a practical question: if 'culture' is so vast an ensemble, where might it be *best* to look for meaning? Should 'culture' be sought through questionnaires, or observed in the uses of shopping malls? Should a study begin by outlining a discourse of dominant meanings (by scrutinizing urban planning records, for instance) or plundering the available archive of popular culture? Where would novels, films and so on (all the textuality that coincides with a relatively limited understanding of culture) fit into a study of urban culture?

An anthropological understanding of culture doesn't simply reorder cultural texts (as might be the case in debates about the validity of treating pop lyrics as 'artistic culture', for instance), it alters the very ground of value. If anthropology is to play a part in rethinking the study of (urban) culture, it is because it allows for a thorough transvaluation of culture. By this I mean that it starts out with a different order of value. As I have been suggesting, I want to treat the 'urban' as a *densely* experienced culture. 'Density', 'thickness' and 'complexity' might also be considered as some of the values that cultural describers would want to promote in any attempt to register the social in the cultural. This is the value that Clifford Geertz privileges in ethnographic work in the hope of generating 'eloquence' from mere occurrence (Geertz 1973: 28). 'Thick description' (the term that Geertz, borrowing from Gilbert Ryle, uses to designate productive ethnographic work) means finely differentiating the registers and modalities of meaning – recognizing irony, for instance, not simply bluntly recording practices and symbols. But if thickness is something to be sought in the business of ethnographic description, can we use it as a value for differentiating source materials; for instance by asking which texts are likely to be the 'thickest', culturally speaking?

Before answering this we might do well to pause. Given the extensiveness of an anthropological understanding of culture, 'thickness' might not be a property of individual texts, but of the *accumulated* field of culture (for instance a multiplicity of 'thin' texts knitted together). While this is often true, the fact that anthropologists like Geertz value certain sorts of *ethnographic* work in terms of thickness should allow us to ask about the thickness of other kinds of cultural accounts not immediately understood as ethnographic. The point I am making is that 'culture' is not simply something that demands explanation (by ethnographers and cultural historians, for example), it is itself a form of explanation and as such can be judged in terms of its ability to register complex and contradictory experience. Given this, it might be that the study of urban culture can recover complex texts (including but not limited to those that have been designated as high culture, novels for instance) for the field of cultural studies, claiming them as forms of 'thick description'. Thick description might be found in a pop lyric, the account of a dream, an act of legislation and so on. An ethnographic perspective doesn't simply revalue texts but performs a thorough transvaluation of cultural texts: the very premise of value changes from aesthetic quality to thickness.

An objection to this blurring (of ethnography and fictional texts and so on) might start out from the claim that anthropologists who practise ethnography do so by attending to empirically 'lived' culture and that they base their findings on evidence. A novelist or a film maker doesn't have to work according to this constraining, or enabling, condition. But to assume that this means anthropologists (or other kinds of social scientists) deal in the actuality of experience, while novelists conjure up fabrications of the imagination, misses out on what fictional and anthropological writing share. Despite the obvious differences in generic conventions, both anthropology and many novels and films attempt to show culture from the 'inside', culture as it is experienced from 'the native's point of view', to quote Malinowski's famous dictum (Malinowski 1922: 25). If one of the goals of ethnographic description is to ascertain what it *feels like* to inhabit certain cultural forms, it might be fair to say that the writers of pop lyrics or novels, for instance, have succeeded in providing just such accounts of urban life.

It has become a reflex within academia, though, to insist on the 'second-orderness' of cultural texts; to insist, for instance, that Joyce's *Ulysses* ([1922] 1971) is not a transparent account of Dublin in the early years of the twentieth century, but a mediation of urban experience through language and literary conventions. In adopting and adapting certain conventions of description and by referencing a whole host of literary and other cultural texts, Joyce's work must be read as a 're-presentation' of Dublin life, relating as much to other works of literature as to the actuality of Dublin life. Such an attitude to texts might well seem to be simply common sense, and the demand that we treat cultural texts as 'representations' is of course a useful inoculation against taking them at face value. It acts as a general warning that we shouldn't treat such accounts of urban life as simply transparent, that we inquire about who is doing the representing, who the representation is directed towards and so on. But if *Ulysses* has an obvious second-orderness about it, is there a form of attention, or description, that doesn't?

For Clifford Geertz, what goes by the name of ethnographic data is clearly not 'first-order' (unmediated) description: 'what we call our data are really our own constructions of other people's constructions of what they and their compatriots are up to' (Geertz 1973: 9). Similarly, what we call 'experience' can't simply be 'first-order' if, as Mills suggests, we inhabit 'second-hand' or second-order worlds. Accounts of experience (even if they are accounts we tell to ourselves), like ethnographic description or complexly constructed novels and films, are all necessarily second-order in that they rely on certain modes of representation. This might include the basic mediation of language, as well as more form-determining elements like genre conventions, narrative patterns and so on.

Now the point of all this is not to bemoan the lack of direct contact with the world, it is rather to raise some questions about how we go about the business of attending to culture. Indeed, one short-circuiting of this argument is to simply say that the world we most intimately and often meet is a world composed of textuality as much as physicality. We need, though, to judge both the problems and the potential of treating culture as representation. On the positive side is the way that the idea of representation sets out as a caution, a warning to tread carefully, to 'look into the mouth of the gift horse'. As far as this goes it might be worth extending such precautionary measures to all forms of description of cultural experience, including our own (after all, the dogmatist's 'mistake' is to simply assume that his or her experience of the world is *the* experience of the world).

But there is a more insidious effect in treating the world as 'representational' – one that is decidedly unhelpful in studying urban culture. The foregrounding of representation often seems to insist that we treat description first and foremost in relation to limited and specific 'worlds' of description: for example, that we treat a detective novel in relation to other detective novels and look to see how it adjusts the conventions of the genre and so on. Of course, the cultural explanation of such adjustments might necessarily need to include a broader attention to the world, but the immediate context has been set. It is this that is problematic for urban cultural studies. It strikes me that one of the main effects of foregrounding the 'representational' is to ring-fence the force and extensiveness of cultural descriptions like detective fiction. A form of attention that continually insists on the representational confines of cultural description might practise, albeit unwittingly, the cultural equivalent of 'traffic calming'. What I am interested in is precisely the obverse of this.

If *everything* that we can communicate is second-order, then first-orderness becomes a 'theoretical fiction'; a nonexistent fantasy used to provoke all kinds of suspicion about the validity and extensiveness of textual meaning. If this is so, then to claim that a specific account of urban life is 'mediated' is misleading, precisely because it might seem to suggest that there are accounts of experience that are not. And if all accounts of experi-ence are mediated or second-ordered, then the issue at stake doesn't have to be pitched at the level of separating fictions from facts (not if both 'rocks' and 'dreams' are things of the world). To necessarily couch talk of urban moder-nity in the language of mediation and representation fails to get to grips with the way in which the culture of the urban presses on us. Mediation or repre-sentation, then, ends up simply including everything in its wake (everything, that is, that we can count as meaningful), and I think that we have a right to be suspicious about the usefulness of such indiscriminate inclusivity. But if we don't treat cultural description as 'representational', how do we treat it? Again, we might want to take as a guide the metaphor that Geertz uses to designate productive ethnography – thickness.

Not only might 'thickness' be a value for producing cultural histories and ethnographies, but it might also be a value to be found in less scholarly accounts of the world. And while we might designate certain descriptions as denser than others, thickness might be found where we least expect it or in those texts that on first glance seem to be either thin on ethnographic detail or provide *unreliable* accounts of urban modernity. Thickness might be another name for an *unresolved* aspect of cultural accounts, an active struggle over meaning. This would suggest that material that is heavily allegorical or symbolic is probably more likely (or at least as likely) to be 'thick' as more passively naturalistic material. Steve Edwards suggests that:

> the figural pulse of a text rises when a thinker attempts to grapple with a difficult ideological problem, when they try to make their conceptions fit awkward, or novel, phenomena. Heavily tropic language can be seen as an index, or symptom, of ideological upheaval.
>
> (Edwards 2001: 38)

This means that we shouldn't just look for ethnographic materials in those descriptions of manners and social propriety that often fill the pages of classic realist fiction; we should also look for it in those more denaturalized and allusive fictions. From this point of view, a detective novel, a symbol-ist poem, a science fiction film or a documentary may all have the potential to provide the cultural historian with ethnographic materials. From this point of view arguments about high culture versus 'mass' culture are short-circuited: the snobbish exclusion of mass culture becomes as myopic as cultural studies' historical aversion to canonical texts.

The fact that such materials (novels, films and so on) often *dramatize* culture also points to another way of locating useful materials for study. The dramatization of culture is a way of figuring the effects and affects of culture: the way that practices and protocols matter or not; of recognizing the *force* of culture. The anthropologist Renato Rosaldo, in his essential book *Culture and Truth: The Remaking of Social Analysis*, suggests that thickness on its own does not tell us how culture *matters*:

> By and large, cultural analysts use not *force* but such terms as *thick description, multivocality, polysemy, richness,* and *texture*. The notion of force, among other things, opens to question the common anthropological assumption that the greatest human import resides in the densest forest of symbols and that analytic detail, or 'cultural depth', equals enhanced explanation of a culture, or 'cultural elaboration'.
>
> (Rosaldo 1993: 2)

Rosaldo provides a much-needed corrective to the assumption that 'thickness' is of itself a sign of how much culture matters. Densely elaborate cultural material without force is, for Rosaldo, of little interest:

> Cultural depth does not always equal cultural elaboration. Think simply of the speaker who is filibustering. The language used can sound elaborate as it heaps word on word, but surely it is not deep. Depth should be separated from the presence or absence of elaboration. By the same token, one-line explanations can be vacuous or pithy. The concept of force calls attention to an enduring intensity in human conduct that can occur with or without the dense elaboration conventionally associated with cultural depth.
>
> (Rosaldo 1993: 20)

In the studies that follow I try and unite both thickness and force and I do this by picking material that *dramatizes* culture. Drama, in the very loose sense that I am using, works to give force to thick culture: it will be my starting point as I endeavour to connect a dramatic figuring of the urban to the thickness and force that is the living aspect of urban culture. My reason for starting out with novels and films is because of their potential for combining thickness with a figuring of the dramatic force of culture (the way aspects of the urban life-world matter).

Chapters and Structure

The *promotion*, so to speak, of cultural texts from work in need of analysis

to work that is *doing* analysis requires an approach that I'm going to call
realist. If the recent history of cultural criticism has meant that so-called
'realist' texts have been subjected to anti-realist forms of attention (based
on a refusal to treat them as windows on the world), the project here is a
partial reversal of this approach. The various items I pursue probably fall
into a range of categories, from pseudo-documentary (the film *Battle of
Algiers*) to expressionistic (the short story 'The Man of the Crowd'), from
popular genre fiction (crime fiction and science fiction) to the layout of
shops. Some of these may well be called 'realist' while others would be
hard pressed to achieve anything approaching this status. However, it is
my methodology that I want to designate as realist. In many ways this is
simply asserting that cultural materials are a product of real-world limits
and pressures: they are elaborate responses to a complexly figured environment. By attending to them in a realist manner I want to be alert to their
descriptive potential to offer a view of culture from the inside. At times it
will mean that I practise a sort of naive literalism, treating texts as akin to
a shopping list of urban experience. If the argument against this approach
is to remind me that novels and films are not the real world, that they are
formal, figural, metaphoric, couched in convention and such like, then my
response would be that I think that urban *experience* inhabits an uncannily
similar realm.

   You may still feel that there is something slightly contradictory about
my approach. Haven't I been at pains to insist on the figural and imaginary
aspects of urban modernity? And doesn't this description of my approach
as 'realist' suggest a more conventional sociohistorical approach? The term
'realist' is meant as a slight provocation, but it is not meant to contradict
what I have said about the lived figuration of the city. There is a consistent
argument here. Realism is used here to describe a mobility that moves,
without too much intellectual impediment, from cultural text to lived actuality and back again. Realism is the convergence of the textual and the
actual. If both the textual and the actual are immersed in networks of imaginative figuration, then the movement from text to actuality is not an
escape from metaphor (for instance), it is simply the mapping of its
extended and extensive life. To enter a sewer might be a more fulsomely
sensual experience than reading about it in a book, but it is not 'free' of the
imaginary universe that makes sewers such particular places (in books, in
films, in cities). Realism seems to me an accurate description of a way of
linking texts to actuality, when the 'real' itself is treated as densely tropological.

   A realist reading might simply mean the forgoing of 'textual niceties'
and an insistent demand to connect texts to contexts in the most direct way
possible. The other side of this means being attentive to the metaphorics of
actual city life, to the effective poetics of streets and shops and so on. Just
as I want to insist on the ethnographic power of texts, I also want to
dislodge the prejudice that the imaginary is not intensely real and effective.

The result of this might be to blur the distinction between text and context in useful ways: one text can become a context for another text, in the same way that a context is also textual. The object of these studies, though, is not to provide the most adequate reading of a film or a story. It is urban culture as a living physical and imaginary world that is the object of this study. Cultural texts are the vehicles that we will take to approach this object. Yet the 'object' might well turn out actually to be made out of these vehicles as well as out of a horrendous variety of other elements.

The topics covered in this book aren't designed to be representative of the field of urban cultural studies, but they are intended to develop the methodologies described above. They are also designed to attend to the central theme of *Cityscapes*: the thickness and force of urban experience as it is animated by movement and rhythm. So in Chapter Two I conduct a 'realist' reading of Edgar Allan Poe's short story 'The Man of the Crowd'. Poe's tale is centrally concerned with the arrangement of urban space and the circulating crowds of the metropolis. Poe's tale is particularly useful as it suggests a form of description that is particularly suited to figuring the illegibility of the city and the restless motion of urban culture. The illegibility of Poe's city also provides instruction into the planned illegibility that was designed to veil the structural unevenness of a rapidly expanding urban centre dedicated to capitalist growth.

Chapter Three concentrates on the physical and desirous realm of the commodity and the 'dream palaces' of consumption designed to frame and activate the commodity's attractions. In terms of rhythmicity, department stores and other shopping environments produce a stuttering orchestration of movement. Constantly propelled and arrested by the commodity, movement is a series of conflicting flows that point to some of the contradictions of commodity culture (its elite 'democratization', for instance). In this chapter I use the idea of the 'phantasmagoric' as a vivid metaphor for describing the new 'palaces and places of consumption' (department stores, street advertising, shop windows and so on). While this has its roots in Marxist theories of the commodity, I aim to demonstrate its usefulness for attending to the peculiarly gendered experience of urban modernity. The phantasmagoria of the commodity also gives rise to a range of new cultural activities (middle-class, female shoplifting, for instance) that can be read as both a symptom and critique of phantasmagoric culture.

In Chapter Four I again offer a 'realist' reading of a particular cultural text. Gillo Pontecorvo's film *The Battle of Algiers* (a filmic account of the struggle by Algerians to liberate Algeria from French colonial rule) has rightly taken its place amongst the central texts of politically committed film making. But it is also a picture of urban structures and urban life at a particular moment of conflict. As such it can be taken as a commentary on colonial spatial arrangements and the historical effects of reconfiguring urban space by colonial domination. To grasp the varied movements and rhythms that animate *The Battle of Algiers*, it is necessary to look at what happened to Algiers as it was re-pressed by colonial rule. The concrete effects of colonialism on the built environment of the city are clearly evident, but to get a sense of their meaning they need to be seen as generating a poetics designed to discriminate between Arab bodies and white French bodies.

In Chapter Five I pursue the idea of treating texts as experiential maps by investigating the fate of the modern detective. Clearly a fictional character, this ubiquitous figure has been a central component of many urban texts. But alongside the shabby suited, hard-drinking and hard-nosed sleuth of the 1940s and 50s, recent decades have witnessed significant variations in this genre. African-American and women writers have taken what might seem like formulaic material and used it to map the city differently. By treating such novels as navigations of actual urban space, they offer experiential maps of urban environments from very particular viewpoints. Here the differences in mappings between the Los Angeles of Philip Marlow (in the novels of Raymond Chandler), the Chicago of V. I. Warshawski (in the novels of Sara Paretsky), the New York of Lincoln Rhyme (in the novels of Jeffery Deaver) and the Los Angeles of Easy Rawlins (in the novels of Walter Mosely) provide material that registers social, spatial and historical differences in particularly vivid and dense ways.

Chapter Six takes as its starting point the Wachowski brothers' film *The Matrix*. By paying particular attention to the actual itineraries of the film, and refusing its mystical invitations, the film can be seen to articulate descriptions of the peculiarly porous urbanism that has occurred since at least the late nineteenth century, with the dual emergence of the railway network and the telegraph. This chapter also allows for a more concentrated inquiry into the history of the present and the way that the most up-to-date aspects of culture often demonstrate some of the most tenacious continuities in the history of urban modernity. Here rhythmanalysis is directed at the movement of information through communicative networks and allows the film to evidence a shift in the metaphorics of the city, namely from the city seen in terms of blood and oxygen to one seen in terms of nerves. *The Matrix* is a striking film, of course, not least for its spectacular picturing of a new sort of urban mobility and the vivid way in which the film's special effects realize this. It is also a film that does productive analytic work while framing this work in a politically conservative vehicle. The extraction of analytic materials from interpretative conservatism points to another productivity of the methodology adopted in this book.

The final chapter returns us firmly to the methodological and theoretical questions that have been driving this book, with a more sustained discussion of the limits and potentials of rhythmanalysis. By focusing explicitly on the work of Henri Lefebvre, the book marks its indebtedness to this work while also explaining the way it extends some of Lefebvre's insights.

The chapter also speculates on the potential of rhythmanalysis to grasp some of the characteristics of modern urban living, particularly in an era when the experience of urbanism might most productively be seen from the contrasting points of view of the refugee and the tourist.

This book is not split into 'theory' and application, nor is it really a historical survey of urban metaphorics. Instead what I want to demonstrate is a range of approaches that foreground complex texts and insist that they access the real city, or the real metaphoricity of the city (which as far as I can tell means the same thing). Many of these chapters might not, at first glace, be centrally identifiable with movement and rhythm. But the point of the book is not to search out speed-driven material but to suggest that rhythmanalysis is a productive framework for viewing urban culture *in general*. Indeed if rhythmanalysis is going to be more than a celebration or condemnation of the fast and brittle motions of the city, it will have to be careful about the prominence it gives to texts that insist on modernity as only a speeding-up. If rhythmanalysis is going to fulfil its descriptive potential, it will need to grasp the most erratic and most tenacious rhythms that animate the modern city.

Chapter Two
Street Scenes – Circulation, Crowds and Modernizing London

The Man of the Crowd

> It was well said of a certain German book that *'es lässt sich nicht lesen'* – it does not permit itself to be read. There are some secrets which do not permit themselves to be told.
>
> (Poe [1840] 1986: 179)

So begins Edgar Allan Poe's 'The Man of the Crowd', thereby foregrounding the theme of illegibility at the heart of modern urban culture. The story, such as it is, is set in the London of the late 1830s and is told from the point of view of a narrator who initially perceives the urban crowd from the vantage of a coffee house window. Looking out on one of London's 'principal thoroughfares' he watches and reads the urban crowd. For him, at least to start with, the crowd is utterly legible. He is, he tells us, 'in one of those happy moods which are so precisely the converse of *ennui*'. Convalescing from a long illness he 'felt a calm but inquisitive interest in every thing'. From his table by the window he begins by seeing an amorphous mass: 'two dense and continuous tides of population were rushing past the door', a 'tumultuous sea of human heads' (180). Having observed the movement and mass of the crowd, he continues by regarding 'with minute interest the innumerable varieties of figure, dress, air, gait, visage, and expression of countenance' within the urban throng.

He reads the different social types in the crowd: 'the tribe of clerks' split into two divisions, the young clerks and the 'steady old fellows' discernible because their 'right ears, long used to pen-holding, had an odd habit of standing off on end' (180–1). He reads 'the race of swell pick-pockets with which all great cities are infested' and the gamblers who have 'more than ordinary extension of the thumb in a direction at angles with the fingers'. He sees 'Jew pedlars, with hawk eyes flashing from the countenances whose every other feature wore only an expression of abject humility', he sees 'modest young girls returning from long and late labor' and 'women of the town . . . putting one in mind of the statue of Lucian, with the surface of Parian marble, and the interior filled with filth'. He notes: children, drunkards, 'pie-men, porters, coal-heavers, sweeps; organ grinders, monkey-exhibitors and ballad mongers; . . . ragged artisans and exhausted laborers of every description' (182–3).

As he builds this taxonomy of an urban crowd, the day turns into night, and with it the vividness of the street scene intensifies; 'as the night deepened, so deepened to me the interest of the scene' (183). Gas lighting 'threw over every thing a fitful and garish lustre'. Sitting in his coffee house, protected from the night by a bow window, the world outside is irregularly spotlit by the glare of artificial light. As the night descends, the crowd is transformed in Poe's description from a 'throng' to a 'mob'. It is the mob that solicits attention, and the attention that Poe's narrator provides is both fascination and disgust; for the mob, it seems, as well as providing an endless spectacle, is both contagious and contaminating. Poe's narrator identifies 'the loathsome and utterly lost leper in rags', and men with 'eyes hideously wild and red . . . who clutched with quivering fingers, as they strode through the crowd, at every object which came within their reach'. A young prostitute 'adept in the dreadful coquetries of her trade' is 'burning with a rabid ambition to be ranked the equal of her elders in vice' (182). Imagined fears of rabies and leprosy stalk the urban environment.

We should stop for a minute. Poe's tale accumulates in description. Its adjectives and metaphors stack up and go to work, pell-mell. And it is here, in the excess of description, that the story resonates across a history of urban imagining. If the city is most obviously an artificial environment, clearly constructed by human effort, then we should take note of the way that natural forces are enlisted for figuring the movement of the crowd. The urban populace is figured as a tidal and stormy sea. We might also note here that such watery metaphors would continue to be used in imagining varied urban populations. The idea of the masses or the crowds or, more belligerently still, foreigners flooding into cities, engulfing them like a force of nature, becomes a dominant trope for articulating anxieties about the urban crowd. In the late 1970s and 80s, fears about immigration in the UK, stirred up by right-wing politicians and press, were continually described using the metaphors of 'flooding' and 'swamping' to characterize the trickle of Commonwealth immigration (see Jackson 1992: 142–4). We should also note that the London of the 1830s is also a cosmopolitan culture evidencing ethnic diversity and the unequal experiences that racism determines. Metaphors of the crowd as 'tidal' work to dedifferentiate urban populations at the same time as they suggest a force unmotivated and uncontrolled by human agency.

The theme of nature is also pursued as a way of categorizing social types within the crowd. Thus Poe's narrator finds his evidence for social difference not in the study of social life, but from the visible 'evidence' of the body. Eyes, skin, hands, gestures – alongside clothing – remain the only signs available to Poe's narrator, and from them he weaves a taxonomy of the urban crowd with what Dana Brand calls 'an affectation of interpretative ease' (Brand 1991: 10). Such ease is dependent on the belief that physiognomy provides the truth of social difference. Such understanding had direct connections to a host of supposedly scientific practices (eugenics, phrenology and so on) that were all based on the assumption that social characteristics were stamped (so to speak) on the body. In the eighteenth and nineteenth century, and gathering particular momentum in the 1840s, the idea that biological structures spoke the truth of the subject (through the size and shape of the features and so on) was used not simply to differentiate between national populations but to differentiate within these populations as well (see Sekula 1986). While this clearly fed the conventional racism of imperialist rule, it also fuelled a more general *racialization* aimed in the direction of class and gender. In Poe's story, eyes are not 'windows to the soul' but 'hawk eyes' showing racial characteristics. An imagined social group becomes a 'tribe' or a 'race'. Prostitutes are seen as bodily filth, however pleasant they look on the surface. Even sticking-out ears are aligned to a social type, although less for biological reasons than for the way they show the effects of clerical practice (keeping pens tucked behind ears). Whether through genealogy, the 'biology of race' or the effects of labour, social character is perceived as written on the body.

But if 'race' is a trope that was deployed extensively across the urban crowd, its articulation as contagion reveals the deep anxiety that social differences provoked. The figuring of the urban crowd as contagious will find its most insistent advocate about 50 years later in the writings of the French psychologist Gustave LeBon. LeBon's book *Psychologie des foules* (translated as *The Crowd*) was enormously influential when it was published in 1895, and in it we can see the leap that connects the racialization of the urban mass to ideas of contagion. For LeBon, 'in a crowd every sentiment and act is contagious to such a degree than an individual readily sacrifices his personal interest to the collective interest' (LeBon [1895] 1995: 30). Such contagion is perceived as belonging to the social character of the crowd itself, which for LeBon embodies 'inferior forms of evolution':

> It will be remarked that among the special characteristics of crowds there are several – such as impulsiveness, irritability, incapacity to reason, the absence of judgement and of the critical spirit, the exaggeration of the sentiments, and others beside – which are almost always observed in beings belonging to inferior forms of evolution – in women, savages, and children for instance.
>
> (LeBon [1895] 1995: 35–6)

To become part of the crowd is to enter into a moral and physical degeneracy, to be infected by 'racial' inferiority. The fact that Poe's story also connects inferiority with contagion suggests that LeBon's urban allegory related to an already deep-seated anxiety about the urban mass. For the narrator of 'The Man of the Crowd' the city is plagued, infested by the crowd. The motley mass that does this infesting are not simply corrupted (prostitutes, criminals and drunkards) they are also perceived as actively corrupting. The fear of the crowd, and the fascination that drives it, acknowledges a double pathology: the crowd as contagious and the narrator luxuriating in the threat of contagion.

Already it should be clear that the short text 'The Man of the Crowd' (less than 10 pages long) registers something of the more general conditions of urban culture *through* the mass of metaphors used to account for the experience of the city. The story so far falls on the side of legibility, even if this is a legibility built on clearly ideological and absurdist foundations. About halfway through Poe's story, legibility gives way to illegibility. The narrator catches sight of an old man, an old man whose 'countenance . . . at once arrested and absorbed' his 'whole attention'. Through 'the wild effects of the light' the narrator sees a 'decrepit old man'. In attempting to fit this man into his taxonomy of urban types, Poe's narrator finds only contradiction and confusion. The man seems to portray 'ideas of vast mental power, of caution, of penuriousness, of avarice, of coolness, of malice, of blood-thirstiness, of triumph, of merriment, of excessive terror, of intense – of supreme despair' (Poe [1840] 1986: 183–4). His clothes are 'filthy and ragged' and yet the linen was of a 'beautiful texture'. Through a rent in the old man's coat the narrator catches sight of a diamond and a dagger. The visible evidence of the old man simply doesn't add up.

It is this obstacle to 'interpretative ease' which decisively alters the entire drift of the narrative. The irreconcilable figure causes the narrator to leave the comfort of the coffee house and take to the streets in pursuit of the 'man of the crowd'. The rest of the story itemizes a walk that takes 24 hours and ends back at the same coffee house he left the day before. The walk takes the reader to a variety of squares. They go to a busy bazaar, where the old man enters 'shop after shop, priced nothing, spoke no word, and looked at all objects with a wild and vacant stare' (185). Once the bazaar was closed the old man retraces his steps and heads towards the theatre district just as the 'audience were thronging from the doors'. Here the old man 'threw himself amid the crowd'. Apart from the endless walking and the perpetual search for, and immersion in, the crowd, there seems to be no rational explanation for the old man's behaviour. Eventually the narrator, 'wearied unto death' (187), gives up the pursuit, suggesting that this is a man who cannot be read.

In struggling to find meaning in the old man's person, the narrator only finds more puzzles. He notes, for instance, that when the old man is walking in less densely populated streets, 'he walked more slowly and with less object than before – more hesitatingly' (184–5). Depression seems to overcome the old man when the urban crowd thins out.

Conversely when the crowd is most dense:

> The old manner of the stranger re-appeared. His chin fell upon his breast, while his eyes rolled wildly from under his knit brows, in every direction, upon those who hemmed him in. He urged his way steadily and perseveringly.
>
> (Poe [1840] 1986: 185)

At one point the narrator notices the old man being touched: 'a shop-keeper, in putting up a shutter, jostled the old man, and at the instant I saw a strong shudder come over his frame' (186). Earlier on in the story the narrator mentions jostling a number of times, most specifically to talk about those with a 'business-like demeanor'. Amongst these he finds minor variations in responses to jostling. Some 'when pushed by fellow wayfarers . . . evidenced no symptom of impatience, but adjusted their clothes and hurried on'. Others, more 'restless in their movements', when 'jostled, they bowed profusely to the jostlers, and appeared overwhelmed with confusion'. No mention of strong shudders here. Alongside this the narrator tells us that these business types 'did not greatly excite my attention', yet of course the old man, with his shuddering response to being jostled, did. Excitement and knowledge animate this story and animate the physical movement of the old man. For the narrator, excitement, which always hovers on the edge of sexual excitement, is provoked by curiosity and a desire to know the world and possess the world as knowledge. For the old man, the arousal (or disgust?) of a more physical knowledge, through contact, is figured much more enigmatically and forcefully and suggests itself as one of the drives propelling him round the city.

But if the 'man of the crowd' doesn't 'allow himself to be read', the wayward path that the old man takes does at least allow another London to become visible, one different from that seen in its 'principle thoroughfare'. For the old man leads the narrator off the tourist map, and takes him to places where respectable men wouldn't normally find themselves. Such places are not the spectacular sites of urban modernity, but the 'nightmare' vision that punctures this dream world and leads to a more troublesome figuring of modernity. The exorbitant use of adjectives registers something of this:

> It was the most noisome quarter of London, where everything wore the worst impress of the most deplorable poverty, and of the most desperate crime. By the dim light of an accidental lamp, tall, antique, worm-eaten, wooden tenements were seen tottering to their fall, in directions so many and capricious that scarce the semblance of a passage was discernible between them. The paving stones lay at random, displaced from their beds by the rankly-growing grass. Horrible filth festered in the damned-up gutters. The whole atmosphere teemed with desolation.
>
> (Poe [1840] 1986: 186–7)

Apart from the facts of description (narrow alleyways and so on) it is the adjectives that do all the work here. Teeming and tottering, the city itself (or at least this part) becomes almost a drunken mob. And here, unsurprisingly perhaps, both characters find themselves in a 'gin palace' (although neither imbibes). This description of what in the nineteenth century would have been called a 'rookery' is crucial to the story and I will return to it below. In many ways, arriving at this tottering scene of desolation ends the story; what is left of the endless circuits around London are passed over swiftly and there is little left in the way of description of either London and its inhabitants or the old man.

Blistering with metaphors, brimful of adjectives, Poe's short story performs a number of crucial operations that will be central to my discussion of urban culture. It insists that metaphor is not something layered over the experience of urban modernity but constitutes the material conditions of that experience. This is one of the reasons why Poe's story was so important for the cultural historian Walter Benjamin in his project to register the emergent culture of modernity in nineteenth-century Paris; a project that David Frisby has usefully termed 'metaphorical materialism' (Frisby 2001: 52). It also figures the city in relation to flows and rhythms. This emphasis on the various speeds of urban circulation was also central to a range of urban literature in the nineteenth century and connected disparate writings such as those of journalists and sanitary engineers. Below I will suggest that, while the foregrounding of 'rhythm' was used by urban commentators in ways often analogous with the demands of urban regulators, the potential of 'rhythmanalysis' to both describe the city and critically investigate it provides generative potential for urban cultural studies.

But Poe's short story has another dimension to it that must be seen to threaten the very premise of *studying* the urban. The story produces fissures in the epistemological basis of urban cultural studies. When Poe's narrator 'enters the field', when he takes to the street (as urban ethnographer), his aim is knowledge. He wants to know this man, understand what he does. And like any good ethnographer he forgoes the comfort of the coffee house for fieldwork. Yet it is precisely here in the street that knowledge is not gained; in fact, for Poe's narrator we might say that the result of his taking to the streets is that his 'interpretative ease' becomes unsettled, undone.

We will need to follow two leads here. The first will be to look at the conditions of urban modernity as they are emerging in London in the first half of the nineteenth century and see how they relate to the legibility and illegibility of the city. The second will be to start to construct a sense of the rhythms and flows of the city and sketch out a rhythmanalysis that can provide a basis for charting the shifts and diversity of the city as it unevenly develops during the nineteenth and twentieth centuries. Rhythmanalysis, as I want to employ it, is a mode of social and cultural description that allows for certain forms of explanation but is not itself explanation. Its job for the moment is to make something of the experience of urban modernity more vivid, and allow for a degree of complexity or multiplicity in describing the city.

London's Modernity

If some of the best writing on urban modernity has concentrated on Paris and Vienna, this is partly because the effects of modernization can be seen so vividly there (see Clark 1984; Rice 1997; Schorske 1981 for examples). Both Paris and Vienna underwent full-scale refashioning in the second half of the nineteenth century. The boulevards of Paris, supplying the city with a network of wide, straight roads, were mostly built between 1853 and 1870 (the period when Baron Haussmann was prefect of Paris). Only a little later, from 1857 into the 1880s, Vienna underwent a period of monumental reconstruction, as the old area of fortification was transformed into a large arterial boulevard (the Ringstrasse) that housed a series of majestic state buildings and gave rise to a spate of apartment building and property speculation. Urban planning in these examples articulated various imperatives: both cities needed ways of allowing a greater circulation of traffic (both people and things); both sought symbolic forms for representing the assent of bourgeois power; and both cities located the threat to social order from inside the city rather than from an invading army.

Paris provides the most compelling example of how these imperatives were combined. Wolfgang Schivelbusch describes the 'Haussmannization' of Paris in the following way:

> The authoritarian, highly structured, even brutal methods with which Haussmann 'renewed' old Paris is often seen only as a modification of the city to make it conform to the counter-revolutionary strategic needs of the Second Empire. It is obvious that the avenues and boulevards were designed to be efficacious army routes, but that function was merely a Bonapartist addendum to the otherwise commercially oriented new system. The form and methodology of Haussmann's street plan was authoritarian and military; its purpose, like the overall intention of Bonapartist regime, was the advancement of the bourgeoisie's business interests.

> (Schivelbusch 1986: 181)

Paris's large network of boulevards allowed wide avenues for increased traffic flow and supplied the stage for spectacular consumption (crucial to an urban plan designed to enhance the circulation of commodities). At the same time the straight boulevards would allow for the speedy movement of troops while dissuading would-be insurrectionists from attempting to erect barricades across the excessively wide streets. What was called at the time 'strategic beautification' (*l'embellissement stratégique*) also supplied Paris with an architecture and a series of public monuments styled from classical references and designed to show the historical importance of the new regime. While the incentives for rebuilding Paris were largely self-promotion on behalf of a social class with wealth and an ideological and material task to perform, a number of other more magnanimous urban achievements were carried out as part of the same urban upheaval. Most important was the attempt to control contagious diseases (cholera especially) via the more systematic expulsion of waste from the city and the construction of a water system free from the contamination of sewage. The network of underground sewers that we glimpsed in *The Third Man*, which were a crucial part of Haussmann's reconfiguring of Paris, were at the time seen as one of the crowning achievements of modernization in both Paris and Vienna.

In London the physical signs of urban modernization are evident earlier in the century, and the modernizing process took place in a much more piecemeal and haphazard fashion than in Paris or Vienna. And this is one of the benefits of looking at London as opposed to those two cities. To look at Paris often means to be seduced by the extent of the newly minted urban vision, and to downplay the more uneven developments of the modern city and the way old forms of urbanism existed side by side with those newly emerging. In Paris traditional artisan and factory worker communities were ousted from the centre, and had to move to crowded and poor areas far away from the new boulevards. Some sections of the population simply fell below the horizon of visibility. In London, at the same time, the worst slum areas existed at the back door of the latest swanky colonnade of shops. To take nineteenth-century London as the scene of urban modernization is to insist on its uneven rhythms and to put those who were, in many ways, residual to the force of capitalist modernity into the foreground of the picture.

In 1842, two years after 'The Man of the Crowd' was published, the twenty-four-year-old Friedrich Engels arrived in London. Soon to become the co-author, with Karl Marx, of the single most important document of the nineteenth century, the *Communist Manifesto*, Engels came to England as something of a reluctant industrialist (his father had sent him to one of the family-owned firms in Manchester). During 1842–4 Engels collected the material that would provide the content for his book of 1845, *The Condition of the Working Class in England*. What is so evident for Engels is that within London's 'immense tangle of streets, there are hundreds and thousands of alleys and courts lined with houses too bad for anyone to live in' (Engels [1845] 1987: 72). 'Close to the splendid houses of the rich', wrote Engels, 'such a lurking place of the bitterest poverty may often be found.' He was referring specifically to 'rookeries' like St Giles ('where everything wore the worst impress of the most deplorable poverty, and of the most desperate crime' as Poe might have it). St Giles was not distanced from the centres of modernization; it was rubbing shoulders with it. (Plate 2.1 shows a 'rookery' similar to St Giles.) It is worth giving some space to Engels' description of St Giles as it corresponds and fills out the description offered by Poe of 'the most noisome quarter of London':

> St Giles is in the midst of the most populous part of the town, surrounded by broad, splendid avenues in which the gay world of London idles about, in the immediate neighbourhood of Oxford Street, Regent Street, of Trafalgar Square and the Strand. It is a disorderly collection of tall, three or four-storied houses, with narrow, crooked, filthy streets, in which there is quite as much life as in the great thoroughfares of the town, except that, here, people of the working class only are to be seen.
>
> (Engels [1845] 1987: 71)

After describing the rotten vegetables for sale in the streets (from the barrows of costermongers), Engels goes further into the warren of streets:

Plate 2.1 Seven Dials, London, George Cruikshank, 1839, illustration for Charles Dickens' *Sketches by Boz*

But all this is nothing in comparison with the dwellings in the narrow courts and alleys between the streets, entered by covered passages between the houses, in which the filth and tottering ruin surpasses all description. Scarcely a whole window-pane can be found, the walls are crumbling, door-posts and window-frames loose and broken, doors of old boards nailed together, or altogether wanting in this thieves' quarter, where no doors are needed, there being nothing to steal. Heaps of garbage and ashes lie in all directions, and the foul liquids emptied before the doors gather in stinking pools. Here live the poorest of the poor, the worst paid workers with thieves and the victims of prostitution indiscriminately huddled together, the majority Irish, or of Irish extraction, and those who have not yet sunk in the whirlpool of moral ruin which surrounds them, sinking daily deeper, losing daily more and more of their power to resist the demoralizing influence of want, filth, and evil surroundings.

(Engels [1845] 1987: 71)

Engels' prose echoes that of Poe's, although Engels, unlike the narrator of 'The Man of the Crowd', offers more of an explanatory perspective, through his interest in social conditions rather than 'social types'. Crucially, Engels shows us that those suffering the worst of the poverty were immigrants from Ireland. St Giles might well have been the setting for Poe's description of a rookery apart from the fact that Poe's narrator tells us the rookery in 'The Man of the Crowd' is located on the 'verge of the city' (Poe [1840] 1986: 186). St Giles and the Seven Dials (another notoriously poor area) weren't on the verge of the city, but abutting its most prestigious streets.

In a commentary on Engels' discussion of the urban environment, Steven Marcus (in an essay tellingly called 'Reading the Illegible') explains how Engels figures the modern city as both readable and illegible at the same time. Crucially, the illegibility of the modern city is seen by Engels as being an articulation of its planning (and not simply a reaction to its scale by those trying to describe it, for instance). The modern city is planned so that the proximity of destitution and expensive shops, the contiguous spaces of filth and brightly sparkling spectacle, can exist side by side without the contradictions being legible (or indeed visible). Modern planning works to veil and disavow the intensity of its unevenness. In Manchester Engels frequently travels from the suburbs to the centre; he knows that behind the façades of street fronts he passes each day lies a reality that he is slowly getting to know. Extracting from Engels' description of the way that the city physically disavows its actuality, Marcus writes:

Those rows of shops, commercial buildings, pubs, warehouses, and factories, different and discriminable as they are, are still ultimately coverings. They function, depending upon the context in which we regard them, as appearances, symbols, or symptoms. They are the visible parts of a larger reality; they both reveal and conceal that reality; they are formations made up of displacements and compromises between antagonistic forces and agencies.

(Marcus 1973: 262)

In London the situation was even more incorrigible. Poe knew London in at least two ways. He knew London as a boy when he went to school in the London suburb of Stoke Newington and later Chelsea in the 1810s, and he knew London through writing. During Poe's time at school London was modernizing in significant ways. The centrepiece of London's moderniza- tion in the first half of the nineteenth century was undoubtedly Regent Street (initially New Street). Built between 1815 and 1823 (which more than covers the period of Poe's residency in London), Regent Street was the physical manifestation of the modernizing impulse of the time (Plate 2.2). A speculative venture that would provide premises for the most expensive shops as well as apartments for the wealthiest of London's bachelors, Regent Street also carved an access route for movement between the area of Westminster and the richly developing suburbs around what is now Regent's Park. John Nash, who was one of the financial speculators involved in the venture, designed the buildings that flanked the street. Classical colonnades swept along the quadrant, providing a continual reference to classicism and the imagined values of antiquity. For Nash it was a way of stitching wealthy but disparate areas of the city together, and thereby making the housing developments he was involved in more desir- able, while veiling over the unsightly fact of impoverished London. In Nash's words, Regent Street was designed to make a 'complete separation between the Streets and Squares occupied by the nobility and gentry, and the narrow streets and meaner Houses occupied by mechanics and the trading parts of the community' (Nash 1828 quoted in Arnold 2000: 88).

As Dana Arnold notes, an emphatic mode of zoning according to class was instituted in the Building Acts 1774 which 'established four different rates of houses by size and grade of materials' (Arnold 2000: 48). For Arnold, 'Regent Street was the fundamental core or backbone of the middle-class presence in London and the zoning of classes was so abrupt that there was virtually no transition between areas' (Arnold 2000: 89). Regent Street, as a road running north-south, protected the wealthy hous- ing to the west of the street from the encroaching poverty of the rookeries of St Giles and the Seven Dials to the east. In Roy Porter's words, 'London's grandest thoroughfare thereby became its social barrier' (Porter 1996: 154). To ensure that Regent Street effectively veiled its proximity to slums and 'common trade', any 'vehicles for the carriage of goods, merchandise, manure soil or other articles' (quoted in Arnold 2000: 89) were to be barred.

But while Poe would have undoubtedly been aware of the emergence of Regent Street, he may or may not have been aware that this piece of urban infrastructure was working to make London even more illegible than

Plate 2.2 The Quadrant, Regent Street, in 1822, from a drawing by T. H. Shepherd, for Ackermann's series of aquatints, Guildhall Library, City of London

previously. Poe, though, also 'knew' London through literature. Charles Dickens' *Sketches by Boz* (Dickens [1839] 1995) was likely to have been one of the main descriptive resources for 'The Man of the Crowd'. Poe wrote an effusive review of an American collection of the sketches (titled *Watkins Tottle, and Other Sketches*) in 1836 and recommended them 'as a study, to those who turn their attention to Magazine writing' (Poe [1836] 1986: 412). *Sketches by Boz* maps a London that would become familiar to Engels. It is a mapping of London that insists on the proximity of spectacular wealth and desperate poverty. At the end of Poe's review, the sketch 'The Gin Shop' is included in its entirety (Plate 2.3). Gin shops, suggests Dickens, 'are invariably numerous and splendid, in precise proportion to the dirt and poverty of the surrounding neighbourhood' (Dickens [1839] 1995: 217). While gin palaces are clearly not as palatial as the hangouts of the well-heeled, Dickens' geography of London makes clear that unevenness is an aspect of such neighbourhoods classed as 'rookeries'. For Dickens the contrast is not simply between poverty and wealth. The contrast between the 'great thoroughfares' (Drury Lane, Holborn and so on) and the 'filth and squalid misery' that adjoin them is also contrasted with the gin shop, which alone seems to offer the possibility of momentarily alleviating the experience of desperate poverty.

Dickens takes as his case study gin shops within the rookeries of St Giles and the Seven Dials. As in Poe and Engels, Dickens is hard-pressed to describe it adequately: 'the filthy and miserable appearance of this part of London can hardly be imagined by those (and there are many such) who have not witnessed it' (Dickens [1839] 1995: 217). Similarly what is stressed is the 'filth everywhere', 'the wretched houses with broken windows

Plate 2.3 The Gin Shop, George Cruikshank, 1839, illustration for Charles Dickens'
Sketches by Boz

patched with rags and paper', and, as in Engels, the preponderance of Irish
Londoners. When Dickens comes upon the gin shop, the description is
almost the same as the one that Poe will provide in 'The Man of the
Crowd': 'you turn a corner, what a change! All is light and brilliancy'
(Dickens [1839] 1995: 217). In Poe's story the narrator embellishes upon
this: 'suddenly a corner was turned, a blaze of light burst upon our sight,
and we stood before one of the huge suburban temples of Intemperance –
one of the palaces of the fiend, Gin' (Poe [1840] 1986: 187).

    However much Poe's mapping of London in the pages of 'The Man of the Crowd' was purely imaginative (or simply casual), it corresponds to the dynamic and illegible configuration of London in the early nineteenth century. The sense of physical distance that Poe's narrator experiences as he moves from 'one of the principal theatres' to the despair of a rookery, needs to be translated as social distance. In fact as Engels tells us: 'in the immediate neighbourhood of Drury Lane Theatre, the second in London, are some of the worst streets in the whole metropolis' (Engels [1845] 1987: 72). To move from Drury Lane to a rookery was merely to turn a corner. The physical spacing of London, as I have been suggesting, didn't correspond to its social spacing and for Engels this was its most emphatic characteristic. Proximity and distance in purely physical terms veil the intimate distance of social class, poverty and wealth, bourgeois propriety and an 'atmosphere teemed with desolation'. Poe's narrator is of course aware that he is being taken about the city in 'a great variety of devious ways' (Poe [1840] 1986: 186), but he can't make head or tail of how such places connect.

The reader of Poe's story is invited, at the end, to speculate about the unreadability of this man of the crowd. 'This old man', the narrator tells us, 'is the type and genius of deep crime' (Poe [1840] 1986: 188). But what is his crime? Is he a pickpocket, a procurer of female or male flesh, a frotteur (a person who gets sexual pleasure from rubbing against someone or something) or a social explorer wearing an intricate form of disguise? If, however, we pass up on this invitation to guess the social type of the old man (a form of attention from which the narrator can't escape), we might find better questions to ask. For instance, it becomes clear that it isn't only the social type of the old man that is illegible; just as unreadable is his movement about the city. And it is the old man's 'way of operating' in the city that I want to discuss in the next section. For now it might be enough to suggest that the old man's crime is the same as Friedrich Engels': both insist on the unevenness of development within the city, both juxtapose the theatre and the rookery, and press that juxtaposition on the reader. And both do so by navigating the city in 'a great variety of devious ways'. It is the meandering, erratic and wayward nature of the old man's movement around the city that for the narrator is impenetrable, but is also the source for presenting another urban modernity, of starting to suggest the dissonance of the polyphonic city.

Uncanny Echoes

One reason for this chapter's concentration on Poe's 'The Man of the Crowd' is because of the particular way its urban imaginary echoes through so much literature about the city and the urban crowd in the nineteenth and twentieth century. This isn't to place Poe's story as an originary precursor or claim that it was exceptionally influential; Hoffmann's 'The Cousin's Picture Window' figures the city crowds in some similar ways and was written nearly 20 years before Poe's (Hoffmann [1822] 1992). Hoffmann's story, though, pictures its Berlin crowd as predominantly female and his urban ethnographer looks out through a window because he is paralysed. The similarities and dissimilarities, though, are telling and prefigure a cinematic way of looking (the window as camera and screen), with Poe's mobile spectator problematizing the epistemological value of movement. The connections between Poe and Hoffmann suggest that looking at distinct chains of influence is not the issue here; more crucial is to recognize the themes that reverberate through the literature on the city, which find themselves so vividly condensed in 'The Man of the Crowd'.

Poe's story did however circulate as a specific text, but this was as much a cause for confusion as for clarity. The French poet Baudelaire translated the story in 1856 and in his 1863 essay 'The Painter of Modern Life' he used Poe's text as a vivid exemplar of the figure of the *flâneur* – an urban wanderer for whom 'curiosity has become a fatal, irresistible passion!' (Baudelaire [1863] 1964: 7). For Baudelaire, *flânerie* was an indispensable modality for reading urban modernity, it allowed a form of spectatorship that was simultaneously both detached and immersed in the rhythms of the crowd:

> For the perfect *flâneur*, for the passionate spectator, it is an immense joy to set up house in the heart of the multitude, amid the ebb and flow of movement, in the midst of the fugitive and the infinite. To be away from home and yet to feel oneself everywhere at home; to see the world, to be at the centre of the world, and yet to remain hidden from the world – such are a few of the slightest pleasures of those independent, passionate, impartial natures which the tongue can but clumsily define.
>
> (Baudelaire [1863] 1964: 9)

Baudelaire imagines the *flâneur* as a rhythmanalyst, simultaneously both inside and outside the rhythmicity of the city.

Walter Benjamin, writing in the 1930s, used Baudelaire's writing as his guide to the prehistory of urban modernity as it emerges in the nineteenth century. He too gives Poe's story a central role. But for Benjamin it is unclear who exactly the 'passionate spectator' is: is it the convalescent following the unknown old man, or is it the old man himself? In his first essay on Baudelaire and urban modernity, Benjamin assumes that it is the old man (and assumes that this is the same for Baudelaire). In this reading, the *flâneur* (old man) is abandoned to the rhythms of the city and thus takes on the same condition as the commodity: 'the intoxication to which the *flâneur* surrenders is the intoxication of the commodity around which surges the stream of customers' (Benjamin [1938] 1983: 55). For Benjamin this form of *flânerie* is about to become extinct as the old man's haunts (bazaars in particular) are about to be replaced by more organized and spectacular consumption. The following year Benjamin rewrote his essay on Baudelaire and this time the *flâneur* is no longer the 'man of the crowd' but the convalescent who attempts to shadow the old man. This time *flânerie* offers a distinctive view of the city because it is undertaken by a class that is facing historical extinction:

> There was also the *flâneur* who demanded elbow room and was unwilling to forego the life of a gentleman of leisure. Let the many attend to their daily affairs; the man of leisure can indulge in the perambulations of the *flâneur* only if as such he is already out of place.
>
> (Benjamin [1939] 1983: 129)

For both essays Poe's story is important because of its intense focus on circulation, movement and the pace of movement. But, perhaps more crucially, the story is historically placed to capture urban rhythms that are about to be cast into oblivion as they are replaced by the marching beat of capitalist modernization. It is as an outmoded figure, a figure on the edge of extinction, that *flânerie*, either in the shape of the old man or Poe's narrator, offers a critical perspective on modernity. It provides another rhythm, another circulatory system, that in its proximity to the newly emerging rhythms of urban modernity can work to make vivid the organizing pace of modernity.

Edgar Allan Poe's short story chimes with a host of other work to which it has no direct relationship. For instance, Marx's description of the lumpenproletariat (a 'class' which is only a class for Marx because of its antagonisms to other classes – it has no identity for itself) is uncannily similar to Poe's description of the urban crowds that populate the city at the end of the day, just as daylight is being replaced by the 'garish lustre' of the gas lamps. This is Marx describing a motley assortment of bohemians who he denounces as the anti-revolutionary or counter-revolutionary forces mobilized by Louis Bonaparte in the middle of the nineteenth century:

> Alongside decayed *roués* with dubious means of subsistence and of dubious origin, alongside ruined and adventurous offshoots of the bourgeoisie, were vagabonds, discharged soldiers, discharged jailbirds, escaped galley slaves, swindlers, mountebanks, *lazzaroni* [Italian lumpenproletariat], pickpockets, tricksters, gamblers, *maquereaus* [procurers], brothel keepers, porters, *literati*, organ-grinders, rag-pickers, knife grinders, tinkers, beggars – in short, the whole indefinite, disintegrated mass, thrown hither and thither, which the French term *la bohème*.
>
> (Marx [1852] 1968: 136–7)

Commenting on this passage, Peter Stallybrass and Allon White (1986: 129) suggest that for Marx this group are 'the object of disgust and fascination'. While Marx works to condemn them for their historical role on the side of the bourgeoisie, 'it is this very group which stimulates his linguistic productivity'. In this, Marx's writing is echoing an urban imaginary (which would also include Poe's text) that expends an exorbitant amount of linguistic energy describing the very thing that it wants to expel. For Stallybrass and White, this is part of a general economy that mixes fear and fascination in relation to the 'Other', in this case social groups not seen as having propriety within the city. As they suggest, the disgust that is at the root of such description is accompanied by fascination that is evidenced by the excess attention that such 'rogue elements' receive: 'disgust always bears the imprint of desire. These low domains, apparently expelled as "Other", return as objects of nostalgia, longing and fascination' (191). This mixing of fear and fascination is the hallmark of two related genres, psychoanalysis and the modern gothic. So it is perhaps no surprise to find elements of Poe's story mirrored in Robert Louis Stevenson's gothic tale of urban wandering 'The Strange Case of Dr Jekyll and Mr Hyde' and Sigmund Freud's essay on the uncanny.

Stevenson's tale, at least in its representation of Edward Hyde, bears many similarities with Poe's story. It too is concerned with the perambulations around London of an 'unreadable' man. The story, of course, ends up revealing that Hyde is the repressed 'pleasure principle' within the morally upright figure of Dr Henry Jekyll: a 'base' double, released from moral restraint, with the help of drugs, to 'spring headlong into a sea of liberty' (Stevenson [1886] 1992: 146). It is in the descriptions of Hyde by those who meet him that most connects with the figure of the old man in 'The Man of the Crowd'. The range of contradictions that describe the old man in Poe's story disqualify him from the social categories employed by the narrator. In Stevenson's story Hyde provokes similarly paradoxical characterizations:

> The problem he was thus debating as he walked was one of a class that is rarely solved. My Hyde was pale and dwarfish; he gave an impression of deformity without any nameable malformation, he had a displeasing smile, he had borne himself to the lawyer with a sort of murderous mixture of timidity and boldness, and he spoke with a husky, whispering and somewhat broken voice, all of these were points against him; but not all of these together could explain the hitherto unknown disgust, loathing and fear with which Mr Utterson regarded him.
>
> (Stevenson [1886] 1992: 108–9)

This 'murderous mixture of timidity and boldness' is a contradiction that relates to the description of the 'The Man of the Crowd', who conveyed ideas of 'merriment, of excessive terror, of intense – of extreme despair' (Poe [1840] 1986: 184). In critical readings of Stevenson's story, much has been made of the fact that the story of Jekyll and Hyde is a story of an exclusively male bourgeois community, who repress sexuality in general and same-sex sexuality in particular. Elaine Showalter finds a range of tropes in Stevenson's story that would have been commonly understood as codings of homosexuality. For instance, when Utterson finally breaks into Jekyll's 'private closet', he finds a mirror: 'the mirror testifies not only to Jekyll's scandalously unmanly narcissism, but also to the sense of the mask and the Other that has made the mirror an obsessive symbol in homosexual literature' (Showalter 1992: 111). In Poe's story, would the mention of the old man's clothes and the presence of a diamond and a dagger similarly suggest a clandestine world of homosexual cruising? More pertinently, perhaps, is Showalter's insistence that a homophobic representation is written into the characterization of Hyde through metaphor: 'the metaphors associated with Hyde are those of abnormality, criminality, disease, contagion, and death' (112). Both Poe's and Stevenson's story wrestle with the difficulty of trying to describe the old man and Hyde; there is something 'unspeakable' about them that can only be gestured at through the layering of contradictory descriptions. And for Showalter 'unspeakable' is *the* 'code word of Victorian homosexuality' (112).

Whether a case can be made for Poe's tale figuring the old man as homosexual is, I think, uncertain. It is, however, suggestive. In figuring the old man as contradictory, placing unresolved clues as to his purpose (the glimpsed dagger and diamond) and leaving unexplained the 'strong shudder' that the old man performs as he jostles the shopkeeper, Poe creates space for endless speculation. If that speculation turns towards sexuality, this may well be because there is little else that can be offered to explain the peculiarly driven manner by which the old man is propelled through the city.

Poe's peripatetic tale is filled with circular meanderings. As well as figuring a labyrinthine city where socially distanced spaces are physically close, it continually takes us back to certain places. In this it seems to provide a useful foreshadowing of an urban emotion that would be made famous in Sigmund Freud's essay 'The "Uncanny" '. This is Freud in Italy, caught in a spatial web of repetition:

As I was walking, one hot summer afternoon, through the deserted streets of a provincial town in Italy which was unknown to me, I found myself in a quarter of whose character I could not long remain in doubt. Nothing but painted women were to be seen at the windows of the small houses, and I hastened to leave the narrow street at the next turning. But after having wandered about for a time without inquiring my way, I suddenly found myself back in the same street, where my presence was now beginning to excite attention. I hurried away once more, only to arrive by another *détour* at the same place yet a third time. Now, however, a feeling overcame me which I can only describe as uncanny, and I was glad enough to find myself back at the piazza I had left a short while before, without any further voyages of discovery.

(Freud [1919] 1985: 356)

For Freud uncanny feelings are provoked by a compulsion to repeat, a compulsion related most directly to the death drive. The sexual content of Freud's meanderings goes uncommented on. Of course, where Freud keeps returning to is not without note; the very fact that his is return to a space of sexuality should alert us to the connection between sexuality and space, and to note the sexual drive as one among many propulsions that animate and rhythm the city.

The enduring vividness of Poe's story is enhanced by all these other writings that seem to accrue out of the same material matrix that generates 'The Man of the Crowd'. I have suggested that Poe's story is not an explanation of the modernizing impulses of the city, but itself a symptom of the illegibility that is being planned into the modern metropolis. Similarly, the desire that drives both the old man and the narrator (and what erotics of knowledge is he driven by?) is itself illegible within the narrative, as it was no doubt within the environs of the city. Here legibility is not an option: any definitive interpretation of the story (and by extension, of the city) cuts down the productive plurality that the story suggestively figures. Rhythmanalysis (both in the story and in reading the story) is about plural, multiple rhythms, their dissonances and harmonies. In figuring an illegible urbanism navigated by a man whose purpose is similarly illegible, harmonies and dissonances begin to suggest themselves, if only as questions.

Was the commodity-driven city that was emerging in the early nineteenth century in or out of step with the veiled sexuality of the city? Was the inordinate trouble that urban modernizing went to, in attempting to hide the savage unevenness of its ambition, similar to the trouble it went to veil the sexual rhythmicity of the city? Or was the force of capitalism primarily directed at inhibiting the visibility of class differences, rendering the city as an illegible palimpsest of economic divisiveness?

Poe's story is an example of the tenacity of an urban imaginary that continually figures the city as a site of uncanny 'sexual' encounters (or the vividly 'absent' lack of them), an arena of the most modern and the most arcane and a territory where 'social outcasts' lurk. Poe's London is a heterogeneous city where difference disrupts the cultural and social management performed by the physical geography of the city.

Chapter Three
City of Attractions –
Commodities, Shopping and
Consumer Choreography

Window Displays and Choreographed Shopping

Some windows seem built for looking out of, some for looking into and some for both. The café window in Poe's story functioned for looking out into the street, as did the window in Henri Lefebvre's Paris apartment (mentioned in Chapter One). But the café window in 'The Man of the Crowd' also offered the opportunity, the invitation for looking in. To be looked at, to be seen relaxing and luxuriating, is the view from the other side of the window, unwritten in Poe's story. The narrator of Poe's story looks out from the bow window on the ground floor of a hotel, into the bustling London street. In the early part of the nineteenth century, the period when Poe was in London, the hotels located in the West End of London were the province of wealthy young bachelors who displayed themselves in the bow and bay windows of the exclusive clubs and coffee houses that the hotels housed. These institutions were the bastions of male privilege, where the large windows offered the opportunity to see and be seen, and to watch yourself being watched. In her book on gender and urban space in London in the early nineteenth century, the architectural historian Jane Rendell demonstrates how 'ground-floor bow windows in clubs [and hotels] provide places to display exclusivity to the public street' (Rendell 2002: 64). Yet the elite masculinity on display in Regency London will soon be challenged by even more alluring visions that will significantly feminize the modern city. Yet this feminizing of the city also continues by other means the masculine privilege of the city: it both reconfigures and continues the asymmetry of gendered relations.

The vision of exclusivity that Poe's narrator might offer the passer-by in the early nineteenth century will be more perfectly realized in other windows later in the century. In the shop windows of department stores and the exclusive shops of arcades and streets dedicated to luxury goods, seduction and exclusivity worked hand in hand as metropolitan cities gave themselves over to the circulation and display of commodities. By the second half of the nineteenth century, the play of attractions, the forms of solicitation and seduction (the inviting, enticing, inciting and exciting of the urban dweller), would take on a certain overarching orchestration. The commodity in all its forms would provide an overwhelming pulsation, a tempo of attraction and distraction for the rhythm of the city.

In this sense the shop window display vividly exemplifies 'the city of attractions'. But display windows are accompanied by other attractions all clamouring for attention: posters and billboards, myriad forms of illumination, countless signs pointing, encouraging, warning. Later, of course, even the most surreal and extravagant shop display will be hard-pressed to compete with neon and video, and the endless phantasmagoria of television. But for now (from the late nineteenth century and into the first decades of the twentieth), the shop window will be 'the proscenium for visual intoxication, the site of seduction for consumer desire' (Frieberg 1993: 65), where mannequins perform 'a mute solicitation of the passerby's gaze' (Gronberg 1998: 82). It is the shop window and its relation to the street that will be our entry into the city of attractions, into the choreography and spatial organization of the consumer city.

The shop window in the form that we experience it today was the beneficiary of a number of new technological developments. It was transformed with the introduction of large sheets of glass (only technically achievable from the mid-nineteenth century) and it constantly benefited from new lighting technologies. As Wolfgang Schivelbusch suggests:

> What we think of as night life includes this nocturnal round of business, pleasure and illumination. It derives its own, special atmosphere from the light that falls onto the pavements and streets from shops (especially those selling luxury goods), cafés and restaurants, light that is intended to attract passers-by and potential customers. It is advertising light – commercialised festive illumination – in contrast to street light, the lighting of a policed order.
>
> (Schivelbusch 1995: 142)

Light and glass combine to form a physical and phantasmagoric spectacle that is the condition for a new form of urban visuality. The illuminated transparency mobilizes an advertising technique designed to fuel desire rather than satisfaction. Jean Baudrillard, for instance, notes that: 'whether as packaging, window or partition, glass is the basis of a transparency without transition: we see, but cannot touch. The message is universal and abstract. A shop window is both magical and frustrating – the strategy of advertising in epitome' (Baudrillard [1968] 1996: 42). It is this immaterial materiality that ushers in a new theatricality to the city:

The more the streets could supply potential customers, the more the shops opened up to them. The display window, that began to develop as an independent part of the shop around the middle of the eighteenth century, was the scene of this interchange. While previously it had been little more than an ordinary window that permitted people to see into and out of the shop, it now became a glassed-in stage on which an advertising show was presented.

(Schivelbusch 1995: 146)

The shop window as stage points to a staged theatricality that is distinct from the participatory and impromptu theatre of older forms of urban drama, where the drama is conducted between human social agents. The shop window stages this drama as a spectacle in which objects become social actors.

Window displays, advertising posters and other elements of a burgeoning commodity culture superceded, but didn't obliterate, the cultural attractions of an earlier period of urban history. For instance, in both the seventeenth and eighteenth century, the Vauxhall pleasure gardens had been a feature of fashionable leisure in London (see Ogborn 1998). Other pleasure gardens followed, and by the middle of the nineteenth century Cremorne Gardens in London's Chelsea was a centre of leisure, day and night. These gardens were modern, commercial ventures, which combined organized entertainments with the improvisations of sexually charged sociability. Cremorne supplied gas-lit, open-air dancing, fireworks, balloon displays, theatre and a place to forge sexual liaisons (Nead 2000: 109–46). Its closure in 1878 marked the demise of the pleasure garden as the privileged space of commodified leisure in the city, which coincided with a period that saw the opening of a large number of department stores. The various amusements of the gardens continue but as separate elements of urban leisure, scattered across the city. This is not to say that the growth of one caused the ruin of the other, merely that the image of a modern space of concentrated and spectacular consumption was, by the late nineteenth century, more likely to be found in the example of the department store than elsewhere.

Similarly in Paris, the image of streets given over to street performers seems to have been replaced with the names of the largest department stores; Bon Marché, Galleries Lafayette, Grands Magasins du Printemps and so on (Plate 3.1). In the early nineteenth century, the central attraction of the city street was more likely to have been a carnivalesque spectacle on the street. Describing the Parisian streets of the 1830s, Siegfried Kracauer writes:

The boulevard du Temple, for example . . . was the scene of a perpetual fair. Was it not a source of ever recurring delight to wander through the throng that surrounded the sword-swallowers, the human skeletons, the

Plate 3.1 Galeries Lafayette, Paris: the art nouveau glass dome and staircase were built in 1912

dwarfs, the giantesses; to watch an exhibition of performing fleas, then a learned dog parading his knowledge, then a young girl apparently being roasted alive?

(Kracauer [1937] 1972: 21)

Such descriptions might still accord with a certain flavour of city life, with its buskers and theatrical displays, but the point is that this is no longer the paradigm for spectacular attractions.

I am using the phrase 'city of attractions' in a way analogous to its use by the film historian Tom Gunning when he designates aspects of early cinema as a 'cinema of attractions' (Gunning [1986] 2000). By using the term 'attraction', Gunning, as well as nodding towards Sergei Eisenstein's theory of a 'montage of attractions' (Eisenstein [1923] 1977), wants to highlight exhibitionism, the use of erotic address and the materiality of display as essential ingredients in early cinema. For Gunning the cinema of attractions 'displays its visibility, willing to rupture a self-enclosed fictional world for a chance to solicit the attention of the spectator' (Gunning [1986] 2000: 230). To take this notion of 'attraction' as the focus for city life in the late nineteenth century and on into the twentieth, is to recognize the commodity as it takes its most urban form (department stores) and its most vivid means of expression (advertising). 'Attraction' seems to capture the play of force, seduction and aggression – the push and pull of the spectacular culture of the commodity. The shop windows of department stores will act as our entry into these new 'technologies' of consumption.

Émile Zola's 1883 novel *Au bonheur des dames* (translated as *The Ladies Paradise*) provides the classic *mise en scène* for consumer desire. In its opening pages it describes a young woman, Denise, arriving in Paris from the provinces with her two brothers and going in search of their uncle. A large draper's shop, which was the typical foundation of most department stores, transfixes them. 'Stopped short' and 'astonished' they gaze as the shop workers adjust the window displays and arrange the 'mountain of cheap goods' in the main entrance to the shop. For Denise the sight of this shop made 'her heart swell, and kept her excited, interested, and oblivious of everything else' (Zola [1883] 1992: 6). Walking alongside the façade, they are drawn to each tableau presented by the windows. But it is the sight of an array of dresses against a background of lace that has Denise 'rooted to the spot with admiration':

At the back a large sash of Bruges lace, of considerable value, was spread out like an altar-veil, with its two white wings extended; there were flounces of Alençon point, grouped in garlands; then from the top to the bottom fluttered, like a fall of snow, a cloud of lace of every description – Malines, Honiton, Valenciennes, Brussels, and Venetian-point. On each side the heavy columns were draped with cloth, making the background appear still more distant. And the dresses were in this sort of chapel raised to the worship of woman's beauty and grace.

(Zola [1883] 1992: 7–8)

Zola's description of the shop as a whole, and the windows in particular, vividly foregrounds a number of elements central to the display techniques of the department store. Alongside the insistence on luxury and expensive commodities is the inclusion of bargains to tempt frugal customers. Coupled with the concentration on the particular (*this* dress, *that* hat) is the excess of the general (the 'cloud of lace', the 'mountain' of goods). Zola's emphatic use of religious motifs (altar, chapel, worship) to describe this unmistakably secular display vividly connects with the ambiguous connotations that commercial culture seemed to elicit.

The choreography of shopping – the rush for bargains and the arrest of movement, as potential consumers are rooted to the spot, as they gaze in awe at the luxurious displays – needs to be emphasized. The invitation to identify passionately with material commodities, and the presumed benefits that owning them might realize, makes the display techniques of shop windows, advertising posters and shop interiors more than simply an inventory of available goods. In being 'rooted to the spot' by the luxurious display of a shop window, commodity displays might be seen as *hailing* individuals (in an analogous way to hailing a cab). For the Marxist theorist Louis Althusser, ideology was more than a set of false beliefs; it was the process by which individuals recognized themselves (and became constituted) as subjects. Althusser describes this recognition as an almost involuntary response to being hailed by ideology:

> Ideology 'acts' or 'functions' in such a way that it 'recruits' subjects among the individuals (it recruits them all), or 'transforms' the individuals into subjects (it transforms them all) by the very precise operation which I have called *interpellation* or hailing, and which can be imagined along the lines of the most commonplace everyday police (or other) hailing: 'Hey, you there!'
>
> Assuming that the theoretical scene I have imagined takes place in the street, the hailed individual will turn round. By this mere one-hundred-and-eighty-degree physical conversion, he becomes a *subject*. Why? Because he has recognized that the hail was 'really' addressed to him, and that 'it was *really him* who was hailed' (and not someone else).

(Althusser 1971: 174)

Althusser's description of ideology offers some suggestive parallels with the experience of commodity culture and its rhythms of movement. As a theory of ideology, however, Althusser's description is problematic (for instance, he seems to suggest that it is only by recognizing ourselves as subjects of state power that individuals are constituted as subjects). This is not the place to delve into the theory of ideology. It is as a description of the continual *rhythmic interruption* performed by commercial culture that I want to use Althusser's theory of ideological hailing, and for this I need to recode it. The police's 'Hey, you there!' needs to be replaced by the 'Hey, you there!' performed in the countless advertising hoardings of a city and the numerous window displays of department stores. (In fact as a head-turning performance such displays might yield better results than the hailing by police and other agencies of the state – after all when the police are doing the hailing, the last thing you want to believe is that it really is you being hailed.) It is Althusser's notion of recruitment and recognition that powerfully connect to the passionate involvement between spectator and commodity.

The idea of the department store as a temple or cathedral for a thoroughly 'disenchanted' secular culture, which worships material goods, is a persistent analogy for modern shopping and one familiar to the late nineteenth century. Similarly the juxtaposition of isolated and unique commodities with the stacks of standardized goods tells something of the way individualism is sold within capitalist culture. The commodity signals the contradictions of a mass individualism, where those with the means to purchase can be unified in their singularity. In other words, commodity culture sells you specific benefits ('this product will change your life and will make you into a unique individual') on condition that it does so as a mass product.

The department store's contradictions, as it fluctuates between uniqueness and mass, as well as its secular religiosity, is well described by the cultural historian Christoph Asendorf:

> On the one hand, an element of the old representational architecture, a reminiscence of a castle's round towers, and on the other an attempt to create little islands of calm in the middle of the teeming current, where the customers can prepare themselves for new excursions across the sea of commodities. The differentiated arrangements of space bundles and scatters perception in a well-calculated relation. In the construction of churches and palaces there is a comparable organization of space, only in this case it is oriented around a single point, altar, or throne, while the main thing in the department store is to put every commodity upon a throne for display to all customers.
>
> (Asendorf 1993: 99)

Asendorf brings together these elements and relates them to the sense of tempo that department store shopping articulates. This sense of both calm and teeming conditions relates specifically to the rhythm of shopping and the kind of passionate contemplation and frenzied activity that modern shopping solicits (a variety of different hailings).

As such, we can see shop windows and shop interiors as techniques that both organize and disorganize the attention of consumers. In Zola's case the shop window arrests the gaze of the young Denise, soliciting her attention and stopping her in her tracks. Stopping and starting seems to characterize the rhythm of the shoppers' movements (even if in this case it is the nascent window shopper). The orchestration of department stores, both outside and in, combined fast-paced movement and halting contemplation. The hurried and excited rush of shoppers clamouring for bargains, the restless flow of consumers (potential or actual), who move swiftly from one delight to the next, are juxtaposed with the moments of spellbound intoxication as shoppers are brought to a standstill. The rhythm of this new form of shopping might be seen as characteristically syncopated; a rhythm neither simply fast nor slow, but uneven and continually interrupted. Chaotic and regulated, fluid and fragmented, the rhythm of shopping displays vivid contradictions.

Using a slightly different analogy, Michael Miller finds the same uneven rhythms in the shop the Bon Marché:

> Part opera, part theatre, part museum, Boucicaut's [the shop's proprietor] eclectic extravaganza did not disappoint those who came for a show. Merchandise heaped upon merchandise was a sight all its own. Bargain counters outside entryways produced a crush at the doors that attracted still larger crowds, thus creating for all the sensation of a happening without and within. Inside the spectacle of flowing crowds intensified, orchestrated by barred passages, by cheap, tempting goods on the first floor that brought still another crush to the store's most observable arena, and by a false disorder that forced shoppers to travel the breadth of the House.
>
> (Miller 1981: 168)

The teeming flow of shoppers corresponds to the teeming arrangement of goods, while the spellbound awe that arrests Denise is focused on commodities picked out and sanctified amongst the tumult. On the one hand the mass (mass consumption, mass production), on the other the singular altars dedicated to the exquisite and rarified product. Together such display strategies orchestrate the varied rhythms of shopping.

Continual stopping and starting, the uneven rhythm of consumer movements, is not necessarily the overreaching desire of nineteenth-century social propriety. Writing about the 1860s (a time that sees the consolidation of the department store as a cultural form) feminist cultural historians like Lynne Walker and Lynda Nead describe how movement and rhythm was a peculiarly significant, yet complex, issue for women:

> Middle-class women were commonly chaperoned in the 1860s, although some respectable women walked alone in the streets of London. Either way the formula was to keep the eyes downcast, to dress neither too

much out of fashion nor too fashionably, and not to dally to look in shop
windows or watch the life of the street.

(Walker 1995: 75)

Yet dallying, of course, is precisely what 'cathedrals of consumption' invite
you to do. The advice for virtuous women venturing out into the streets
alone (mainly from popular magazines of the time) was to maintain a
purposeful pace and not to be slowed by the distractions surrounding
them. Writing in 1862, Eliza Lynn Linton delineates the necessary protocols
for keeping women 'safe':

> If she knows how to walk in the streets, self-possessed and quietly, with
> not too lagging and not too swift a step; if she avoids lounging about the
> shop-windows, and resolutely foregoes even the most tempting
> displays of finery; if she can attain that enviable street-talent, and pass
> men without looking at them yet all the while seeing them . . . she is for
> the most part as safe as if planting tulips and crocuses in her own
> garden.
>
> (Linton cited in Nead 2000: 66)

The demand of this piece of advice requires a complex performance that
negotiates speed (not too fast, not too slow) and visual awareness (to look,
but not to be seen looking at the looker). Such advice on female propriety
flies in the face of the more instrumental demand to look, gape and gawk
at the wonders on display in shop windows. Of course the slippage that is
continually made is between material objects and sexual desire. In both
instances (in negotiating the gaze of men, and in refusing or capitulating to
the gaze of things) it is 'passion' that is at stake. And in this sense the regulating and organizing of passion, as well as the deregulating and disorganizing of passion, is an ambiguous, yet defining characteristic of urban
modernity.

The Push and Pull of the Commodity

For Asendorf, window displays can be seen as organizers of passion:

> The department store accomplishes the perfect organization of passions,
> beginning with the configuration of the display windows. The goods are
> so arranged that they 'enchant' and 'captivate' – even the most modest
> stocking or glove is presented as if it is covering a tempting body, as if
> it were there only to lend expression to the beauty of every female shop-
> per, a beauty that is completely untouched by the burdens of daily life.
>
> (Asendorf 1993: 102)

Yet we might also say that passions and perceptions are simultaneously being disorganized by the display practices of department stores. In nineteenth-century literature it became something of a commonplace to describe the effects and affects of commodity culture as a form of intoxication. Intoxication suggests the unbinding of the senses, of passion and desire unleashed, and it is this that suggests that the very phrase 'organization of passions' itself rests on a contradiction: a passionate self, in the eyes of Victorian probity, is a disorganized self. In as much as nineteenth-century decorum and propriety placed enormous value on the taming of passion and the control of sensuality, any address to sensual passions could well be seen as an invitation to impropriety, thereby disorganizing forms of social regulation. That passions were being disorganized (or unleashed), or that this is what seemed to be happening, is made evident by the intense attention that was aimed at the female shoplifter, by psychiatrists, retailers and the police.

As Michael Miller points out in his study of the Bon Marché, 'what particularly struck this generation of psychiatrists [in the 1870s and 80s] was both the sheer number of kleptomaniacs arrested in department stores and the fact that so few of these were incited to steal elsewhere' (Miller 1981: 201). What shocked the keepers of moral and social propriety was not that shoplifting should happen, but that the practitioners should be relatively wealthy women. Working-class theft was not the same kind of problem as bourgeois theft; it was simpler to explain if not eradicate. Theft by 'respectable' women was problematic, not least because it seemingly could not be explained in terms of material need.

Kleptomania as a diagnosed malady was invented as a partial solution to middle-class and upper-class female shoplifting. If these women were not driven by need or greed (already having a relative excess of wealth), one way of explaining it was to pathologize their actions. Like hysteria, kleptomania was initially seen as biological – linked to the specificity of the female body. Elaine Abelson (1989: 187) describes this explanation in terms of women being 'diseased by their own sexuality'. For the medical fraternity, kleptomania, as a specifically female disorder, was diagnosed as a symptom of 'uterine disease'. Thus it was treated as one of the more spectacular effects of menopause, menstruation, lactation or ovulation (Abelson 1989: 186–7).

The conjuncture of femininity (naturalized as biology), a desire for sensuality and repressed sexuality, soon provided the familiar contours for explanation. That this might also trouble the account of femininity that such an explanation relied on or that it might result in moral blame being levelled at the shop owners does not seem to worry unduly either medicine or retailing. The idea that sexual frustration only needed the trigger of conspicuous consumption for women to loose their grip on social decorum puts in play more disruptive elements. One is the phenomenal power of commodity culture, the other, the presumed energies of female sexuality that might be unleashed once social decorum was fractured. Dr Legrand du Saulle, who coined the term 'department store thefts' in 1883, claimed that:

> Women of all sorts, drawn to these elegant surroundings by instincts native to their sex, fascinated by so many rash provocations, dazzled by the abundance of trinkets and lace, find themselves overtaken by a sudden, unpremeditated, almost savage impulse.
>
> (Legrand du Saulle quoted in Miller 1981: 202)

This conflation of 'savage' energies, female sexuality and lack of control is the same conflation that we saw in the previous chapter in the work of Gustave LeBon. Seen from the perspective of the female shoplifter, this is not the simple surrendering to an instinct kept in check by social decorum, rather it seems to respond to a need and a promise. On the one hand the promise of sensual luxury, and on the other a need for bodily desires left unsatisfied by the conditions of bourgeois marriage:

> When I grab some silk, then I am just as if I were drunk. I tremble, although not from fear because the sordidness of what I have just done does not occur to me at all; I only think of one thing: to go into a corner where I can rustle it at my ease, which gives me voluptuous sensations even stronger than those I feel with the father of my children.
>
> (Quoted in Miller 1981: 204)

Here, though, the example is of a working-class woman, the eroticism articulated by kleptomania is focused on a singular item, silk. Gaëtan Gatian de Clérambault, a psychiatrist employed by the Paris police, made a number of studies of women shoplifters who stole silk from department stores. The case studies repeated a central motif: the women stole the crisp new silk, masturbated with the silk and then threw the cloth away (Doy 2002: 107–11). Such cases give the impression of department stores as, potentially, the stage for female sexual frenzy, of unbound passions.

The second explanation, which was less well received, was the idea that it was the shops themselves that were to blame for the moral lassitude engendered. The extreme class-bias shown in cases of shoplifting worked on the assumption that middle-class female shoplifting can't be based on something as tawdry as greed. Indeed, as Miller goes on to describe, the logic of bourgeois women's shoplifting resulted in a recognition of the powerful force of commodity culture: 'If kleptomaniacs committed so many thefts in department stores, then it was not only because they were predisposed to steal but because the department stores created the conditions for them to do so' (Miller 1981: 202). In some ways this argument was not altogether distinct from the argument that suggested that these wealthy women shoplifters were ill: both rested on a notion of women as vulnerable to passion. What both explanations fail to suggest is that women might be neither lost to the lure of the commodity nor prisoner to the 'savage' impulses of their sex, but instead purposefully engaged in a dialogue with the commodified femininity being circulated by the department store.

If window displays could entice, they could also incite, and such incitement wasn't necessarily erotic or surreptitious. The incitement could be exuberantly political, locked in critical dialogue with the insistent gendering of commodity culture. This, at any rate, might be one reading of an event that took place in London in 1912. On 1 March 1912 the Women's Social and Political Union (the militant voice of the suffragette movement) smashed nearly 400 shop windows in London's West End. For Mr Lasenby Liberty (owner of the department store Liberty's) the attack was incomprehensible, the women were smashing 'the very shrines at which they worship' (Liberty quoted in Rappaport 2000: 215). That the passionate intensities offered by the shop displays could be perceived as a prison of femininity, while at the same time affording new pleasures to women consumers, points to the contradictory power of commercial culture.

In Alfred Döblin's novel of 1929 *Berlin Alexanderplatz*, a desire to smash the shop windows of luxury shops and department stores introduces us to the antihero of the novel. When Franz Biberkopf is first released from Tegel Prison and finds himself once more in the centre of Berlin, he first sees the 'hundreds of polished window-panes' that front the expensive department stores of the Friedrichstrasse. For Biberkopf they are an invitation to violence: 'let 'em blaze away', he says, 'are they going to make you afraid or something, why you can smash 'em up, can't you, what's the matter with 'em, they're polished clean, that's all' (Döblin [1929] 1996: 5). For Biberkopf the display windows evoke a world of sexual and material allure that insistently mocks his sexual and material shortcomings. These displays promoting the latest fashions are, for Biberkopf, a simulation of a world hollowed out: 'wax figures stood in the show-windows, in suits, overcoats, with skirts, with shoes and stockings. Outside everything was moving, but – back of it – there was nothing' (Döblin [1929] 1996: 5).

Berlin Alexanderplatz was written during the Weimar Republic at a time of excessive commercialization in urban Germany. At the time Döblin was writing, the first international congress of window dressers was held in Leipzig (1928) and the Alliance of German Window Dressers was formed (1925). In 1930 there were 6000 window dressers in Germany (Ward 2001: 201). As Janet Ward shows in *Weimar Surfaces*, the shop windows and shop architecture of Berlin and elsewhere was being thought of as a technology of persuasion. Shop fronts were designed to sweep you into their embrace: 'the store window, in particular, as the primary mise-en-scène of the designs and desires of Weimar consumerism, was host to the daily (and especially nightly) acts of seduction that occurred on the city street' (Ward 2001: 197). Against what was a concerted play of sexual and economic seduction, the idea that such shops also seemed to invite violent and criminal responses is hardly surprising.

Perhaps the ultimate representation of the attraction and distraction of the commodity in urban culture is not to be found in novels or theories of capitalism, but in a shop window display. In 1932, instead of using the display techniques of window dressing to emphasize the magic and wonder of specific commodities, a Berlin department store simply displayed the frenzied desire for consumption (Ward 2001: 217–18). This window staged a tableau where all that the viewer sees are the backs of female mannequins dressed in street clothes (coats, hats and so on) clambering over each other in an attempt to get to the goods. With the mannequins pushing, struggling, tugging and falling over each other, this was a humorous yet violent staging of consumer desire coded as 'woman'. With hardly a glimpse of any of the actual items for sale in the shop, the mannequins seem to become one single clamourous body whose energies are directed unblinkingly towards consumption.

Refashioning and Reshaping the City

The new domains of shopping that emerged in the second half of the nineteenth century and continue into the present can be seen to indicate a general spectacularization of the urban; they are symptoms of commercial impulses governing the city. The innovations and invitations of consumer culture are vividly apparent in the vast range of advertising forms, from posters to posed mannequins, and in the lavish array of shopping environments. What is more surreptitious and requires another telling is the way that emergent consumer culture rearranges the social space of the city. The spatial refashioning that is accomplished by modern commercial culture is part of much larger shifts brought about by modernity. Such shifts in social space, as we will see in the next chapter, are particularly devastating when recognized as the consequences of colonialism and neocolonialism. For now it is the refashioning of the public and private realms that is the focus. We would do well, though, not to think of these terms as either stable or fixed to specific attitudes, practices and spaces, but instead to think of them as changing and changeable, contested and defended. As such, boundaries between what counts as public space and private space are not systematically dismantled and rearranged, rather they are confused and blurred. Social space, in uneven and specific ways, becomes porous.

Richard Sennett, in his book *The Fall of Public Man*, surveys the shift in ideas of public space and provides a quick snapshot of the revolutionary innovations of the department store:

the store was based on three novel ideas. The markup on each item would be small, but the volume of goods sold large. The prices of goods would be fixed, and plainly marked. Anyone could enter his shop and browse around, without feeling an obligation to buy.

(Sennett 1986: 141).

The consequences of such innovations are crucial for Sennett and they signal a transformation in characteristic forms of public behaviour and public life. For Sennett the marketplace or the bazaar was (and still is in many places) premised on an involvement in the process of exchange, informally instituted in the rituals of haggling over the price of goods. As Sennett puts it 'haggling and its attendant rituals are the most ordinary instances of everyday theatre in a city' (142). If, for Sennett, the public space of the marketplace is theatrical, this is, to a large extent, done away with in the department store, because 'dramaturgy takes time'. A commercial culture based on 'low markup, high volume', that is, on speeding up the flow of goods and profits, 'had therefore to do away with such theatrical behavior' (142). In the period that sees the emergence of the department store, then, something is changing about the very nature of public life, its rhythms and its forms of sociability.

This isn't the replacement of the public by the private but a sort of emptying of the public, an obliteration of its traditional characteristics, which are to be replaced by a thinner and more instrumental sociality. In another way, however, private and public were increasingly blurred by the gendered associations that these terms had in the social imaginary. If public and private have their synecdoches in the corresponding images of the street and the home, then they also had their gendered representatives who inhabited such space. Women 'belonged' in the private, while the public sphere 'belonged' to men. As a generation of feminist cultural historians have shown, this certainly didn't mean a kind of symmetrical distribution of social space or indeed that actual women simply kept to the private and weren't present in public. Rather it suggests the kind of structural mindset that could make women's presence in public seem at odds with the existing spatial order. Of course 'respectable' women did enter the public realm, and while attempts to curtail their freedom took various forms (chaperones to prevent gentlewomen from experiencing monadic mobility), women's circumscribed freedoms included charitable work that allowed (limited) access to a number of urban spaces not under the propriety of bourgeois respectability.

The terms 'public' and 'private' interrelate on at least three levels. On one level public/private articulate a sense of social access and inclusion: it is public space that parades its inclusiveness; it is the private where the principle is exclusion. On another level public/private have tended to designate a phenomenology of space: public space has tended towards exterior, outside space, while private space has connotations of bounded, enclosed space. While there are too many exceptions to see such spatial differences as rule-governed (private parks, public buildings), it is the connotative sense that matters most. It is this connotative aspect that links these terms to a psychology of space – private as psychological interiority, and public as exhibition and performance of exterior persona. Thirdly, public and private signify protocols of behaviour: what is appropriate behaviour in private might not be deemed so in a public space, and vice versa. The ground for the interrelation of these three levels is history, and it is in history where the peculiar grafting of meanings has been achieved.

The instability of the terms 'public' and 'private' haunts the history of the modern city. We can see this today when entering a shopping mall; the mall appears to be a convincingly public realm, yet shopping malls are invariably privately owned and often policed by private security firms. The mere semblance of publicness becomes glaringly apparent when we notice the way that homeless men and women are refused access to such spaces. On a more phenomenological level, to walk around a shopping mall is to find oneself in an outdoors that is also an indoor environment. We may walk along the 'streets' of shop windows, surrounded by palm trees and piped music, warm within a temperate climate, while outside it is raining and grey. Outside, once more, in the cold and rain, giant hoardings picturing sunbathing couples, intimate interiors and romantic 'private' moments continually puncture the urban environment, forcing the 'private' into the public sphere. The refashioning of public and private space is a much-debated topic and has consequences for a range of social and cultural issues. Any porosity between private and public, then, has to take into consideration the changing nature of what counts as private and public in the first place.

The idea that the open streets of cities were unfit for the gentlewomen of the nineteenth century, for instance, suggests that private and public is not simply a category of place, but is linked to other categories as well, such that to be both a woman and to be public was fraught with problems. Elizabeth Wilson argues that the moral anxiety that accompanied prostitution was so prevalent that the merging of 'woman' with 'prostitute' almost became inevitable; 'Prostitutes and prostitution recur continually in the discussion of urban life, until it almost seems as though to be a woman – an individual, not part of a family or kin group – in the city, is to become a prostitute – a public woman' (Wilson 1991: 8). In France such a connection was reinforced through the vernacular term for a prostitute, *femme publique*, in Britain by the term 'streetwalker'.

Feminist approaches to the city are invaluable for supplying a critical scepticism that interrupts the gendered associations of 'public' and 'private' spaces as they are reconfigured by the emergence of the arcade, the department store and the mall. The very asymmetry of the couplings (private/public, home/street, feminine/masculine) and the instability of the way they are grafted together (private/home/feminine) suggest that it is only by grounded historical inquiry that such connections will become visible. Feminist scholarship also seems to suggest that rather than discarding the kinds of insights supplied by Benjamin (and his literary host Baudelaire), a sceptical pursuit of their analogies, a pursuit that always has to imagine that women's experience often falls outside the realm of available representations, will be the most productive route. Thus feminism, as an approach to cultural history, is an act of critical reading, unpicking the seams of patriarchy, so to speak. But it also strives to recover and rescue women's experience from the condescension of patriarchal history.

The two tasks that run concurrently for feminist cultural historians, then, are the deconstruction of patriarchal culture and the reconstruction of its missing ingredients. Of course this coupling is itself problematic: recon-struction in any exhaustive sense may well be impossible due to the exten-siveness of patriarchal representation. Mica Nava (1996: 38), for instance, says that she began her study of department stores 'to argue against those theorists who defined modernity of the late nineteenth and early twentieth centuries as a public stage from which women were excluded'. But, in conducting her study, it shifted to become a 'genealogy of absence', a study of the way women's modernity had been disavowed in the histories of modernity (including those by some feminist historians). What Nava finds is that in placing women in the foreground of modernity, another history of modernity becomes possible, one much more ambiguous and fragile than the one provided by the major/male poets and theorists of the modern. For Nava this modernity is to be found in the new spaces where women were allowed to roam (department stores, libraries, galleries, teashops, hotels and so on); it was to be found in the work that connected women to urban space (charity work, shop work, clerical work and so on). Nava also suggests that the suffragette movement, rather than seeming to be a threat to commercial culture, was perceived as an opportunity:

> In England, as in the United States, the high point of the department store coincided with the peak years of suffragette militancy. The owners of the department stores were well aware of the importance of the move-ment and several manufactured, displayed and supplied a wide range of goods – from tea services to outer garments – in purple, white and green, the symbolic colours of the struggle. They perceived their inno-vations in retailing as part of the same modernising process as women's emancipation and saw no conflict of interest between women's growing independence and the economic success of the stores.
>
> (Nava 1996: 55)

One particular North American store, Wanamaker's, actually gave women time off during suffrage parades (56).

Seeing modernity in this light usefully feminizes modernity itself and makes some of the interpretations of emerging urban forms interestingly unsettled. For instance, one of the most distinctive forerunners to the department store and the shopping mall were the arcades of the early nine-teenth century. These spaces turned outdoor public space into something like a semi-domestic interior. Walter Benjamin took the arcades to be part of a crucial prehistory to urban modernity, offering both a taste of the future and a reminder of its renegaded promises. From 1928 till his death in 1940, Benjamin collected material relating to the emergence of Paris as the 'capital of the nineteenth century' for a project he called the *Passagenwerk* or *Passagenarbeit*. Quoting from an early nineteenth-century guidebook, the *Illustrated Guide to Paris*, Walter Benjamin writes:

> These arcades, a recent invention of industrial luxury, are glass-roofed, marble-paneled corridors extending through whole blocks of buildings, whose owners have joined together for such enterprises. Lining both sides of these corridors, which get their light from above, are the most elegant shops, so that the *passage* [arcade] is a city, a world in miniature.
>
> (Benjamin [1935] 1999: 3)

A product of the new glass and iron technology, arcades were built in cities across Europe, the United States and Australia (Plate 3.2). Although many of these have since been destroyed, the arcades in metropolitan centres like Brussels, Paris and Milan still provide a major focus for commercial activity (for full international listings see Geist 1983). Built throughout the nineteenth century, 'the arcades were a cross between a street and an *intérieur*' (Benjamin [1938] 1983: 37).

Benjamin sees these new social spaces as home to a particular form of masculine sauntering (*flânerie*):

> The street becomes a dwelling for the *flâneur*; he is as much at home among the façades of houses as a citizen is in his four walls. To him the shiny, enamelled signs of businesses are at least as good a wall ornament as an oil painting to a bourgeois in his salon. The walls are the desk against which he presses his notebooks; news-stands are his libraries and the terraces of cafés are the balconies from which he looks down on his household after his work is done.
>
> (Benjamin [1938] 1983: 37)

The analogy of street to home is, as we should expect, riven with gendered associations. If the domestic sphere was discursively nominated as female and the street as male, the transformation of the street into an *intérieur* should suggest a general feminization of the urban, even if it is only at the symbolic level. However, the distribution of difference between home and street, private and public, masculine and feminine is not symmetrical, and here the particularity of feeling 'at home' in the arcade suggests the masculine mastery of urban space. Indeed the arcades, a cornucopia of luxury commodities, were a place where women had an uncertain status.

For instance, Burlington Arcade in London, an early arcade built in 1818, was a space where women were often proprietors, consumers and commodities simultaneously. Jane Rendell's research on the Burlington Arcade has shown that the women using the arcade in the early nineteenth century fell into various categories; shop workers, shop owners, shoppers

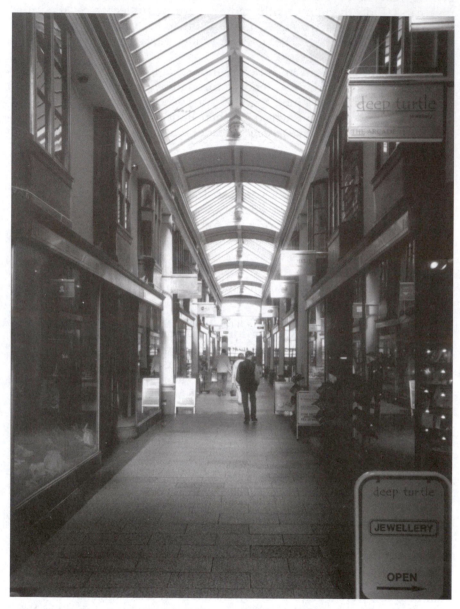

Plate 3.2 The Lower Arcade, Bristol, built 1824–25; architects James and Thomas Foster (photograph by the author)

and high-class prostitutes (working-class prostitutes were barred from entering the arcade) (Rendell 1996). Using the feminist philosopher Luce Irigaray to reconceive Marxist political economy, Rendell (1996: 224) suggests that 'women are the commodities in patriarchal exchange'. In the light of this, the dedication of arcades to commodity culture might inevitably impact on women's status within the space. It is the prostitute who most vividly fills the role of commodity, but because women are identified as commodities (wives, mothers and daughters as well as prostitutes), all women are potentially in danger of being mistaken for prostitutes within patriarchy. 'By far the most pervasive gendered representation is, and was, the prostitute, a figure with whom all women who occupied the arcade were conflated' (Rendell 1996: 227). But she also warns us that 'our knowledge of female experience is obscured historically through the construction of gendered systems of representation' (225).

The role of women in relation to commodity culture is filled with ambiguity, a circumscribed freedom, enhancing the exoticness of commercial space. Yet exoticness was also the role that the commodity had to play, and in many department stores the commodity was linked materially to imperial trade routes, the circulation of exoticness as a commodity. While most department stores in Britain had dedicated 'oriental' departments, specific shops emerged with the sole intention of being purveyors of exoticness. Liberty's in London specialized in Turkish embroidery, Indian silks and pyjamas, Persian bronzes, Japanese vases, Arab smoking rooms and so on. It advertised itself as 'importers from India, China and Japan' (Adburgham 1975: 35) and flourished alongside the cognoscenti's enthusiasm for Moorish culture or Japanese style. Shops, like Liberty's, decked their interiors in an opulent overabundance of carpets and silks, decorative objects and furniture. For the cultural historian Rosalind Williams, this was a crucial aspect of the commodity spectacle:

> The décor represents an attempt to express visions of distant places in concrete terms. It is a style which may without due flippancy be called the chaotic-exotic. But within one exhibit not chaos but repetition is often employed to numb the spectator even further.
>
> (Williams 1982: 69)

But Liberty's points to other forms of circulation as well. In 1878, with a staff of just 12 people, it is interesting to note that this included a Japanese salesman, Haro Kerossake. Urban modernity, especially in imperial, cosmopolitan centres like London, was fuelled by and helped to fuel global networks of imperial consumption. It points to an urban reality that by the second half of the nineteenth century was insistently multicultural. As Jonathan Schneer writes in his book *London 1900: The Imperial Metropolis*:

The empire, formal and informal, likewise contributed to the capital's cosmopolitan character. From Asia came Indians, Malaysians, Chinese, and Japanese. Like the Irish and the Jews they tended to live and work in the rookeries and slums, the ghetto which took up a good portion of East London. Twenty thousand 'Malay and Lascar' dockers and sailors passed through this part of the city annually, many making it their home base. Along the Limehouse Causeway and adjoining streets there was a small Chinatown. Scattered throughout the poorer sections of the imperial metropolis there was also a sprinkling of African and West Indian immigrants.

(Schneer 1999: 8)

Colonial and imperialist ambitions refashion the city in a variety of ways, not least through the migrant traffic of people, the global circulation of bodies. As we will see in the next chapter, the spatial distribution of cultural and ethnic enclaves is a vivid indication of the structural inequality of colonial urbanism.

Entering a department store often meant leaving the drab, workaday world to encounter the fantastic realm of the commodity. At times this meant being cast into a geographically distinct world. To enter a department store could mean not simply stepping off the relatively public space of the street to enter another, more insistently commodified space, it could also mean stepping into another culture. But this 'other culture' is also pervasive in the imperial capital itself, in the population who labour and the circulation of imperial commodities. In this sense colonialism is not something that takes place (literally) 'over there' (in Africa, say), it is also something that fashions out space within Western metropolitan centres ('back here' or 'over there', depending on where you are situated).

Residual Rhythms

To be seduced by the spectacularity of such wondrous sights as the exterior and interior of the Bon Marché, Macy's, Selfridge's or Liberty's is hardly surprising, but it shouldn't be allowed to eclipse the thoroughly heterogeneous practices of urban modernity. The potential of rhythmanalysis lies in its ability to attend to multiple rhythms and polyphonic orchestrations. The department store, as we have seen, simultaneously encouraged the rapid circulation of bodies and goods, as well as arresting the attention, movement and passions of consumers. It was an element that encouraged an uneven global circulation of 'exotic' commodities and migrant citizens. Yet a rhythmanalysis of urban modernity needs to extend attention beyond the glamour of *emerging* and *dominating* cultural forms to take account of the tenacious persistence of more established practices (the corner shop as well as internet shopping, so to speak). To attend to the range of what Raymond Williams (1977: 121–7) called 'the dominant, residual, and emergent' aspects of culture provides an insistently polyrhythmic perspective on the city.

It is true that modern shopping and its associated forms of publicity quickly succeeded in creating or colonizing the most visited and fashionable areas of the modern city. Urban planning went to considerable lengths to further the desirability and thereby the class exclusivity of particular shopping areas. Written into the planning of Regent Street, for instance, were rules forbidding the use of the street for any practices that were not in keeping with the exclusively gentrified demeanour of the street (Hobhouse 1975: 33). Yet, as mentioned in Chapter Two, fashionable streets invariably seemed to feed into notoriously impoverished areas. A form of gentrification, linking city planning with the interests of high street shops, worked to evict impoverished citizens and their practices from proximity to the newly emerging 'cathedrals of consumption'. Church Lane in London, for instance, a street consisting of low-rent housing, second-hand furniture shops and the like, which connected to the prestigious Oxford Street, was demolished in 1877 (Plate 3.3). Commentators at the time were in no doubt as to which forces were exerted in bringing about its demise:

> Church Lane stood condemned as an unwholesome, over-crowded thoroughfare, and the houses on either side are now almost entirely destroyed, and the inhabitants have been compelled to migrate to other more distant and less convenient parts of the metropolis. This lane was certainly one of the worst streets in the neighbourhood, but it stood in disagreeable proximity to New Oxford Street, and the tax-payers of that important thoroughfare had to be conciliated.
>
> (Thomson and Smith [1877] 1994: 128)

A growing spectacle of consumption, while not obliterating the slower recycling practices of selling second-hand furniture, was striving to put such practices and their rhythmicity at a distance, ousting them from their closeness to the intoxicating circulation of more commodified goods.

The emergence of department stores necessarily meant that blocks of shops were devoured to make room for the new retail leviathans. Within a few years of setting up shop in Oxford Street in 1902, Bourne and Hollingsworth had expanded into a department store and had swallowed up a vast array of neighbourhood shops. It is worth listing what had to be removed to make way for this *one* department store:

> 1 pub; a brothel; 1 dairy; 1 private residence; a branch of Finch's; a wholesale lace merchant; a barber; a nest of Polish tailors; a coffee house; a sweet shop; a carpet layer; Doan's Backache Pills; a costume manufacturer; a cigarette factory (Savory's); a wholesale milliner; a wholesale blouse maker (Frances); a retail milliner; a wine-merchant's cellar; a music publisher; a soda water manufacturer; a musical instrument shop

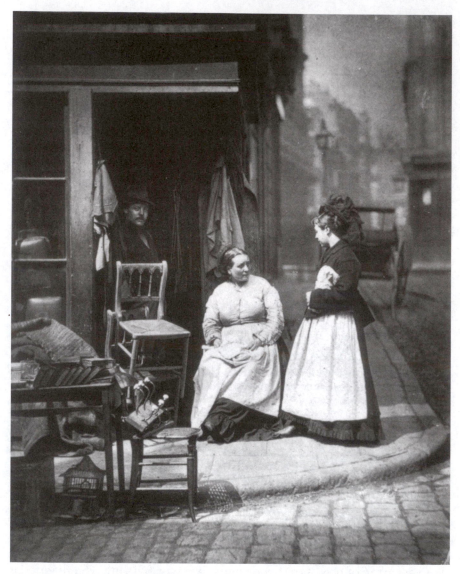

Plate 3.3 Second-hand furniture shop, Church Lane 1877 (just prior to demolition), John Thomson

(German); a jeweller; a baby linen manufacturer; a palmist; a wallpaper merchant; a beauty parlour; an estate agent; British headquarters, New Columbia Gramophone Co.; 2 solicitors; 1 chapel.

(Hollingsworth cited in Adburgham 1979: 169–70)

It is also worth noting that Bourne and Hollingsworth wasn't the only department store in Oxford Street at this point, nor was it the biggest. If the diversity of the shops and manufacturers listed above gave way to large-scale business interests, this doesn't mean that these smaller and seemingly idiosyncratic businesses simply disappeared. What it meant was that a form of spatial zoning resulted that pushed smaller concerns further from the metropolitan centre. It also suggests that various immigrant communities (the Polish tailors represented in a racist image as congregating in a nest) were being pushed out of prime commercial sites.

There is, of course, a range of cultural and spatial effects that result from the emergence of the department store and other forms of industrialized shopping. On the one hand, main street or high street shopping takes on a much more homogeneous flavour. This tendency continues into the present, where shopping malls and retail parks provide habitat for only the most dominant brands. Yet this is clearly not the only form of exchange practised in cities. Once off the high street or out of the mall and the streets manifest something of the heterogeneity that existed prior to Bourne and Hollingsworth. Wallpaper merchants and soda water manufacturers might be few and far between but the range of independent beauty parlours, 'alternative' therapy shops, second-hand clothes stores, delis and so on are constantly evident. One point to note, then, is the spatial specificity of different forms of exchange. The other point to note is the tenacity of seemingly outmoded practices of circulation.

Perhaps surprisingly, at the very moment that department stores were consolidating their new dominions and their financial dominance, other forms of circulation (forms that could hardly be conceived of as modern) actually increased in number. As James Winter (1993: 109) notes: 'the proportion of street traders to central city population increased by something like 25 percent between 1851 and 1911, despite the rapid development of large-scale retailing operations in the last quarter of the century' (Plate 3.4). Any account of modern shopping that doesn't also register the persistence and growth in such smaller scale and more impromptu forms of circulation is only going to show one side of the urban rhythmicity of commodity exchange (see Highmore 2002). Costermongers (street sellers) and mudlarks (collectors of useable trash from the mud of tidal rivers) might be relegated to the past, but the car-boot sale and the internet marketplace are very much in the present. The second-hand furniture shop might not be a stone's throw from the Fifth Avenue shops, but it hasn't disappeared either – it has relocated. The impromptu street stalls set up by the homeless on the pavements of cities around the world is the underside of department store life. It provides a glimpse of an economics that tries to cater to the needs of those whose access to resources is actively and savagely restricted.

Today's modern cities, like their predecessors, are characterized by plural rhythms and a range of circulatory patterns. Shopping malls are

Plate 3.4 The cheap fish of St Giles (London's costermongers), 1877, John Thomson

now often perched on the edge of cities, attached by the umbilical cords of arterial roads and motorways and accompanied by large-scale parking. But the local urban neighbourhood is often characterized as much by second-hand shops and small retailers as by supermarkets. Writing about the modernization of Paris by Baron Haussmann, T. J. Clark insists that 'Haussmann's modernity had been built by evicting the working class of Paris from the centre of the city, and putting it down on the hill of Belleville or the plains of La Villette, where the moon was still most often the only street light available' (Clark 1984: 23). Modernization is, as you might expect, uneven, but it is actively uneven, it works to expel, to distance, as much as it works to choreograph the movements of those it interpolates. Clark's words emphasize the unevenness of technological resources and the divergent spatiality and access to their benefits and limits. Modernity, if it is going to remain a meaningful approach to contemporary urban culture, will need to include these more residual cultures, these more socially hidden spaces, alongside the glamour and clamour of the new.

The coexistence of two distinct spatialities, however, is not always hidden. At times the juxtaposition of cultural space and the emphatic vividness of uneven development is insisted upon by urban planners and civic managers. The colonial city is often structured on the insistence of cultural contrast. In the next chapter I am going to look at the city of Algiers. But rather than start with the colonial conquest of the city, I want to begin on the eve of decolonization in the 1950s. The point of starting here is to remind us that the critical investigation of urbanism is not something that emerges in the corridors of academia – the critical work of decolonizing the city is carried out in the street and at the cost of many thousands of lives.

Chapter Four
Colonial Spacing – Control and Conflict in the Colonial and Neocolonial City

---

> In the mountains our work is always easier
>   (unidentified French general – from *The Battle of Algiers*)

The Battle of Algiers

The Italian director Gillo Pontecorvo's 1966 film *The Battle of Algiers* was filmed in the Algerian city of Algiers (al-Jaza'ir) in the years immediately following Algerian independence – 5 July 1962. An Algerian-Italian co-production (the Casbah film company in Algiers and Igor Films in Rome), the film centres on an intense period of fighting in Algiers, a time when the Algerian National Liberation Front (the FLN – *Front de Libération Nationale*) were involved in a bloody war with the French paratroopers who had been sent into Algeria to supplement the occupying army and gendarmerie (Plate 4.1). The film is structured around the torture of an FLN member in 1957, who, brutalized into submission by the paras, gives up the FLN leaders hiding in the Casbah. Djafar, alias Saari Kader (played by Saadi Yacef, who actually was the FLN leader represented by Djafar/Kader), and others are arrested; Ali la Pointe, an FLN lieutenant and subsequent hero of the liberation war, is killed by the paras. The FLN is effectively silenced in Algiers, and the general strike that they organized has been crushed. Thus the film centres on a moment of defeat, a liberation guerrilla organization overcome by the superior strength of a national army. As one of the arrested FLN leaders puts it when questioned about the 'cowardliness' of using guerrilla tactics: 'of course, if we had your airplanes it would be a lot easier for us' (Solinas 1973: 122). Larbi Ben M'Hidi, the FLN leader being questioned, was later found dead in prison – 'suicided'. The film's epilogue, though, is of the almost spontaneous overflow of Algerians, out

70

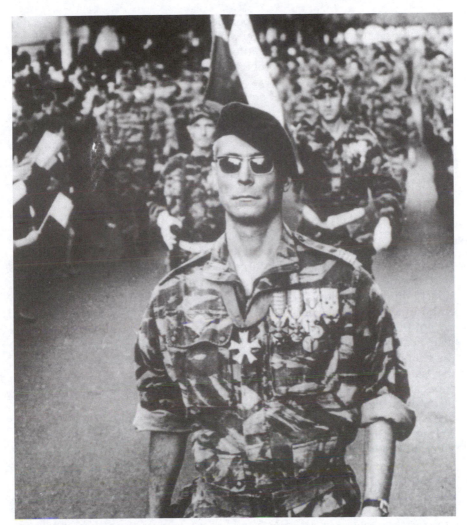

Plate 4.1 French colonial paratroopers arrive in Algiers led by Colonel Mathieu: scene from *The Battle of Algiers*

of the Casbah and into the European quarters in 1960, and the eventual liberation in 1962.

Filmed with only one professional actor (Jean Martin playing the para Colonel Mathieu), it included members of the FLN, farmers, tourists and others amongst the cast. The film was the result of a collective and political act of remembering by the newly liberated Algerians involved in the film. Pontecorvo was invited to direct the film as a left-wing film maker who would be sympathetic to the FLN's fight, and he and the writer Franco

Solinas spent a year interviewing people involved in the struggle. Yet the film is by no means a hagiography of FLN leaders; it follows in exacting detail the actual events of the battle (see, for instance, Horne 1977) and details the bombing by FLN members of civilian Europeans as they congregate in cafés and milk bars.

Pontecorvo has claimed that he 'wanted the audience to identify with a *choral* protagonist – with the hope, the pain, the joy of an entire people' (Pontecorvo interviewed in Solinas 1973: 166–7). The point of concentrating on the defeat of the 'Battle of Algiers', from a production that is committed to the cause of decolonization, is paradoxically to reinforce the historical inevitability of the liberation movement: 'the movement will keep on, nothing will be able to stop it, no matter what blows the organization which originally propelled it may receive' (Pontecorvo in Solinas 1973: 165–6). But while the Algerian people are the collective protagonists of the film (figured most insistently in the various crowd scenes), it is the physical *mise en scène* of the film, the city of Algiers, that articulates and supplies the rhythmic orchestration of the film. Continually moving between the Casbah (the Algerian enclave of the city) and the European quarters, the film highlights a colonial city that is a physical, social and architectural embodiment of French-Algerian colonialism. Indeed, the spatial articulation of the film is one of its most significant features and foregrounds the historical and geographical inevitability of the liberation struggle. Many of the shots are filmed on the steps of the Casbah, near or at the point where the Casbah feeds into the European quarters of the city. Many of these shots are of angry and desolated Algerian crowds amassing ready to burst through the spatial apartheid of the city.

To move from the nineteenth-century European focus of the previous chapters to the Algerian liberation in the mid-twentieth century may seem like a jarring jump-cut. Yet this leap into North Africa (to the Maghreb, the land of the sunset) and the turbulent period of decolonization that marks the period after the Second World War neither leaves the nineteenth century behind nor manages to escape Europe. Algiers is a city shaped and divided by a colonial urbanism that impacted on the city throughout most of the nineteenth and twentieth centuries. Algiers, in the period of the film (mainly 1954–57), and from 1871 to 1962, was a North African city that was administratively a *département* of France (this colonial policy was designated as 'attachment'). This chapter is about the historical density of some of the scenes from the film, and will require us to spill out, historically, from the events of 1956/7 into the past and the future. We need history, the history of colonial urbanism, to begin to register the spatiality of the film and figure the continual neocolonial articulation of urban space.

There are two scenes that I want to pay particular attention to in this chapter. One of them (chronologically first in the film) is a scene where three Muslim women, members of the FLN, are seen removing their veils, dyeing and cutting their hair and dressing themselves in European clothing. The scenes immediately prior to this 'unveiling' depicted the bombing of the Casbah by French Algerians (*pied noirs*), and the removal of the dead from the rubble of the ruined houses (Plate 4.2). The women are going to avenge the dead by placing bombs in the European city. They need to pass as European so that they can pass the heavily policed checkpoints that are scrutinizing all Muslims. Their disguise as European is what allows them mobility in an embattled city. As they are preparing their costumes, the music that is heard on the soundtrack is a *baba saleem*, an Arabic music form with an insistent percussive beat that sounds like a synchronized, collective, racing heartbeat.

The second scene is almost an inversion of the first: instead of a tiny number of Algerian women 'passing' as European, leaving the Casbah to move into the European quarters, the scene is of a vast undisguised army of paratroopers collecting on the borders of the Casbah, ready to invade it. The script sets the scene as one of uncanny stillness that then explodes in a systematic and total invasion:

Plate 4.2 The bombed Casbah: scene from *The Battle of Algiers*

To the south, the mountains and the Casbah, situated halfway along the
coast. The Casbah, still, inert, expectant, on this first day of the strike [the
general strike organized by the FLN] . . .
The paratroopers are already at their places, one after another, at equal
distances like links of a very long chain, strung through every alley,
spreading to every sidestreet, twisting through the squares, climbing up
the stairways, dividing, rejoining, and lengthening again. The silence is
perfect; the camouflaged immobile forms seem to be part of the landscape.
Then a brief and sharp hiss, a hundred whistles together.
A signal releases the still forms: the attack begins.

                                                    (Solinas 1973: 101–2)

As soon as the whistle has been sounded, the music begins. In contrast to
the breathless urgency of the *baba saleem*, there is a staccato military beat of
snare drums. Against the ad hoc tactics of the determined but melancholic
Algerian women, there is the orchestrated efficiency of the paras.

These scenes together, and others throughout the film, concentrate our
attention on the border zones. These zones, because they are contact and
conflict zones, suggest how different elements of the city are rhythmed by
the force of colonial urbanism. The improvised and guerrilla methods of
the FLN women as they negotiate the military checkpoints at the entrances
and exits of the Casbah are set against the paras' collective and highly regi-
mented invasion of the Casbah. The restless urgency of the *baba saleem*
contrasts with the military efficiency of the marching music. The collectiv-
ity of the Casbah is revealed as a social network rhythmed by the mutual
needs and support of its inhabitants: the mass of paras is rhythmed by the
machinic regimentation of the occupying force. The dissonance produced
by these conflicting rhythms, as we move across the border zones at the
perimeter of the Casbah, is the dissonance of an urban colonialism that is
nearing the point of collapse.

Spatial Politics and Colonial Urbanism

Reading Franco Solinas's screenplay for *The Battle of Algiers*, it is clear that
one of the key elements to the film was juxtaposing the expressive differences between the Casbah and the European quarters of the city. An early
scene that elliptically returns us to the start of the liberation war, the
moment when the FLN asks Algerians to unite in the struggle for national
independence (1954), is made up of a montage of 'Views of the Casbah' and
'Views of the European City'. The screenplay itemizes the Casbah as
'compressed humanity, swarming in the alleyways, on the steps, in the
cafes, in the Arab baths, in the mosques, and in the markets; a tangle of
voices, gestures, faces, veiled women, eyes' (Solinas 1973: 9). 'The
European city', on the other hand, was 'reinforced concrete, asphalt, steel,

lights, shop windows, buildings, automobiles. A steady rhythm of efficiency, music, cordiality, an apéritif' (9). It is this juxtaposition of difference that is not simply key to the film but key to figuring the complexity of colonial spatial politics as it impacted on the urban fabric and practices of Algiers. We need to pay attention to the visual and aural register of the film to get some sense of the differences that might be involved, but we also need to work historically to see what happened in the colonial period that produced this unbridgeable and stark contrast in the urban form.

As the screenplay suggests, rhythms are going to be important here. The 'steady rhythm of efficiency' of the European city, contrasted with the 'swarming' and 'tangle' of the Casbah, does, in many ways, echo the language of colonial urbanism. This isn't to claim that the film makers were caught in a web of colonial ideology, rather, it is to recognize how colonial tropes – steadiness and efficiency versus disordered tangles and 'swarming' and 'compressed humanity' – had become concretized in the city itself. To take just the simple fact of housing density: in the mid-1950s European housing in Algiers consisted of a density of 1.2 people per room, whereas for Algerians it was almost triple the density at 3.4 people per room (Çelik 1997: 111). We would also need to include the 'unofficial' housing in the shantytowns (*bidonvilles*) that had been accumulating on the outskirts of Algiers since the 1920s and on the edges of the Casbah in the 1950s, which resulted in a situation where over 40 per cent 'of the native population lived in squatter settlements' (Çelik 1997: 110). 'Swarming' and 'compression' had an actuality.

The orchestration of these varied urban conditions, their conflicting rhythms and the dissonances they generate, is articulated by a politics of rhythm that seems to establish certain spaces of the city as crucial zones, where rhythmic dissonances are at their most intense. Robert Stam, writing about the film, describes the historical inevitability of the Casbah's revolutionary role in the following terms:

> The choreographed surging movements of the demonstrators, for example, are edited almost musically to give the impression of growing strength. The subliminal metaphor of convergent streams organizes the editing. At one point a tributary effect is created, as we are shown the point of intersection of two Casbah streets. The demonstrators arrive first on the right. Then the camera pans left to show the demonstrators arriving on the left. Then the two groups join arms and rush toward the camera, giving the spectator a feeling of swelling relentless force. . . . Throughout *The Battle of Algiers* one feels this revolutionary pressure. Even the checkpoints become a kind of microcosm of the colonial situation. The people approach the checkpoints, the number of people builds up, they get impatient, and one has the sense that colonial repression cannot hold them back forever.
>
> (Stam 1975: 20–1)

Whether the river metaphor is actually present in the film to the degree
that Stam seems to suggest is perhaps beside the point, although it has
certainly become the way that Pontecorvo has understood his reason for
concentrating on a moment of defeat (see Pontecorvo's interview in
Solinas 1973: 165). Stam, however, does usefully alert us to the importance
of two borderland spaces that are hugely significant in the film: the French
military checkpoints and the steps and streets leading out of (and, of
course, into) the Casbah. These borderlands between the Casbah and the
European city require historicizing so that the revolutionary transformation of Algiers (the 'explosion' of Algiers) isn't seen simply as the result of
a few insurgents, but as a consequence of how groups of colonized people
respond to the whole social and urban process of a particular brand of
colonialism.

   This urban process begins with the initial colonial occupation by France
in 1830 (the eventual conquest of the Algerian interior didn't occur until
1845). The fact that Algeria has a history of colonization prior to French
occupation shouldn't distract us from the specificity of this European occupation. To begin with, French occupation asserted itself within Algiers as a
military force, and the urban planners responsible were military engineers.
The most significant moment of this initial colonial urbanism was the
constitution of the Place d'Armes in the 1830s, which was soon renamed
the Place du Gouvernement. The establishment of this vast square,
designed specifically for the massing of troops, involved the demolition of
the al-Sayyida Mosque, as well as a number of houses and shops (Çelik
1997: 26–8). It also signals the beginning of an urban practice that refashioned the areas around the Casbah into wide, straight, French-style boulevards. Thus, much of Algiers was savagely reconfigured by the imposition
of broad and easily policed streets. As Zeynep Çelik puts it: 'the boulevards
encircled the casbah and signified the surrender of the original residents of
Algiers to the French – literally and metaphorically' (Çelik 1997: 37). Such
urbanism is at once militaristic and technological, monumental and
economically driven – the boulevards were, as in Paris, a showcase for the
more expensive shops, the buildings were a monument to (colonial) state
authority and the streets were an efficient corridor for the movement of
goods, workers and troops. As well as imposing an urban form on Algiers,
colonial urbanism also deposes and destroys the urban forms that signal
the culture of the colonized, which in this case was the demolition of the
mosque, the destruction of Algerian shops and the general sense of remaking Algerian space as French space.

   Alongside this practice of demolition and construction is a practice of
isolation that is simultaneously cultural and physical. What distinguishes
colonial urbanism from the sort of technological modernizing impulse that
was practised in Paris at the same time was the separation of the European
city from the 'Arab' or 'Islamic' one. The isolation of the Casbah operated
as a sign of controlled exoticism and a reminder of imperial achievement.

The spectacular juxtaposition of 'two cities' performed an aesthetic and social comparison that was evidently meant to work in favour of the culture of the colonizers: on one side was imperial order, on the other side 'native' disorder. (British colonialism effected an analogous spatial 'apartheid' in Delhi in the 1920s, where it established a separate but adjoining 'administrative city' designated as New Delhi – see King 1976; Evenson 1989: 145–56.) A crucial tool in establishing these differences, and thereby supplying an alibi for colonial rule, was the newly emerging tourist industry. Consider this, for instance, from a tourist guidebook of 1908: 'the Casbah whose houses are jammed one on top of another guides one's gaze toward the European city with its marvellous gardens, open, vast boulevards, full of animation, and its stylish apartments' (cited in DeRoo 1998: 156). The presumed chaos of the Casbah ends up supplying nothing more (and nothing less) than a vivid contrast to the 'marvel' that is the French city.

Rebecca DeRoo suggests that the production of Algiers as two cities was a structuring principal of the postcard industry, which was a significant component in remaking Algiers as a destination for European tourists. The postcards, along with tourist guidebooks, portray the boulevards of the French quarter as an achievement of a civilizing mission and the Casbah as merely the expression of indigenous charm (Plates 4.3 and 4.4). For example, in the view of the French quarter in Plate 4.3, emphasis

Plate 4.3 Postcard: Alger, Le Rampes et les Quais (author's collection)

Plate 4.4 Postcard: Alger, Rue de Tombouctou (author's collection)

is placed on the engineering feat of the boulevards and ramps: the view is positioned so that we not only see the scale and stretch of the boulevard, but also the layers of colonnades that seem to hold the road in place. On the other hand, the scene of the Casbah in Plate 4.4 concentrates on the 'exotic' inhabitants, refusing us a view that could take in the architectural achievement of the site. Of the hundreds of different postcards produced for tourist consumption in Algiers, the vast majority are of urban views: 'city views of French administration, commercial centres, and leisure activities [that] reinforce a comfortable separation between the civilized metropole and the indigenous population' (DeRoo 1998: 147). These postcard views include both images of the Casbah and the European sections of the city, the difference being that while the images of the European quarters include the occasional Muslim, the images of the Casbah are totally free of Europeans. A sizeable proportion of the postcards produced in the early twentieth century were of 'types' – a spurious ethnological imagery of different Algerian practices and occupations. Needless to say, these were entirely made up of indigenous Arabs and Berbers.

Postcards of Algiers and Algerians were produced in France and sold in Algiers; their postal destination was invariably to be sent back to France. Malek Alloula, in *The Colonial Harem*, his study of the postcards depicting the phantasm of the harem, notes the restless movement involved in the colonial tourist postcard:

[The postcard] straddles two spaces: the one it represents and the one it will reach. It marks out the peregrinations of the tourist, the successive postings of the soldier, the territorial spread of the colonist. It sublimates the spirit of the stopover and the sense of place; it is an act of unrelenting aggression against sedentariness.

(Alloula 1986: 4)

As far as this goes, the colonial mission of dehistoricizing colonized people, making them seem timeless and outside the processes of modernization, also works to absent them from the *urban* process. In comparison to the presumed global mobility and modernizing mission of the European colonizer, the Algerians and the Casbah are represented as static and timeless.

To recognize that this image of the Casbah was ideological and used for supplying an inverse image of Europe is merely to recognize how colonialism works via material practices that were both physical and imaginary at one and the same time. What needs stressing, however, is the ambiguity that was the result of this process of urbanism. If colonial urbanism worked to render the Casbah as an isolated, exotic site that was outside modernity, then in the end it was the very isolation of the Casbah that made it such an effective centre for resistance during the war of liberation, even to the point where the FLN referred to it as the 'autonomous zone'. Çelik, for instance, notes how the lack of any state care of the Casbah meant that impromptu community action became the only source for the maintenance of the buildings. Thus the 'private' world of the Casbah turned into a space where: 'the residents of the Casbah, the heights of al-Jaza'ir left untouched by the colonizers, spoke back by turning in upon themselves, consolidating their unity, tightening and redefining their own mechanisms of maintenance and control over the public and private spaces of their neighborhoods' (Çelik 2000: 164).

The moment in *The Battle of Algiers* when the French paras invade the

Casbah has to be seen in relation to these urban processes. It is precisely because the Casbah has become a force of sustained and substantial resistance that it takes such a massive force to try to suppress it. Yet this substantiation of the Casbah as resistance is precisely an effect of colonial urbanism and its process of isolation. The architectural properties of the Casbah (which we detail in the next section) became properties that could accommodate: 'a whole series of secret passages leading from one house to another, bomb factories, caches and virtually undiscoverable hiding-places concealed behind false walls' (Horne 1977: 184). Thus the initial properties of the Casbah could be adapted to ends unimagined by the original builders. Colonial urbanism produced the Casbah as a 'private sphere', a process fully in keeping with the exclusion of the vast majority of Algerians from the public sphere. The Algerians responded by turning the Casbah into a 'counter public sphere' or an 'oppositional public sphere' (see Kluge 1981 for the use of these terms) – a place for the emergence of an Algerian public. The film ends as that public emerges to claim Algiers.

Passing

This ending to *The Battle of Algiers* is the 'spontaneous' (that is, not directed by the FLN) resurgence of Algerian resistance to colonial occupation in 1960. After a day of demonstrations parading makeshift Algerian flags and battling with the tanks and militia of the occupying force, the demonstrators return to the Casbah. This is the moment when, for Pontecorvo and others, the historical mission of the people of Algeria is recognized: they can no longer do anything except take their independence. As night falls and the streets are cleared, we hear the voice of a journalist claiming: 'now calm has returned, although from the Casbah continue to be heard those cries . . . incoherent, rhythmic, nightmarish cries' (Solinas 1973: 158). The journalist is referring to the trilling calls (*ju-ju*) of Algerian women that have been a tenacious presence throughout the film.

Colonial representation has consistently perceived the Casbah as female, or more precisely as a veiled Moorish woman. Writing in a tourist guide in 1906, one Pierre Batail could describe the entirety of the Casbah as if it were a veiled woman: 'the Casbah . . . still has the same mysterious atmosphere. It still resembles the Moorish women whose veils only allow their eyes to be seen. There are still the same low doors that never open' (cited in DeRoo 1998: 147). One can only wonder what the reference to low doors refers to in this context. The colonial imagination perceived and depicted the Casbah as full of mystery, and that mystery was fundamentally female and sexualized.

It is worth pausing for a moment to take a note of how the Casbah was indigenously gendered before pursuing the colonial imagination in these matters. Our guide is, again, Zeynep Çelik:

Regardless of the family's income or size of the building, the houses of the Casbah closed themselves to the street and turned onto a courtyard surrounded by elaborate arcades. The geographic and topographic conditions of Algiers added another element to the houses of the Casbah: rooftop terraces. In contrast to the interiorized courtyards and relatively contrived rooms of the houses, the terraces opened up to neighbors, to the city, to the sea – to the world. The concern for privacy, so dominant in defining the street facades, disintegrated at roof level. It was this alternative realm that the women of Algiers claimed for them-selves – as a place of work, socialization, and recreation; indeed, a much more pleasant place than the restricted streets below. The Casbah thus became divided into two realms: on top, occupying the expanse of the entire city, were the women; at the bottom were the narrow streets belonging to the men.

(Çelik 1996: 130)

Indeed the 'dense configuration of the casbah made it possible to pass from one terrace to the other and visit other homes without having to use the street' (Çelik 1997: 19). The spatiality of the Casbah is an articulation of Muslim culture and designates specific spaces (the most internal rooms of the house, the courtyard and rooftops) as female. This, as we will see, is not inscribed as immutable law but as an expression of cultural practice: it reflects a gendered division, a division which can simultaneously be inter-preted and practised as providing a relatively autonomous arena for Muslim women, or as a practice of isolation and control. Neither Muslim culture nor the practices of Muslim women are static entities, rather, it is how they change, and what they change in relation to, that is crucial here.

The colonial imagination assumed two approaches towards Algerian women: on the one hand it rendered them as a uniform, undifferentiated mass; on the other it exercised an obsessive desire to unveil them. The first of these is well described in Assia Djebar's words as the 'anonymity of exoticism' (Djebar [1980] 1999: 135), an anonymity produced because the exclusive interest for the colonial subject is in Algerian women's visible differences *from* European (non-Muslim) women. In this all that is seen is the uniformity of the *haïk* (the white cloth that veils Muslim women's bodies) rather than the modifications and variations of design that consti-tute the wearing of the *haïk*, which would have been evident to other resi-dents of the Casbah (both female and male) (see Macey 2000: 403–9). The 'unveiling' of Algerian women by colonial tourism is well documented in Malek Alloula's study of postcards, *The Colonial Harem*, where he analyses the 'erotic-ethnographic' picturing of 'Moorish women' in various states of undress. For Alloula the endless picturing of unveiled Muslim women (and Islam is a culture that prohibits the figural depiction of the human body) 'is an immense *compensatory undertaking*, an imaginary revenge upon what had been inaccessible until then: the world of Algerian women'

(Alloula 1986: 122). We should read this in two ways. Firstly as a reminder of the aggression of colonialism as it is exercised on colonized women ('offered up, body and soul, these *algériennes* are the metaphorical equivalent of trophies, of war booty'); secondly, though, it points to an understanding of women's veiling in Algiers (and this was not a practice that was customary outside Algerian urban centres) as a purposeful refusal of the culture of the colonizer, a deliberate opposition to the regime of colonialism.

It is the deliberate and dialogic use of the veil that is described in one of the most important documents of the Algerian war. Frantz Fanon's *A Dying Colonialism* was written and published during the war and when it was published in France in 1959 it was called *L'An cinq de la révolution algérienne* (The fifth year of the Algerian revolution). The French title declares the author's commitment to the cause of the FLN. The first chapter was titled 'Algeria Unveiled', or, as David Macey suggests, offering a more literal translation – 'Algeria Unveils Herself' (Macey 2000: 402), and describes how Algerian women had become part of the revolutionary struggle and, in the process, how ideas about women and femininity were being revolutionized. The theme of how an anti-colonial, socialist revolution has and will challenge and reconfigure family relationships, traditional practices and the private sphere more generally were the themes of his book. In relation to Algerian women and the veil, it raises some problematic issues. Fanon seems at times, for instance, to suggest that the outcome of anti-colonial liberation will be the adoption of European-style ideas about dress and the visibility of women's bodies.

Yet Fanon describes a tactical process that relates the veil to notions of urban mobility within colonial and decolonizing culture. Fanon, for instance, recognizes how both the adoption of European clothing *and* the wearing of the *haïk* could be used for tactical purposes to aid movement through a heavily controlled city and thereby aid the struggle:

> There is thus a historic dynamism of the veil that is very concretely perceptible in the development of colonization in Algeria. In the beginning, the veil was a mechanism of resistance, but its value for the social group remained very strong. The veil was worn because tradition demanded the rigid separation of the sexes, but also because the occupier *was bent on unveiling Algeria*. In the second phase, the mutation occurred in connection with the Revolution and under special circumstances. The veil was abandoned in the course of revolutionary action. What had been used to block the psychological or political offensives of the occupier became a means, an instrument. . . . After the 13th May [1957, when veiled women were dragged into public squares to have their veils forcibly removed], the veil was resumed, but stripped once and for all of its exclusively traditional dimension.
>
> (Fanon [1959] 1980: 41)

Algerian women resist colonialism by asserting a traditional form of dress that makes them unavailable for assimilation and colonialist sexual solicitations. Next, they let go of these traditions as their revolutionary consciousness is awakened. But then, when the colonizers enact a policy of forced unveiling, they reveil themselves. No doubt this is all too neat, and Fanon seems blind to the way that Algerian women's refusal of the veil, both before, during and after the revolutionary war, may have been an explicit critique aimed not simply at colonialism, but also at masculinist interpretations of the Koran. Nonetheless, it usefully begins to highlight the pragmatic and tactical nature of clothing and movement in this struggle.

Like many politically engaged intellectuals at the time, Gillo Pontecorvo and Franco Solinas read Fanon, and explicitly cited Fanon's work as a crucial reference for the making of *The Battle of Algiers* (see for instance Said 2000). Nowhere is the reference to Fanon clearer than in the scene in *The Battle of Algiers* where the three Muslim women refashion themselves so that they can pass as European. This scene is a filmic illustration of Fanon's reading of the historic significance of the veil in relation to the Algerian revolution. Yet the scene can be read on at least two levels. As symbolic material it might be read as a revolutionary unveiling, as Muslim women join the struggle and leave behind certain forms of traditional life. Yet there is a more pragmatic reading of the scene: veils are removed, hair is dyed and cut, simply in order to aid the mobility of the women through a heavily policed checkpoint – a checkpoint that was focused on anyone looking Islamic. In this way the wearing or not of the *haïk* is endlessly tactical. It might aid mobility when it was not being worn, but it could also aid the movement of weapons and bombs when it was being worn (the folds of the *haïk* allow for a loose draping, useful for concealing objects). But even this pragmatic register resonates with symbolism: the sacrifice of cutting hair and adorning themselves with lipstick is seen as costly. This is particularly shown by the use of mirrors, as we watch the women watching themselves cutting their long hair and looking regretfully at themselves in the mirror. The shrugging off of tradition, whether it is symbolic, pragmatic or even the result of an awakening revolutionary consciousness, is not performed lightly. At stake, along with lives and freedom, seems to be the very possibility of maintaining continuity with the past. The future, the revolution, will perhaps always be a step into the unknown.

The scene is close to the actual events of 30 September 1956 when Zohra Drif, Djamila Bouhired and Samia Lakhdari planted bombs in the European quarters of the city. In many ways the film follows the overly neat theorizing of Fanon in this account. What we see are three women who seem to be leaving the narrow enclaves of the Casbah to realize their part in the historical mission of a free Algeria. The FLN leader, played by Saadi Yacef, is seen as all-powerful, bringing the women to consciousness in the face of the previous day's bombing of the Casbah. In reality, Drif and

Lakhdari were part of the Algerian educated elite, both were educated within the French system (which only allowed a small number of Algerians to attend French schools), both had their baccalaureates and were studying law at university in Algiers. The idea of the male FLN leaders bringing these women to political consciousness hardly squares with the actuality of these women's lives. Yet even if the reality of the situation was more complex than the film or Fanon allow for, this scene does offer a condensed image of elements that are at stake in the colonial city. In passing through the checkpoints, the three women reveal the fragile nature of colonial racism – indeed the scene reveals the ontological impossibility of the very category of 'race' as a support for such an ideology. What is it precisely that would allow armies of colonizers to discriminate so systematically against a group of people who were supposedly so different from Europeans, the film seems to ask, when the colonizers can't tell them apart from Europeans and when the Algerian women seem so adept at passing as European (Plate 4.5)?

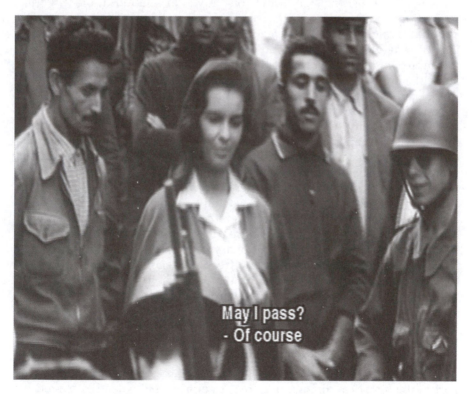

Plate 4.5 FLN operative passing the checkpoint and passing as European: scene from *The Battle of Algiers*

This scene, and the film more generally, reveals the plasticity and unevenness of colonial urban culture. It shows the agility of Algerians in performing various roles in the city, while the paras are shown as not needing such tactical skills. It also reveals the plasticity of the social architecture of the city, especially the Casbah. Rooms and routes in the Casbah that had been reserved for women were renegotiated as practices and roles changed:

> The war of decolonization brought the Casbah to the forefront as a major locus of resistance. In this context, Algerians did not consider the privacy of the family and of women as a sacrosanct issue: resistance fighters were allowed into the houses and onto the rooftops (accessible only through the hearts of houses), facilitating their movements, while other outsiders, including the French forces, were not allowed access. Subsequently, the French forces would blockade the Casbah and occupy not only the streets but also the homes and roof terraces.
>
> (Çelik 1996: 138)

The Casbah, then, is designed for particular uses, which include the separation of male and female space. With its interior courtyards and various navigational possibilities, the Casbah wasn't designed to facilitate a guerrilla campaign, and yet proved to offer a number of tactical possibilities for the FLN. Social architecture, both domestic and public urban space, needs to be seen in relation to social practices that are continually changing and transforming space. For colonial urbanism the isolation of the Casbah was *intended* to provide an alibi for colonialism but ended up producing one of the conditions for colonialism's destruction. Intentionality and design don't lead in any straightforward way to specific effects. Yet the tenacious symbolism of these spaces is not easily obliterated: the gendering of space and its violation continues to be experienced, most extremely when *European male* soldiers violate it.

Michel Foucault provides a useful explanation of how spatiality must be thought about in conjunction with an understanding of social and cultural practices. Using as an example the cooperative factory building designed by the utopian industrialist Jean-Babtiste Godin, Foucault writes:

> The architecture of Godin was clearly intended for the freedom of people. Here was something that manifested the power of ordinary workers to participate in the exercise of their trade. It was a rather important sign and instrument of autonomy for a group of workers. Yet no one could enter or leave the place without being seen by everyone – an aspect of the architecture that could be totally oppressive. But it could only be oppressive if people were prepared to use their own presence in order to watch over others. Let's imagine a community of unlimited sexual practices that might be established there. It would once again

become a place of freedom. I think it is somewhat arbitrary to try to dissociate the effective practice of freedom by people, the practice of social relations, and the spatial distributions in which they find themselves. If they are separated, they become impossible to understand. Each can only be understood through the other.

(Foucault 1984: 246)

Foucault's example takes us to a world distinct from both the colonially planned quarters of Algiers and the Casbah. Yet, his insistence that a description of space that ignores the practices of social relations will be unable to grasp the complex actualization of space at a specific historical moment is important for both these spaces. It shows how urban space is always relatively open to being used in a variety of ways and how its meanings are always, potentially at least, available for contestation. For instance, the isolation of the Casbah could be seen as a policy of colonial aloofness, providing respect for the colonized and so on – this, at any rate, was the way that colonial administrators wanted it to be perceived. To reveal such a practice as part and parcel of a fundamental refusal to grant Algerians civic and civil rights was the outcome of another practice, the practice of decolonization. In analogous ways the gendered spaces and the gendered practices of the Casbah could be remade in ways that allowed for a variety of actualizations.

Neocolonial Urban Experiences

Colonial and anti-colonial urban experience highlight a problem that has been at the centre of this book from the start; namely, the inextricable convergence of the imagination and hard facticity of urban life. If French occupiers in Algiers lived a life whereby the Casbah was simultaneously disorderly, authentic, mysterious, unsettling, unhygienic and exotic, this imaginary realm cannot be disentangled from *their* physical experience of the Casbah or the colonial urbanism that was practised on the Casbah and in relation to the Casbah. The inhabitants of the Casbah operated in ways that were constantly and simultaneously both symbolic and practical. Such operations are always a convergence – symbolic activities always constitute a physical presence just as physical activities offer symbolic (or potentially symbolic) resonances. The use of varying dress codes by female FLN activists, for instance, is simultaneously practical (an aid to mobility, a way of concealing weapons) and symbolic (depicting Europe or Islam and the connotations that accompany them).

Henri Lefebvre usefully describes the simultaneity of this double register when he talks about the lived aspect of space as 'representational space'. For Lefebvre the separation of 'experience' and 'representation' are clearly not sensible distinctions. Yet he will claim that 'representations of space', for example those representations instantiated by urban planners, architects and the like, rarely correspond with the experience of space. Lefebvre understands social practice (living) as a representational activity, but refuses to treat representation as a 'second-order activity' (they are rarely the representation of something *else*). Representation is the name he gives to an activity that we have been describing as the simultaneity of symbolic and practical activity – it is perhaps another word to describe the thickness of culture that is always practical and symbolic. For Lefebvre one of the crucial distinctions to be made is between the activities of those who have the social power to generate space ('representations of space') and those, with more limited resources, who are faced with living in already constructed spaces ('representational space' or 'spaces of representation'). Representation is a social practice that is dynamic and contested and constitutes a struggle over and within space.

We can get a sense of how Lefebvre understands this when he designates 'representational spaces' as: 'space as directly *lived* through its associated images and symbols, and hence the space of "inhabitants" and "users" ' (Lefebvre [1974] 1991: 39). At first this may seem to be a contradictory statement – surely to live directly is at odds with living through images and symbols? For Lefebvre, however, there is no such contradiction because experience in any meaningful sense is the experience of life as it is interlaced with symbols and images. What Lefebvre is pointing to, though, is our ability to appropriate space culturally when we are not in the position to control or generate actual physical space. Thus he goes on to describe representational space: 'this is the dominated – and hence passively experienced – space which the imagination seeks to change and appropriate. It overlays physical space, making symbolic use of its objects', it is spatial experience that is 'linked to the clandestine or underground side of life' (Lefebvre [1974] 1991: 39 and 33). Here, in the context of the history of the Casbah, we may want to suggest that such use of space doesn't remain in the realm of the imagination and that symbolic use is always and at the same time practical, physical use. We might also want to note that the 'passivity' of this experience (and by passivity Lefebvre seems to mean simply not being able to generate space actively) can, and often does, lead to an active engagement with the physical conditions of space.

The significance of Lefebvre's understanding of space, which according to Edward Soja is characterized by an insistence 'that each mode of thinking about space, each "field" of human spatiality – the physical, the mental, the social – be seen as simultaneously real and imagined, concrete and abstract, material and metaphorical' (Soja 1996: 64–5), is crucial for our understanding of colonial urbanism. But it is also significant for our understanding of the experience of space *after* decolonization. More pertinently, perhaps, we might want to say that decolonization is an incomplete project. Not only do we need to be wary of assuming that the overthrow of one colonial rule will simply bring about liberatory urban space (and the

history of Algeria since 1962 should emphatically encourage such wari-
ness), we also need to register the wider spatial implications of colonialism
that we are still living through. The experience of Algerians living in France
might give us an insight into something of the 'representational spaces' of
neocolonialism.

This is the 'Algerian' writer Zimba Kerdjou describing her childhood in
Alès, in the south of France:

> The town where I live, Alès, is a nice, quiet place. I've always lived there.
> My earliest childhood years were spent amidst enormous tower blocks
> which, at the time, children living in other apartment blocks called
> Chicago, as if this was a more suitable name than 'Les Cévennes'.
> Although the district was less poor than Le Chaâba [an Arabic name
> designating an Algerian shanty town on the outskirts of Lyons], as
> described by Azouz Begag, during the 1970s it, too, was a little piece of
> Algeria in the heart of France . . . For this reason, outsiders have never
> been able to describe the reality of everyday life in my district.
>   (Kerdjou cited in Hargreaves 1995: 90)

Kerdjou is describing an urban district in southern France where poor
housing complexes, inhabited by families who have migrated (sometimes
several generations previously), are described in relation to a variety of
spaces (various places in France, Chicago, Algeria). One important thing to
note though is that this place is not 'like' Algeria; more complexly and
more experientially, it was 'a little piece of Algeria', existing in France. In
physical terms it is clear that we are not dealing with a space that was in
Algeria, nor are we dealing with a space that was somehow analogous to
Algeria. It *was* Algeria, in the sense that cultural practices could constitute
it as such.

Neocolonial space operates in surprisingly similar ways to colonial
space, in that it is animated by juxtapositions of unevenly valued cultures
that are 'spatially contiguous but culturally disparate' (Hargreaves 1995:
91). To move between the Casbah and the French quarters of Algiers in the
years prior to decolonization was to move across cultural worlds even
though the physical space traversed might only be a few metres. In a more
general culture of neocolonialism, people who are perceived as 'immigrants' experience such dissonances continually. Zimba Kerdjou, for
instance, describes her school life within the French education system:

> Even at primary school, most of us were of Algerian origin, and our
> absence when Muslim festivals took place was a way of asserting our
> Arab culture. The distinction between Algerian and Arab meant nothing
> to us. Algeria was basically a piece of countryside to which each family
> returned during the summer holidays, but it was also a kind of ideal land.
>   (Kerdjou cited in Hargreaves 1995: 90)

Migration within neocolonial spatiality is not a singular act; it is performed daily (and yearly) as children 'migrate' from home to school and back again. As Alec Hargreaves suggests, 'though school and home were only a few hundred metres apart, in journeying between them each child migrated daily between profoundly different cultural universes' (Hargreaves 1995: 91).

There are a number of points to be made here about neocolonial urban space. Firstly, that the symbolic, imaginary appropriation of space needs to be thought of as a cultural practice that is simultaneously physical and imaginary. Kerdjou, for instance, is writing about the physical practice of upholding the Muslim calendar within a culture (and in this France is not dissimilar to Britain) that seems unable to recognize either the value of 'other' cultures or the continuity of its colonial inheritance. Recently a law was passed in France banning the wearing of Islamic headscarves, the *hijab*, as well as other 'ostentatious' religious dress in schools. At present, though, it seems that only Muslim girls are being excluded from French schools. We need to think of these spaces as neocolonial rather than simply multicultural because of the conditions within which these cultural contacts occur. It is not that one child is experiencing more cultural diversity than another, but that the experience is of cultural diversity that is unequally valued in both symbolic and physical ways. Alongside the racism that might accompany the cultural practices of following the Islam religion, we need to think about the cultural and economic discriminations that impact on cultural space. Algerians migrating to what, before 1962, was meant to be just another part of France, ended up living in the worst housing conditions in France. Indeed, one common experience of migration was the feeling of having swapped poverty in Algeria for poverty in France, while simultaneously suffering a deep nostalgia for home. One of the largest *bidonvilles* in either France or Algeria was an Algerian 'squatter' camp in the Nanterre suburb of Paris (Plate 4.6). This is where the writer Brahim Benaïcha grew up, having left Algeria at the age of eight in 1960. Benaïcha describes how he used to pretend that he lived in a block of flats and how his attempts at close friendships with his classmates always floundered when it came to visits to friends' homes:

> They were nice to me, and some of them invited me home. I always found a pretext for refusing the invitation. It wasn't that I didn't want to go home with them, but because sooner or later I would have to return the hospitality – and there could be no question of my taking them back to the shanty-town. I knew what they thought about places like that.
>
> (Benaïcha cited in Hargreaves 1995: 96)

Representational space is necessarily limited because it can't overcome the larger spatial practices of neocolonial urbanism (without, that is, a successful revolutionary campaign). Nonetheless, Benaïcha remembers

Plate 4.6 *Bidonville* in Nanterre, near Paris, in 1973, Marc Garanger, SAIF, 2004

another side to his French *bidonville* childhood: 'what has it given us during
the last ten years? It has enabled us to preserve our language, our religion,
our identity. It has enabled us to remain ourselves amid all the tempestu-
ous clashes of civilisations through which we have been' (Benaïcha cited in
Hargreaves 1995: 95). The *bidonvilles* in Algiers during the years of the war
for independence were the most visible sign of the inequality of housing
practices. They can and should be seen as an exercise of colonial spatial
exclusion, but at the same time they became a space for crucial information
exchange, fortifying and unifying the opposition movement:

> in the summer of 1956, refugees from the burned and bombed villages
> of Mitija (at the foot of the Atlas mountains) and Kabylia flocked to the
> Mahieddine settlement, the most extensive *bidonvilles* of Algiers. Their
> stories mixed with those of the urban resistance, complementing each
> other and unifying the struggle.
>
> (Çelik 1997: 211)

In the next chapter I want to explore the cultural unevenness of the city within North American detective novels. It might seem to be a long way away from the world of *The Battle of Algiers* and the real-world struggles of colonialism, decolonization and neocolonialism. In other ways, however, the kind of emphatic yet surreptitious cultural divisions that are articulated by spatial practices of isolation and the production of community will continue to be the focus. In particular the theme of movement and mobility and, perhaps more crucially, the limits that are placed on movement will allow us to access the very different neocolonial urban space of North America.

Chapter Five
Urban Noir – Mobility and Movement in Detective Fiction

Gumshoe Culture

In his acerbic essay 'The Simple Art of Murder', the crime novelist Raymond Chandler set out to draw distinctions between the then dominant English variety of detective fiction, often set in rambling country houses and featuring unflappably logical detectives, and the characteristically hard-boiled urban version of crime fiction that was emerging in North America. Chandler is, of course, a novelist of the hard-boiled school. He assesses the plot in a novel by the English author Agatha Christie as 'guaranteed to knock the keenest mind for a loop. Only a halfwit could guess it' (Chandler 1950: 325). 'The English', writes Chandler, 'may not always be the best writers in the world, but they are incomparably the best dull writers' (326). For Chandler it is the North American novelist Dashiell Hammett who reanimated the detective genre because he 'took murder out of the Venetian vase and dropped it into the alley' (330). Chandler's criticism of English detective fiction is motivated by a diagnosis of the genre as feminized – the focus on Christie and vases, for instance, is deliberately chosen (see Light 1991 for an extensive discussion of Christie as a conservative modernist who dialogically responds to the overmasculinzed culture of post First World War England). Chandler's remedy to feminization was Hammett's prose.

Hammett, who in the 1910s and 20s worked as an operative for the Pinkerton National Detective Agency (Frisby 2001), set his novels in an urban world of violence, street-speak, tough machismo and fatally attractive women and sinister, shadowy corruption. Both Hammett and Chandler describe the city in, to use Dennis Porter's phrase, an 'anti-picturesque' manner (Porter 1990: 86–7); a description of urban landscape that, instead of revealing aesthetically uplifting visual scenes, concentrates on the seedy dereliction and destitution of the city. For Chandler, though, such fiction requires redemption: 'down these mean streets a man must go who is not himself mean, who is neither tarnished nor afraid' (Chandler 1950: 333). The detective, for Chandler, must have a moral anchor, an incorruptible core. Alongside this, the hard-boiled detective deploys a fierce vernacular; he 'talks as the man of his age talks, that is, with rude wit, a lively sense of the grotesque, a disgust for sham, and a contempt for pettiness' (330).

Chandler's celebration of the realist drive in urban detective fiction has fared well, and hard-boiled detective literature provides one of the most robust genres for attending to the complexity of the contemporary city. His injunction that crime writers should create detectives with unswerving moral rectitude, however, has fared less well. So too has his implicit insistence that detectives are necessarily men. The aesthetics and ethics of the hard-boiled detective genre, its vivid anti-picturesque figuring of the city and the moral ambiguity of the detective will provide the background scenery for the investigation that follows. But I have a more specific aim in mind in dedicating this chapter to detective fiction. Here I want to use detective fiction as an optic for refracting themes around mobility, movement and access within the city. After all, the classic hard-boiled detective is a 'gumshoe', stealthily and silently (gumshoes are rubber-soled overshoes) trailing suspects through the city streets. The ability to move, often unnoticed, through the city, the knack of reading the streets and interiors of the city, these are the skills that mark the classic detective of urban *noir*. But what happens to these private investigators, these street readers, when their mobility is impaired, when they don't easily or invisibly occupy and roam the city? In what follows I want to concentrate on the detectives who Chandler couldn't or didn't imagine.

The three novelists that I'm using inhabit the genre of crime fiction, but in doing so they inflect its conventions in particular ways. The mobility of the classic gumshoe was premised on an ability to appear as 'universal man' (déclassé and generally unmarked in appearance). This mobility coincided with the fact that public space, and the private space of the privileged, was accessible to a rugged-jawed, white-skinned, suit-wearing man in ways that it wasn't to non-whites and women. This means that Sara Paretsky's detective fiction, for instance, featuring the female private investigator V. I. Warshawski, will necessarily articulate a different mobility within the city. It should register something of the socially differentiated access and movement within urban space. So too should Walter Mosley's novels about African-American protagonist Easy Rawlins, who, working via an informal trade in 'favours', solves, but rarely resolves, crime in Los Angeles. The third series of novels features the quadriplegic criminalist Lincoln Rhyme. Bedridden in the first novel, then wheelchair-bound after that, his limited physical mobility is enhanced and extended by a number of technical devices and his extensive forensic knowledge of the city. Rhyme investigates the gruesome world of serial killers, and he does this partly through a cipher figure: a beautiful and arthritic female investigator.

These various investigators, though, are not of course simply representative of women, African-Americans or those with limited mobility. Rather, within the constraints of the generic conventions and in the particularity of the inflections that these novels necessarily perform, *something* of the social and cultural differences of urban mobility can be registered.

Writers, especially writers of genre fiction, are also readers. Their knowledge of the conventions of a genre is evident in their reading and rereading of the classic monuments of the genre. Genre fiction is mimicry and difference. We find the recognizable in a worldscape peopled with wise-cracking, tough-talking investigators and opaque and sneaky suspects. But we also discover distinction in the peculiar traits of the detective that make them different from previous protagonists. It is in this process of rereading through writing that we gain access to a subtle differentiation that registers distinct social and cultural differences. Michel de Certeau's evocative description of reading is useful here. He offers a number of analogies for the process of reading, and while he has in mind readers who *don't* find an outlet for their reading in actual writing, his suggestive descriptions can be productively extended to include genre fiction writing. Readers, de Certeau suggests, are like people who rent a furnished apartment: 'renters make comparable changes in an apartment they furnish with their acts and memories', as do pedestrians 'in the streets they will fill with the forests of their desires and goals' (de Certeau 1984: xxi). De Certeau is alerting us to the way that people inflect their 'second-hand worlds' to accommodate something of their particular needs and desires, how they subtly alter the culture that they have to 'make do with' and how they secrete meanings into activities that seemingly have no place for them.

Genre fiction registers a process of adjustment as authors variously inhabit a second-hand literary world and make it accommodate different articulations of the city. As Tony Bennett suggests:

> The point of locating Conan-Doyle's Sherlock Holmes stories and Chandler's Philip Marlowe novels in the detective fiction genre is thus not to identify a fundamental commonality between them to be accounted for in terms of similarities in their underlying social conditions. Rather, it is to pinpoint those aspects in which they most manifestly differ – their differing representations of the city, for example – as the most pertinent focal points for social and historical inquiry.
>
> (Bennett 1990: 101)

For Bennett it is the historical differences within the 'family resemblance' of genre that point to changes in urban experience and alterations in the conceptualization of the city. For this chapter, though, it will be the simultaneous variety of articulations of the hard-boiled crime story that will act as a barometer for registering a range of experiences and attitudes towards the city that are marked by social difference. But before we can look at the particularity of these various inflections, these subtle inhabitations, we need to put in place the worldscape of the classic hard-boiled detective.

Hard-boiled Detectives in the City of Night

Crime novels are tours of the city, but they are tours that take you off the tourist map, which is one of the reasons why Walter Benjamin claimed Poe's 'The Man of the Crowd' (discussed in Chapter Two) as 'something like the X-ray picture of a detective story' (Benjamin [1938] 1983: 48). Location is the sine qua non of detective fiction; poorly lit alleyways, offices at night, derelict buildings set in overgrown wastelands, expensive houses and hotels. The detective has to navigate across a city animated by social distinctions and divided by social antagonisms. Detective fiction, in its hard-boiled state, is peculiarly adept at registering a city cast in shadows, peopled by secretive and complexly motivated forces. 'Shadowing' is, of course, the favoured metaphor for what is often the bread and butter work of the private detective (both actual and imaginary). In his study of the Pinkerton Detective Agency (founded in Chicago in 1850 and now part of the international Securitas company), David Frisby shows how information gathering was structured around two roles: the 'shadow' and the 'roper'. Shadows watched and followed people: ropers gathered information by gaining the confidence of unwitting informants (roping them in). Both roles, although very different, rely on a specific kind of invisibility:

> The shadow should not be visible to the shadowed, but the task is to create vision. The 'shadow' is not visible but is preoccupied with the visible. The eye is capable of surveying unobserved, which is a constituent element of surveillance. The 'roper' collects knowledge and information through social interaction. The acquisition of information and knowledge is secured by direct (but hidden) means. The roper is visible but his or her intention is *hidden* or *invisible*.
>
> (Frisby 2001: 64)

The detective is required to access both space and information and to do so invisibly. It is hardly surprising then that one of the most highly valued attributes for detectives was their ability to *mix* with a wide variety of social types, to not seem out of place within the city's varied social and cultural geography. Mobility and access is premised on being able to blend in with rouges and ruffians, lowlife and high society, moving across social space without drawing attention to yourself. Such chameleon-like ability was not, however, available to all. In a culture where the racial and gendered geography of the city marked out spaces of prohibition and confinement, the ability to roam was itself a mark of distinction. The real-life operatives in the Pinkerton Detective Agency often only excelled in passing themselves off

within a fairly limited range of social classes. Yet their fictionalized counterpart is granted almost unlimited 'freedom to roam'. A key accoutrement
for this ability to navigate across this fragmented and socially divided city
is clothing. Marlowe, as paradigmatic of the hard-boiled investigator,
wears a slightly dishevelled suit (Plate 5.1). This allows him access to a
wide range of social spaces. The suit, crucially, has no equivalent in female
attire, nor is it a costume that can perform to the same effect for his African-
American counterpart. Of course, fictionalized hard-boiled detectives often
don't go unnoticed and much of the action is precisely because they
purposefully refuse to abide by the social propriety of a particular place.
But the very fact that these hard-boiled Caucasian men *can* charm or force
their way into all manner of social spaces attests to a relationship between
mobility and social privilege. For instance, at the start of Chandler's 1940
novel, *Farewell, My Lovely*, Philip Marlowe and Moose Malloy enter a Los
Angeles bar only to be told 'No white folks, brother'; they then force their
way in. In 1940s America it is impossible to imagine a reverse situation –
African-Americans forcing their way into white-only clubs or women
accessing these sites of male drinking.

When Chester Himes wrote his version of the African-American hard-

Plate 5.1 Dick Powell (right) as Philip Marlowe in *Murder, My Sweet*, RKO, 1944

boiled crime novel in 1957, he set the narrative in New York City. In *A Rage in Harlem* (originally titled *For Love of Imabelle*), his first in a cycle of novels featuring the appropriately named cops Coffin Ed Johnson and Grave Digger Jones, the plot is almost entirely confined to the streets of Harlem (Himes [1957] 1985). The spacing of the city is limited, and the freedom of movement enjoyed by Marlowe is severely truncated for the black protagonists. Indeed, in its dizzying denouement, the narrative signals chaos via a frantic drive in a hearse that takes the narrative, momentarily, out of Harlem and downtown into mid-Manhattan, that is, white New York. Any control the black characters can maintain over their destiny is limited to the neighbourhood of Harlem; out of this 'ethnic enclave', they are in danger, out of control.

Allan Pinkerton (founder of the Pinkerton National Detective Agency) had employed the first female Pinkerton operative in 1856, and had the intention of creating a department of female detectives in Philadelphia in 1876 (Frisby 2001: 70). The number of female detectives, however, remained minuscule and attempts to enlarge the number were continually blocked within the company. Moreover, the role assigned to female operatives was heavily demarcated: while men were employed for a variety of operations, women were more specifically accorded the role of roper. The perceived dexterity of the female operative was at a verbal rather than a spatial level. In the fictional world, the first female detective was created in 1861 and although fictional women detectives might well seem to outnumber their real-life equivalents, the female detective's world is one that has often been spatially circumscribed. For instance, in the mid-1930s, at about the time when the male hard-boiled genre was being inaugurated, one of the most persistent worldscapes for the female investigator was the enclosed and closeted world of the all-female college or convent (Munt 1994: 10).

Already we can begin to see that detective fiction (and aspects of the reality of private detection) figures a complex relationship between space and knowledge and that movement itself articulates social and cultural differences. But although the classic hard-boiled detective has been white and male, the hard-boiled narrative doesn't utilize the perspective of an all-seeing, all-knowing universal subject. The characteristic perspective for hard-boiled fiction is first person narration by the detective; a narration that manages only to piece together a series of very partial views, and where the narrator stumbles through an illegible series of events, often being deceived by those around him. Knowledge, even in the midst of privileged mobility, is situated, and while the hard-boiled detective might very well be able to roam, he is, for all that, relatively powerless in the face of the institutional corruption of the powerful and wealthy. First person narration flags the partiality of any particular view of events, mainly because it always has to foreground the very act of viewing. Yet something like a truth always unfurls, and because the hard-boiled detective is able to move across the city and also uncover the corruption that is at the heart of the city, he has been taken to offer some critical purchase on the modern city.

Writing about Raymond Chandler's fiction and his hard-boiled detective Philip Marlowe, Fredric Jameson suggests that, 'as an involuntary explorer of the society, Marlowe visits either those places you don't look at or those you can't look at: the anonymous or the wealthy and secretive' (Jameson 1970: 630). Thus the detective novel, by ranging across diverse sites, makes visible the social and economic unevenness of the city. For Jameson the picaresque mobility of Chandler's novels, their episodic movement across seemingly disconnected social spaces, is not a mere generic characteristic but a response to something fundamental about the modern city: 'The detective's journey is episodic because of the fragmentary, atomistic nature of the society he moves through' (Jameson 1970: 633). The hard-boiled detective is a vehicle for travelling across a city that has lost its coherence, and for Jameson it is significant that Chandler's fiction is based in Los Angeles, the very epitome of incoherent urbanism:

> Los Angeles is already a kind of microcosm and forecast of the country as whole: a new centerless city, in which the various classes have lost touch with each other because each is isolated in his own geographical compartment. . . . Since there is no longer a privileged experience in which the whole of the social superstructure can be grasped, a figure must be invented who can be superimposed on the society as a whole, whose routine and life-pattern serve somehow to tie its separate and isolated parts together.
>
> (Jameson 1970: 629)

On the one hand, then, these separate domains of wealth and poverty are brought into contact with each other; on the other hand, it is precisely the spaces that lie between them that will be the sovereign territory of the hard-boiled private eye. The view from the window, from the waiting car, the scene set in the corridors between offices, in hotel lobbies, these offer the best places and views for revealing truths about modern life.

Jameson notes that Chandler's novels constantly view the world from the perspective of spatial liminality (in-between-ness) and that this view reveals the social shoddiness of a seemingly affluent society:

> The shabby anonymity which is the meeting place between luxurious private lives that stand side by side like closed monads, behind the doors of the private apartments: a dreariness of waiting rooms and public bus stations, of the neglected places of collective living that fill up the interstices between the privileged compartments of collective living.
>
> (Jameson 1970: 626)

This poverty of social space reflects and refracts an aspect of urban life within advancing capitalist society, and this is the depth of its alienation. In these anonymous spaces our collective life is atomistic: in these places we are actively constituted as strangers.

The classic hard-boiled detectives don't offer solutions to overcome such conditions, nor do they provide radical critiques of capitalism. What they do offer is a reading of urban culture that moves across its divisions and catches glimpses of the city 'caught unawares':

> Out of the apartment houses come women who should be young but have faces of stale beer; men with pulled-down hats and quick eyes that look the street over behind the cupped hand that shields the match flame; worn intellectuals with cigarette coughs and no money in the bank; fly cops with granite faces and unwavering eyes; cokies and coke peddlers; people who look like nothing in particular and know it, and once in a while even men that actually go to work. But they come out early, when the wide cracked sidewalks are empty and still have dew on them.
>
> (Chandler [1943] 1977: 60)

For the most part, such descriptions avoid sentimentality and provide a view 'from the side': just when you least expect it you catch a glimpse of an obvious truism – during working hours the streets belong more convincingly to those who don't work. These descriptive insights are the situated maps of the hard-boiled detective. But precisely because they are situated by the particular perceptions of a protagonist, the hard-boiled genre seems to insist on its endless potential to be reimagined, simply by providing a new protagonist to inhabit the narrator's position.

Rawlins' Los Angeles

Walter Mosley's series of hard-boiled novels, featuring the African-American Easy Rawlins, articulate issues of mobility in conjunction with the theme of a racist and racialized city. Published in the 1990s, the series chronicles a period of North American history from the late 1930s into the mid-1960s. This period witnessed the massive migration of African-Americans from the rural south (Mississippi, Alabama, Texas and so on) to the urban centres in the north (Chicago and Washington, for instance) and on the west coast (Los Angeles and San Francisco). As Nicolas Lemann describes it:

> Between 1910 and 1970, six and a half million black Americans moved from the South to the North; five million of them moved after 1940, during the time of the mechanization of cotton farming. In 1970, when

the migration ended, black America was only half Southern, and less than a quarter rural; 'urban' had become a euphemism for 'black.' The black migration was one of the largest and most rapid mass internal movements of people in history – perhaps *the* greatest not caused by the immediate threat of execution or starvation.

(Lemann 1991: 6)

The Easy Rawlins novels are set against this backdrop of mass migration. The first novel that Mosley wrote was *Gone Fishin'*, although it was only published after the success of four other Easy Rawlins novels. The novel introduces us to Easy Rawlins (Ezekiel Porterhouse Rawlins) at the age of 19 and living in the Fifth Ward (an African-American ghetto) in Houston, Texas in the late 1930s. Having grown up on a sharecropper's farm, Rawlins now ekes out a precarious living in Houston. By the end of the book, though, he has moved to Dallas, where he then joins the US army to fight in the Second World War. *Devil in a Blue Dress* (1990) finds Rawlins owning a house in the Watts district of Los Angeles in 1948: bought, we may assume, through the government loans and mortgage arrangements available to ex-servicemen. Like many African-Americans migrating from the south, Rawlins works in the military and civil aviation industry in LA; that is, until he is fired. It is his need to find money for his mortgage repayments that provides the motivation for his first investigative work.

Unlike the private investigators such as Chandler's Philip Marlowe or Dashiell Hammett's Sam Spade, Easy Rawlins is not a professional detective. His investigative work is informal and based on mutually dependent social relationships rather than a money economy. Money, for Rawlins, is the lucky find, the unplanned payoff for the ethically and socially ambiguous work that he gets involved in. The Easy Rawlins novels invoke a world of urban community that continues the social practices originally fabricated in a southern rural culture:

I was in the business of favors. I'd do something for somebody, like find a missing husband or figure out who's been breaking into so-and-so's store, and then maybe they could do me a good turn one day. It was a real country way of doing business. At that time almost everybody in my neighborhood had come from the country around southern Texas and Louisiana.

(Mosley 1995: 196)

Easy Rawlins operates in the areas of Watts and Compton, the predominantly African-American enclaves of Los Angeles. To some extent this is his urban world. Yet in this urban space Rawlins is answerable to the administrative demands of government and police, even if there is a degree of relative autonomy. Mosely's protagonist, Easy Rawlins, is something of a liminal figure, a black man working as an investigator for white clients (often because he has no choice) who use him because they don't have access to the black neighbourhoods of LA. Rawlins navigates LA as an emphatically racialized space, a space where he plays out the social contradictions of his situation. Access and movement are foregrounded in a way that suggests that the geographical mobilities of the city are thoroughly racialized. For instance, one of the demands made on Rawlins comes from people (mainly white, or representative of white power) who, while they might have the authority to move through south central Los Angeles, have little access to the information that African-American culture harbours. So Rawlins will be asked to find out what is going on in black society:

> I knew when he called me mister that the LAPD needed my services again. Every once in a while the law sent over one of their few black representatives to ask me to go into the places where they could never go. I was worth a precinct full of detectives when the cops needed the word in the ghetto.
>
> (Mosley 1995: 428)

The predominantly white police force may be able to enter Watts but they can't enter invisibly and therefore they have no access to the roper's knowledge. Easy Rawlins can access this level of knowledge in Watts, but in other parts of the city his mobility, his freedom to roam, is severely truncated:

> I drove across town to La Brea then straight north to Hollywood. The canyon road was narrow and winding but there was no traffic at all. We hadn't even seen a police car on the ride and that was fine with me, because the police have white slavery on the brain when it comes to colored men and white women.
>
> (Mosley 1995: 82)

Mosley's novels articulate the complexity of urban mobility, but they also problematize the idea of taking mobility simply as a sign of privilege. Any cursory comparison between recreational tourists and sociopolitical refugees will vividly demonstrate the unevenness of different forms of movement as well as implicitly alerting us to the precariousness that, for many, is signalled by the term 'home'. As Tim Cresswell has put it, mobility 'is not inherently implicated in any form of domination or resistance', while at the same time there is 'no mobility outside of power' (Cresswell 2001: 20). The other side of mobility, stasis, is just as much riven with the complexities and contradictions of power. And this is, partly, what Walter Mosely's Easy Rawlins novels present. If the movement of Rawlins demonstrates the difficult mobilities of an African-American man through the various enclaves of Los Angeles, the notion of home is also a central motif.

Home has not been an essential ingredient for the classic hard-boiled crime novel. More recently, though, an idea of home and a feeling for home have become constituent elements in hard-boiled detective fiction by women. For instance, in Sue Grafton's 'alphabet series' (*A is for Alibi, B is for Burglar* and so on), which features the private investigator Kinsey Millhone, home is not simply a base *from which* Millhone conducts her investigations, it is also the site of action and deep emotional investments. The very scale of the apartment, tiny and perched on top of a garage, provides continuity with Millhone's childhood, when, as an orphan, she lived with her aunt in a mobile home. In the bourgeois world of Chief Medical Examiner Dr Kay Scarpetta, in a fiction series by Patricia Cornwell, her large Richmond home figures partly to reveal the precariousness of her achievements. Her home is where she entertains her closest friends, where she reveals her culinary skills. It is fitted with every kind of security device and yet is constantly invaded by psychopathic killers. Home is a precarious achievement for Rawlins too, but for reasons that have a different historical depth. Rawlins' attachment to home, as ownership of private space, is deep and persuasive and couched in passionate language: 'I loved going home. Maybe it was that I was raised on a sharecropper's farm or that I never owned anything until I bought that house, but I loved my little home' (Mosley 1995: 12).

The passion that Rawlins has for his house is not on account of its grandeur or because it relates to childhood memories:

> The house itself was small. Just a living room, a bedroom, and a kitchen. The bathroom didn't even have a shower and the back yard was no larger than a child's rubber pool. But that house meant more to me than any woman I ever knew. I loved her and I was jealous of her and if the bank sent the country marshal to take her from me I might have come at him with a rifle rather than give her up.
>
> (Mosley 1995: 12)

Rawlins' house figures as a sign of fixity, an immobility that signals a different kind of luxury; the luxury of stasis, of not having to keep on moving on. But this stasis is hard work to maintain:

> When I was a poor man, and landless, all I worried about was a place for the night and food to eat; you really didn't need much for that. A friend would always stand me a meal, and there were plenty of women who would let me sleep with them. But when I got that mortgage I found I needed more than just friendship.
>
> (Mosley 1995: 20)

Throughout the novels, mobility and stasis are juxtaposed and infiltrate each other. Rawlins struggles, through the novels, to achieve a material existence that will provide security and fixity for him and his family.

The impossibility that the novels demonstrate is not just the impossibility of free movement through the city for those who are 'racially' marked, but also the contradictions between being African-American and being a middle-class homeowner during this period. The idea of stasis becomes the almost impossible dream of the books. If the books articulate the racially uneven mobility of urban space, they do much to stop any simple equivalence being made between social privilege and excessive mobility. This is achieved because the historical memory of the great migration is never far from sight:

> California was like heaven for the southern Negro. People told stories of how you could eat fruit right off the trees and get enough work to retire one day. The stories were true for the most part but the truth wasn't like the dream. Life was still hard in L. A. and if you worked every day you still found yourself on the bottom.
>
> (Mosley 1995: 25–6)

The novels know that movement isn't only a sign of power; it can be, and has been, a sign of powerlessness. Having to constantly move to find work, living a transient existence, has often been the option of those lowest on the social scale. The luxury of tourism is that home is literally just around the corner (or just a flight away). Mosley's novels recognize the power and importance of house and home, but they also inflect this in racialized ways. The question of stasis (the security of living space, the security of static employment) is a question that Mosley pitches historically: how were African-American's going to live the urban dream of America? In other words, just how were they to become middle class? The impossibility of being able to answer this question affirmatively is given its clearest possible historical statement in the Watts riots of 1965. The fact that in 1992 Watts was once more the scene of riots might well suggest that this question is still a burning issue.

Warshawski's Chicago

Sara Paretsky's V. I. Warshawski series began life over 20 years ago with the publication of *Indemnity Only* (Paretsky [1982] 1993). Warshawski's territory is Chicago and the novels constantly crisscross this unevenly developed city; from the mansions on the gold coast to the impoverished blue-collar housing of south Chicago; from the financial district containing the insurance companies that are her biggest clients, to the newly gentrifying areas where her offices are situated. Warshawski is a private detective, who once trained to be a lawyer, but it is clear she doesn't like being answerable to others or working in bureaucracies. She makes most of her money from doing fairly standard fraud investigation for big insurance clients, but she also does freelance work. The novels are nearly always based on these freelance cases but inevitably what starts out as a missing person's case, for instance, is found to be embroiled in the corruption of the corporate world.

The outcome of many of the stories is the revelation of the systematic and brutal nature of corporate fraud. It is the scale of this fraud set against the vulnerability of those who are the victims of corporate corruption that presents something of the world-view of the novels. The novels expose the corruption and ascertain culpability, but the cost is usually high. In a world of highly systematic corruption, specific individuals are often impotent in their efforts to get redress; Warshawski's endeavours, then, might be read as compensatory in regard to this, offering us an image of a woman who can right corporate wrongs. With a modicum of physical power but little or no institutional power, Warshawski achieves her results through tenacity, guile and foolhardiness.

Throughout the course of the novels something of the recent urban history of Chicago is revealed. By being a low-renter, Warshawski has to find premises that are near enough her main clients (who occupy the downtown financial part of the Loop) but are still cheap enough for her to rent. At the start of the series, Warshawski's office is in a once-opulent but now rundown building in the South Loop. But this building is set for demolition as developers move into the area. By *Hard Time* (1999) she has been priced out of the downtown area and has had to find offices further out of the Loop. She moves into a converted warehouse in a relatively low-rent neighbourhood, with a friend who is a sculptor. Here, though, the same forces that priced her out of the Loop are threatening this area:

> When we moved in, the area was still a grimy no-man's-land between the Latino neighborhood farther west and a slick Yuppie area nearer the lake. At that time bodegas and palm readers vied with music stores for the few retail spaces in what had been an industrial zone. Parking abounded. Even though the Yuppies are starting to move in, building espresso bars and boutiques, we still have plenty of collapsing buildings and drunks. I was against further gentrification – I didn't want to see my rent skyrocket when the current lease expired.
>
> (Paretsky 2002: 49)

Gentrification is the dynamo of urban uneven development and a number of urban geographers have demonstrated the way that it is structurally reliant on processes of systematic neglect (Smith 1996; Zukin 1982, for instance). Rather than seeing gentrification as the solution to urban blight, gentrification needs to be seen as a process that is dependent on neglect and lack of investment. Seen as a process, the gentrification of one area will, *at some point*, correspond to related disinvestments in another area (the cycle is thereby constantly repeatable). As Rosalyn Deutsche puts it, there is a 'concealed relationship between processes such as gentrification and those of abandonment. The decline of neighborhoods, rather than being corrected by gentrification, is in fact its precondition' (Deutsche 1996: 75). But as Paretsky suggests, gentrification is a cultural as well as an economic process: it is boutiques, espresso bars and art studios that are the material signifiers that herald rising property prices. Contradictorily, then, the vanguard of gentrification is often made up of people who are in search of cheap rent (particularly artists) but whose cultural connotations suggest aspiring middle-class values (see Zukin 1982 for an exemplary study of how this worked in lower Manhattan). Warshawski, at least, is aware of her qualified complicity and culpability in this process: 'now the bars and the palm-readers of Humboldt Park are giving way to coffee bars and workout clubs as Generation X-ers move in. I could hardly criticize them: I'd helped start the gentrifying wave' (Paretsky 1999: 45).

While the relatively fixed points of the novels (office and home) are both on the cusp of unaffordable gentrification, the investigations take us across a more varied landscape. In the novel *Toxic Shock* (originally titled *Blood Shot* in the US), Warshawski is drawn back to her childhood neighbourhood of industrial south Chicago. Working, somewhat unwillingly, for a childhood friend, she returns to the streets of her childhood:

> South Chicago itself looked moribund, its life frozen somewhere around the time of World War II. When I drove past the main business area I saw that most of the stores had Spanish names now. Other than that they looked much as they had when I was a little girl. Their grimy concrete walls still framed tawdry window displays of white nylon communion dresses, vinyl shoes, plastic furniture.
>
> (Paretsky [1988] 1990: 34)

The underdevelopment of this area is signalled via the ethnicity of its inhabitants: south Chicago had always been poor but the whole area is now facing dereliction as its thriving industrial base closed down. Warshawski's memory of the East European enclaves, the working conditions within the locality, and the industrial landscape of her childhood is thus a political memory:

> I could remember when eighteen thousand men poured from those tidy little homes every day into the South Works, Wisconsin Steel, the Ford assembly plant, or the Xerxes solvent factory. I remember when every piece of trim was painted fresh every second spring and new Buicks or Oldsmobiles were an autumn commonplace.
>
> (Paretsky [1988] 1990: 11)

What were once the pristine housing tracts of relatively prosperous blue-collar workers have now become an area ready to submerge into destitution. Such dereliction is mirrored by the physical condition of old workers who suffer incapacitating and chronic illnesses after working in the Xerxes factory. Exploitation, then, takes many forms and the health of workers as well as the ecological sustainability of the city is ridden over in the interests of capital. When Paretsky crosses town to talk to the wealthy owners of the factory, she finds them in their Lake Drive mansions in the north, bought, it becomes clear, from profits whose cost was the systematic ruination of the bodies of factory workers.

As many commentators have noted (for example Munt 1994; Plain 2001), the Warshawski novels are filled with the details of what Warshawski is wearing, and about her changes of clothes throughout the day (which are frequent). At first glance they might be explained according to Roland Barthes' notion of 'reality effects', where details 'seem to correspond to a kind of narrative *luxury*, lavish to the point of offering many "futile" details and thereby increasing the cost of narrative information' (Barthes [1967] 1988: 141). Yet, as well as being 'reality effects', they also articulate specific aspects of urban culture. Sally Munt, after suggesting that Paretsky's focus on clothing might be read as commenting on the performativity of gender, offers what she calls a mundane reason for the focus: 'could Warshawski's constant need to change her clothes be a reflection of the many identities necessary to her survival as a woman in a multi-roled and predominantly masculine environment?' (Munt 1994: 47).

Warshawski's masquerade is continually stressed as she insists that appropriate clothing (along with physical fitness) is an essential accompaniment and accomplishment for the female detective: 'by nine I had done my exercises. Skipping a run, I dressed for the corporate world in a tailored navy suit that was supposed to make me look imposing and competent' (Paretsky [1988] 1990: 48). In this Paretsky is recognizing that her job will always involve elements of the roper's craft: the ability to convince someone that you are in the proper place and they should talk to you. This is a necessity even when involved in shadowing. The class mobility that Chandler's Marlowe could utilize by wearing a suit that was applicable across town is unavailable to Warshawski: how she dresses to talk to families within the working-class and ethnic enclaves of south Chicago is different from what she wears to gain access to the corporate culture within the Loop or the wealthy families of Chicago's 'gold coast'. The suggestion is of a canny operative, with a good deal of know-how and an ability to judge the performativity required in a range of social situations. But it is a knowledge specific to her situation as a female operative and makes visible the unsymmetrical divisions of gender performance in the city.

Alongside this gendered knowledge, clothes function in a way that is not always immediately apparent. For instance, early in *Toxic Shock* we find Warshawski bemoaning the state of her clothes as she begins her investigation into the Xerxes factory:

I walked slowly back down the long hall to my car, absentmindedly stepping in an oozy patch that plastered sludge firmly to my right shoe. I cursed loudly – I'd paid over a hundred dollars for those pumps. As I sat in the car trying to scrape it clean, I got oil sludge on my skirt. Feeling outraged with the world, I threw the shoe petulantly into the backseat and changed back into my running gear.

(Paretsky [1988] 1990: 55)

Of course a hundred dollars is not small change (certainly not in the mid-1980s), yet its significance in the novel seems disproportionate in relation to other narrative elements. But Warshawski is the daughter of immigrant parents and, although they are both dead, their lives and their values continually haunt her. Shoes, we discover, are the one item of clothing that her mother always insisted must be of the highest quality, preferably Italian and handmade. Thus clothing is the continuation of the past into the present, a reminder of her immigrant mother's struggle to bring up Victoria Warshawski within the often xenophobic culture of south Chicago.

In moving about this unevenly developed city, Warshawski navigates the gendering of capital and class as it is given spatial form. This is most vividly expressed by the excessive attention to dress, to a wardrobe that functions antithetically to Marlowe's shabby suit: whereas the man's suit provides Marlowe with the accoutrements of a universal masculinity, allowing him a degree of invisibility in most surroundings, Warshawski's clothes either facilitate or prevent access to these same spaces. In Paretsky's novels, Warshawski is continually changing her clothes, using a complex and mobile masquerade to help her negotiate the city. But it's a fragile masquerade that can leave her being chased across industrial wasteland in high heels and an evening dress, or trying to gatecrash a posh party in a sweatshirt.

This ambivalence, where the same item of clothing can either help or hamper her mobility, is echoed in the way that clothing, for Warshawski, simultaneously speaks of her professional cunning and her attachment to the past. The black crease-resistant dress and the expensive Italian shoes, kept in the back of the car in the same way you might keep a raincoat and walking boots, are tools of her professional life. Keeping them to hand and constantly changing dress codes is the necessary tactic for a female private investigator crossing a socially divided city that is insistently articulated by gender. Yet, as well as being a tactical accomplishment, clothes (especially shoes) signal an attachment to the memory of her mother and her mother's struggle in the impoverished and often racist environment of industrial south Chicago.

Rhyme's New York

Movement and knowledge are inseparably tied together in the fictions of forensic experts. Paradoxically, though, much of the spatial and mobile investigation of forensics takes place within the confines of the laboratory and the dissection table. This idea of roaming urban space while remaining 'locked' in the forensic and pathologist lab is given an emphatic twist in the Lincoln Rhyme crime series written by Jeffery Deaver. The reader of this series first meets Lincoln Rhyme in the novel *The Bone Collector*. At this point Rhyme has been a quadriplegic for three and a half years after a roof caves in on him at a crime scene, and he is trying to find someone to help him kill himself. Former head of forensics for the New York Police Department (NYPD), Rhyme is paralysed from the neck down: 'he could move his head and neck, his shoulders slightly. The only fluke was that the crushing oak beam had spared a single, minuscule strand of motor neuron. Which allowed him to move his left ring finger' (Deaver 1997: 34).

Like many series based around forensic procedures, the Lincoln Rhyme novels centre on psychopathic serial murderers and professional killers; sociopaths who are remarkable in their cunning and the lengths they go to fulfil their morbid desires. All the killers in the novels are scrupulous about not leaving physical evidence at crime scenes: gloves are worn, of course, but also floors are swept; discarded materials are generic and untraceable; shoe soles are smooth and so on. The challenge for the forensic scientist or criminalist (as Rhyme is called) is to make something out of the motley evidence available: a bit of grime, a strand of thread. Dirt is Rhyme's specialism:

> DAs and reporters and juries loved obvious clues. Bloody gloves, knives, recently fired guns, love letters, semen and fingerprints. But Lincoln Rhyme's favorite evidence was trace – the dust and effluence at crime scenes, so easily overlooked by perps.
>
> (Deaver 1997: 135)

For Rhyme there is never a lack of evidence. A firm believer in the French forensic scientist Edmond Locard's 'exchange principle', Rhyme maintains that 'whenever two human beings come in contact, something from one is exchanged to the other, and vice versa. Maybe dust, blood, skin cells, dirt, fibers, metallic residue' (Deaver 1997: 136).

Dirt is tied to the geography of the city; it is place-specific. It is by analysing trace elements that Rhyme finds out, not who the killer is, but, more importantly, where the killer is, or where the next victim is being kept. The city of dirt becomes a readable entity to Rhyme, who had spent years, prior to his injury, walking around New York collecting soil samples and compiling databases from the material. He has also studied the history and geology of New York. Reading dirt becomes an activity that reveals a human geology, which turns the city into an archaeological palimpsest, recording the impact of human settlement on the soggy landmass of Manhattan:

He [Rhyme] said to Hoddleston, "The dirt has a high moisture content and's loaded with feldspar and quartz sand."
"I remember you always like your dirt, Lincoln."
"Useful, soil is," he said, then continued. "Very little rock and none of it blasted or chipped, no limestone or Manhattan mica schist. So we're looking downtown. And from the amount of old wood particles, probably closer to Canal Street."
North of Twenty-seventh Street the bedrock lies close to the surface of Manhattan. South of that, the ground is dirt, sand, and clay, and it's very damp. When the sandhogs were digging the subways years ago the soupy ground around Canal Street would flood the shaft. Twice a day all work had to cease while the tunnel was pumped out and the walls shored up with timber, which over the years had rotted away into the soil.

(Deaver 1998: 209–10)

Dirt articulates not simply a geology spanning thousands and thousands of years but also that which, over the course of several hundred years, has shaped that geology. Hundred-year-old subway systems and sewers record the strenuous modernizing impulse of the city and its gargantuan aspirations. This human geology is, of course, unfinished.

For Lincoln Rhyme, confined to his bed or his wheelchair, dirt is a partial liberation from immobility. Analysing the traces of dirt left by one killer, Rhyme's team find: 'Very old oxidized iron flakes, old wood fibers and ash and silicon – looks like glass dust. And the main act is a dark, low-luster mineral in large concentrations – montmorillonite'. Rhyme's mobility, although it is confined to his imagination, ranges across the geological environments of New York:

He sailed over the Columbia University tower, over Central Park with its loam and limestone and wildlife excrement, through the streets of Midtown coated with the residue of the tons of soot that fall upon them daily, the boat basins with their peculiar mix of gasoline, propane and diesel fuel, the decaying parts of the Bronx with their lead paint and old plaster mixed with sawdust and filler.

(Deaver 2002: 166)

This imaginative and historical navigation leads Rhyme to the recent re-developments of Battery Park City: 'clay used as slurry to keep groundwater out of the foundations when construction crews dig deep foundations'; the 'whole area is landfill and it's full of rusted metal and glass trace. And the ash? To clear the old piers down there the builders burned them' (Deaver 2002: 166–7). Battery Park City is an area of luxury apartments and elite 'public' space situated on the lower-west seafront of Manhattan looking out towards the Statue of Liberty. Although the initial plan for Battery

Park in the 1960s was for mixed income housing, by the time the area was developed in the 1980s it had become dedicated to the wealthy. With government working for the interests of private and commercial capital, Battery Park City has been seen as an exemplary symptom of governmental involvement in gentrification, the privatization of public space and the decline of urban democracy (Deutsche 1996: 79–93).

Battery Park City, then, is an actor in the unevenly developing landscape of New York and it is where the 'Ghost' (a wealthy and deadly Chinese smuggler of human cargo) is located. The Ghost's whereabouts are initially determined by the dirt, and this is further specified through finding traces of 'fresh gardening mulch' (an indication that the pseudo-public spaces of this enclave are constantly subjected to beautification) and fibres pointing to the installation of opulent and exclusive carpeting. Battery Park City marks one of many locations in the book. Other locations include Lionel Rhyme's park-side town house, the dirty, overcrowded apartments in Chinatown and the small, impoverished homes in an area of Queens. A human and social geography thus identifies a landscape marked by movements: the movement of landmasses, the movement of peoples. That this is a landscape articulated by the unevenness of power and wealth, and that this unevenness is differentiated along ethnically distinct patterns, is the very bedrock of this potentially critical geography and geology.

Lincoln Rhyme, then, reads the city through its traces. But, of course, it isn't Rhyme who collects these traces; his colleague and eventual lover Amelia Sachs collects them. Rhyme extends himself electronically (via mobile phones, computer links and so on) and through the body of Sachs. Technology and sexuality are the mediations for his mobility. Sachs, a former street cop (or 'portable' in the language of the NYPD), was once a model. She suffers from arthritis and drives fast cars very fast. Sachs is to some extent Rhyme's body: 'you're my legs *and* my eyes, remember' (Deaver 1997: 176). The relationship between Rhyme and Sachs is complex, with Rhyme as the immobile but knowledgeable 'senior' who is deeply in love with Sachs and recognizes her abilities as a criminalist. To begin with, Sachs is an unwilling supplicant who has been press-ganged into being Rhyme's accomplice, but who in the end realizes that Rhyme is the only person who can take her into the deathly world where she feels she needs to go. Mobility here is uncanny, as the immobile Rhyme haunts and controls Sachs' body, moving her, berating her, encouraging her and offering her salvation. Sexuality is the key to knowledge here. Communicating by mobile phone, Rhyme takes an inexperienced Sachs through the procedures of crime scene investigation, which involve fairly horrific operations: 'He was calm and he sounded . . . what? Yes, *that* was the tone. Seductive. He sounds like a lover' (Deaver 1997: 88). As Michel de Certeau suggested, knowledge needs to be questioned about its desire. Describing the planner's view of the world as seen in totalizing panorama, de Certeau asks: 'To what erotics of knowledge does the ecstasy of reading such a cosmos belong?' (de Certeau 1984: 92). The Lincoln Rhyme novels provide a partial answer here, but one that is complicated by the question of mobility: on the one hand, the erotic distribution articulates an active knowing on the side of masculinity and, on the other, a more unconscious intuition on the side of femininity, but it is hard to continue with such a structural opposition for long, given the degree to which mobility is associated with activity and immobility with passivity. The 'erotics of knowledge' is about subjecting and being subjected, but it is also about the frustrations and accessibility of movement.

One particularly inconsistent aspect of these novels is the way that they treat aspects of behavioural science and psychological simulation. For instance, Rhyme is often openly dismissive about the speculative world of psychologists and behaviourists, preferring the hard facticity of physical evidence. Yet he will also encourage Sachs to enter imaginatively the mind of the killer, to imagine being him. The amount of identification and control involved in these scenes almost suggest a composite figure, where Amelia Sachs is a hypersensitive and intelligent cipher who is at times imaginatively inhabited by the forensic expertise of Rhyme and simultaneously the sick violence of the killer: 'suddenly she was filled with a burst of unfocused anger. It nearly took her breath away. "No, wait, Rhyme. It's like his death is secondary. What I really want is to hurt him. I've been betrayed and I want to hurt him bad" ' (Deaver 2002: 150–1). A patriarchal economy that swings inconsistently between scientific knowledge and homicidal violence inhabits the body of Sachs.

The relationship between technology and mobility, a key ingredient in the novels, is also rendered problematic. As one symptom of the contemporary moment, we imagine an urban environment humming with digital electronic messages. For Rhyme dependency on technology has often been total (he was, for instance, on a ventilator for a year). In the second Rhyme novel, *The Coffin Dancer*, Rhyme's environment (his bedroom and forensic laboratory) has a central control system that is voice-activated. The novels witness the technological development of Rhyme, as he becomes a professional criminalist who is also quadriplegic: his computer screen becomes a hub for a range of laboratory operations (looking through an electron microscope for instance, or reading the data from a mass spectrometer). The voice-activating computer allows him to control most of his environment from his wheelchair or bed: 'In truth Rhyme was quite pleased with the system – the lightning-fast computer, a specially made ECU box – environmental control unit – and voice recognition software' (Deaver 1998: 11).

At one point in the novel a pilot (a potential victim for a maniacal hit man) compares her life in the air to his. At first the comparison seems particularly inappropriate, given the intense mobility of flight, yet again the material actuality is often of intense immobility and absolute dependence on technology. At one point the very technology that was designed to allow greater control and extended mobility fails him (the dark irony being that the previous generation of technology wouldn't have). The voice-recognition software that is designed to recognize his voice only recognizes it when the modulations are even, but at this point they are marked by extremes of tension and stress:

> At one time he'd had a mechanical ECU controller and he could use his one working finger to dial the phone. The computer system had replaced that and he now *had* to use the dictation program to call the safe house and tell them that the Dancer was on his way there, dressed as a fireman or rescue worker.
> "Command mode," he said into the microphone. Fighting to stay calm.
> (Deaver 1998: 254)

The computer's response to this appears on Rhyme's screen: '*I did not understand what you just said. Please try again.*' He tries again, trying to keep the anxiety from disturbing his voice patterns. Unable to control the technology at precisely the moment when he is most reliant on it, Rhyme can't warn his colleagues, and one of the people the FBI are supposed to be protecting is killed. A technologically robust city is uneven in its effects and once again the environment disables Rhyme.

Limited Mobilities and Limitless Possibilities

The purpose of these small sketches is not to claim these fictional detective worlds as either 'good' or 'bad' in their depiction of the city. The job of cultural studies isn't simply to pass judgement on the political and social currency of cultural texts, to declare them progressive or reactionary, for instance. Nor is it, I don't think, to set about the more textually limited task of finding instabilities and cultural transgression within them. Or at least I don't think that this is *all* cultural studies is about. Cultural studies is also engaged in attempting a much wider, less pragmatic project: it is, like its anthropological ancestors, trying to register what culture feels like from the inside – what culture is like in terms of density and force, its thick complexities and its animating energies, so to speak. Such an excessive project is probably doomed to failure, doomed to crashing on the rocks of over-generalization or overspecification.

Returning once more to Fredric Jameson's essay on Chandler, it is worth noting what it is about detective fiction that he finds arresting. Unusually, perhaps, Jameson isn't particularly interested in the narrative of detection, the crime and the punishment, or the psychologies of the hunter and the hunted. For Jameson, the detective genre, precisely because it so emphatically places this narrative at the centre, is allowed to describe aspects of the urban world *without having to focus on them*. This inattentive-attention allows the everydayness of the world to be 'half-glimpsed, half-disregarded' in a way that wouldn't be possible if it were elevated to the symbolic centre of the novel. So even though detective fiction is not particularly concerned with the everydayness of the urban (it is after all usually addressing exceptional circumstances and exceptional people), its ability to capture the quality of the urban world is paradoxically greater than those novels that focus explicitly on this everydayness (say, for instance, Joyce's *Ulysses*). 'Indeed', Jameson writes, 'it is as if there are certain moments in life which are accessible only at the price of a certain lack of intellectual focus: like objects at the edge of my field of vision which disappear when I turn to stare at them head-on' (Jameson 1970: 627).

For urban cultural studies this might mean elevating what is marginal in a work to the critical centre. But, unlike deconstructive approaches, the end point is not in undoing the cultural object. Indeed the realist drive of this approach is to move away from the cultural object *as text*, so that it can be used as a way of registering what cities feel like, how they register across the cultural imaginary (which would also include the conventions of genre fiction). It is less a question of these fictions being 'realist' (of judging them in terms of the accuracy of their depiction of actual cities) than providing a 'realist' form of analysis, which might want to attend to all the peculiarities and differences within a particular series and across the various subgenres of detective fiction.

Mobility, movement and access are only one aspect of detective fiction, and detective fiction is only one genre that might be analysed in relation to what it articulates about mobility and the city. Such a focus is always open to accusations of not taking heed of this or that aspect of a work, of wilfully ignoring its more obvious address (for instance I have said relatively little about Deaver's depiction of quadriplegics, or his representation of Chinese people in *The Stone Monkey*). Mobility is, to a degree, a slight topic in detective fiction: in some important ways it is no more central in detective fiction than in any other fictional world. What is helpful, I think, is the usefulness of looking at genre forms and their constant rearticulation and reaccentuation of the themes of mobility, movement and access within a 'secondhand', convention-bound world.

Such an attention to cultural texts requires that we treat them ethnographically, as the texts of native informants. But detective novels are not simply answers to ethnographic questions, or at least if they are, we have lost the questions that are being asked. They are in some senses partial articulations of a living culture, formed via a number of conventions which mean that some things are easier to say than others and some are highly unlikely to be given any prominence within the confines of the genre. I have been suggesting that this genre fiction is a form of analysis of urban mobilities: it is not, of course, an analysis of the same order as a sociology of mobility, or a history of mobility. But this doesn't invalidate it. What these examples of genre fiction provide is access to a real imaginary around issues of mobility. It is precisely because genre fiction authors are working within some of the confines of the conventions of genre that the books seem to articulate vividly some of the force of urban mobility. It is by trying to inhabit this generic world with detectives who are 'marked' by social difference that these social differences take on a vividness that is heightened precisely because it alters the conventions of genre fiction.

In using literature to discover something of the way social differences impact on themes of urban mobility and movement, we benefit from a cultural form that is aligned to the study of complex singularity, and is attuned to the tropological landscape (that is, a landscape experienced simultaneously as both physical and metaphoric) of the city. In this light Michel de Certeau's suggestion that a form of modern ethnography, concerned with the ordinary rather than the exotic, finds a place for itself in literature is crucial:

> As indexes of particulars – the poetic or tragic murmurings of the everyday – ways of operating enter massively into the novel or the short story, most notably into the nineteenth-century realistic novel. They find there a new representational space, that of fiction, populated by everyday virtuosities that science doesn't know what to do with and which become the signatures, easily recognized by readers, of everyone's micro-stories.
>
> (de Certeau 1984: 70)

It is, perhaps surprisingly, the convention-bound world of genre fiction that, I think, supplies some of the most useful ethnographic material. Genre fiction has at least two ways of registering the ordinary: in its distracted gaze on the urban everyday and its adjustments within the genre. By treating literature as practical life, as recounting ways of operating in the world, de Certeau allows us to access the social spaces of the city as negotiated and lived space.

Detective fiction can be a form of critical realism, but this isn't to say that it is realistic, that it registers much of what the world is like to us as we experience it day to day. Or rather it doesn't do this in any straightforward, mimetic way. No doubt part of the pleasure of reading such fictional accounts of urban life is that they compensate for our lack of effect on our surroundings. After all, detectives are often extraordinarily successful in the way they impact on the world around them: industrial corruption is unmasked; the lost are found; death and life accompanies their decision making. But it is because detective fiction operates on such a ludicrously lurid level that it can vividly picture urban antagonisms. The rich and powerful meet the underdogs in a way that is, of course, contrived, but which allows social antagonism to be dramatically foregrounded.

In allowing detective fiction to speak about the varied mobilities of the city, we have been getting such literature to tell us a specific truth (one that is always encountered in its singularity). Mobility is a register of cultural and social difference but one that is never reducible to cultural and social difference as an abstraction. Mobility, movement and access, at the level of lived experience, are always truncated, always limited. Yet how we live and *imagine* this always limited mobility tells us a good deal about the way cultural forces impact on our lives. As far as this goes the fictional detective is a genre that will continue to inflect the uneven landscape of the city in multiple ways. Any new forensic criminalist, any new detective will bring to the genre a particularity and this particularity will have something to say about our abilities and lack of them in negotiating the city.

Chapter Six
Networks – Communication, Information and The Matrix

We have begun to create a new nervous system in society using the advanced communication technology that will enable the social brain to function more effectively. In large contemporary urban complexes, communication networks twist and interlink into a complex which must be something like the nervous system of the brain ... whirling around in these brains are the people and the information. The citizens are like electrons flowing in an electronic brain.

(Kenzo Tange 1966, quoted in Wigley 2001: 104)

'The World that has been Pulled over your Eyes'

Computer screens give off a neon-green illumination reminiscent of an oscilloscope's glow; black Bakelite ring-dial telephones are ever-present. A once-opulent hotel, the Heart o' the City Hotel, lays derelict now that the heart of the city has moved away from the industrial factories and warehouses. Corporate office blocks, with their endless epidermis of mirrored-glass, house thousands of workers in offices and partitioned cubicles. This is the city of the 'matrix' (from the film *The Matrix*) in the year 1999; a city predominantly peopled by office workers, police and cleaners. It is a modern city dedicated to service provision, but filled with anachronisms from a now-defunct past. It is policed by anonymous-looking 'agents' and cops who look as if they have come from the 1950s.

But while this description seems almost like a slice of modern urban actuality – North American or Pacific Rim urbanism, for instance – it soon becomes clear that social verisimilitude is not on offer. The first person we meet is Trinity (Carrie-Anne Moss), trying to locate a useable and untapped telephone landline. In the middle of her search a group of police confront her and try and arrest her. All the police officers are killed within moments, as Trinity displays a range of abilities that are clearly superhuman; she can sprint up walls, seemingly hang effortlessly in the air and jump unfeasible distances. Pursued by 'agents' she finally gets to a public phone box where the telephone is already ringing. A truck driven by the agents is revving up ready to plough into the phone box; Trinity picks up the telephone seconds before the truck destroys the phone box. Trinity has escaped.

Such movement – the superhuman physicality and the disappearance and appearance through communication networks – are explained as we learn that the urban world we are seeing is merely a simulation hiding a more worrying reality of humanity enslaved to machines. This city is 'the Matrix': 'a neural-interactive simulation', a 'computer-generated dream-world' (Wachowski and Wachowski 2001: 38, 41). In other words it is a software program, hardwired and mainlined into the battery-farmed humans to keep them occupied while their bodies are used as an energy supply to fuel the machine-world that dominates the 'real' world. As Morpheus (Laurence Fishburne) puts it:

> The Matrix is everywhere, it is all around us, here even in this room. You can see it out your window or on your television. You feel it when you go to work, or go to church or pay your taxes. It is the world that has been pulled over your eyes to blind you from the truth.
>
> (Wachowski and Wachowski 2001: 28)

Our entrance into the 'real reality', the world outside the Matrix, is via Thomas Anderson (Keanu Reeves), also known as Neo. Anderson works as a software programmer for the Meta CorTechs Company, but in his spare time he is a computer hacker called Neo. Anderson/Neo is searching for something – the answer to the question: what is the Matrix? And as his search bears fruit, he is offered a chance to see behind the simulation, to experience 'the desert of the real'.

Working outside the Matrix is a group of humans who were either born outside slavery (in the city of Zion) or else were liberated from the massive human battery farms where people are suspended in fluids, fed nutrients and digital information, while having their energy supply tapped. The leader of one group is Morpheus, who believes that humankind can only be saved by 'the One' who can transcend the machine code of the Matrix and find liberation from within its programs. To do this the One must confront the agents, 'the sentient programs' who 'can move in and out of any software' while 'still hardwired to their system' (52). The group of hackers or freedom fighters consist of Morpheus, Trinity, Tank, Dozer, Apoc, Cypher, Mouse, Switch and now Neo. They live on a hovercraft that navigates through the vast network of disused sewers underneath the burnt-out carcass of a once-prosperous metropolitan city. The hovercraft is called the *Nebuchadnezzar*: 'this is where we broadcast our pirate signal and hack into the Matrix' (Wachowski and Wachowski 2001: 36). The narrative drive of the film is dedicated to the story of Neo confronting the agents and learning to see through the simulacra and achieve some agency within the Matrix.

There are, then, a number of good reasons for *not* treating the Wachowski brothers' 1999 film *The Matrix* as a text that would be immediately pertinent for the study of urban culture. After all it is plotted around a messianic narrative that tells the story of how Neo (played by Keanu Reeves) becomes the chosen One: the one who might be able to save humankind from the malign dictatorship of machines. The city that is depicted by the film is a vague and generic image of modern postindustrial urbanism, filled with gleaming office blocks and pitted with the ruins of an industrial past, yet this city turns out to be nothing more than a software program that provides a total hallucination, keeping humankind 'occupied' while their bodies are used to power the machinic world. *The Matrix*, then, is not a film about the physical presence or actuality of the city. Nor does it offer anything that would tell us about the future direction of cities; apart, that is, from a paranoid dream of destruction (which is available in any number of other films, from the *Mad Max* cycle to the *Terminator* films).

By not addressing the *physical* city, by casting the city as a program, the film articulates (or at least can be made to articulate) a range of elements that are useful for talking about the *culture* of urbanism at a moment when communication networks and information exchange are widely considered the most important and dynamic forces shaping our experience of urban modernity. Peter Wollen has suggested that 'the cinematic vision of the city which leaves the most lasting impression is really a cartoon and comic-book vision. It is the vision of *Batman Returns*, of *Who Framed Roger Rabbit*, of *Brazil*, of *Blade Runner* and before that of *Metropolis* and *King Kong*' (Wollen 1992: 25). Such films offer imaginative extrapolations of aspects of a film's present-day conditions and project them onto a more vividly articulated life-world. Vivian Sobchack writes that this extrapolation works to provide an expressive cityscape for science fiction films:

> Owing no necessary allegiance to representational verisimilitude, such a metropolis serves as a hypnogogic site where the anxieties, desires and fetishes of a culture's waking world and dream world converge and are resolved into a substantial and systemic architecture.
>
> (Sobchack 1999: 123)

Sobchack's stress on social and cultural *experience* (anxieties and desires) is crucial here, and it is the idea that fantasy texts like *The Matrix* are a *response* to real fantasies that make them vivid articulators of contemporary cultural passions and fears.

Wollen's emphasis on comic-books will, as I hope to show, prove useful here and it is worth noting that the writers and directors of *The Matrix*, the Wachowski brothers, worked for Marvel comics and initially wrote the stories that became the film as comic-books. Of course by claiming that fantasy films are extrapolations of contemporary experience and suggesting that they provide temporary resolutions to the traumas and desires of modernity does not mean that those resolutions or extrapolations are going to be socially and culturally productive or worthwhile. Indeed, the very fact that fantasy films can be seen to work like dreams might well warn us about trying too hard to locate a critical and liberatory politics from the mire of violence, hope and paranoia. The task here, then, is not to assess *The Matrix* in terms of a politics of the city. Instead what I am interested in is how to make this film articulate something of the experience of modern urban culture. In its slow-motion movements (its famous 'bullet-time' sequences) and in the way that people's bodies move, the solid, physical world dissolves into a more fluid, penetrable world. The gift of movement, fluidity, is offered at precisely the same moment as the world is revealed as totally 'held' within the grip of authority. Such a dilemma might tell us what it is like to be a political subject in Western neoliberal democracies at the moment, or it might tell us that there is a difference between the perception of agency and its actuality. These interpretations seem all well and good, but they already move too far away from the text, from the literal text of bodies and places on screen.

The Matrix shows bodies moving in the city, and it shows Neo transforming from sedentary computer programmer into a fantasy of mobility. Offices, screens, telephones and buildings are the day's residues of our urban actuality: flight, fluidity and dissipation are wish fulfilments caught in the historical reality of urban culture.

Method: Historicity and Realism

One of the questions that drives this chapter (and the book as a whole) is the question of how cultural texts register the larger urban culture that they picture and articulate. In this chapter I'm looking to historicize the film *The Matrix*. I should point out that the intention here isn't to give an adequate interpretation of the film; I am more interested in the way the film itself interprets the urban culture of our present. There are themes and issues that belong to the film but won't be dealt with here (for instance the religious symbolism of the film). Nor will I explore the obvious relationship between *The Matrix* and cyberpunk fiction (in the writing of William Gibson, for instance), although such a link would clearly be productive. My main interest is in developing a form of attention, an approach towards the film, that can be thought of as 'realist'. To do this it is important to see reality as inclusive of fantasy, or rather, to see reality as meaningfully saturated by anxieties, desires, fears and hopes. A film, a novel or any piece of cultural text may or may not have a realist mission, it may or may not set out to register mimetically the historical moment of its production. Yet whatever the intentions and pretensions of the makers of cultural objects, it strikes me that for the *study* of cultural texts, a realist mission might be productive, perhaps *especially* for those films that seem to refute trenchantly a world of empirically known facticity. The bedrock of social historical investigations of culture (investigations which this book seeks to pursue and extend) is that *all* culture registers social actuality because all culture can be recognized as a dialogic response to a wider cultural context. In this way the distinction between 'fantasy' and 'realism' is only really a question of genre, and doesn't *necessarily* posit one with a more profound connection to the actual social world. It would, I think, take an empiricist of a particularly ruthless and cruel persuasion not to recognize our everyday reality as meaningful precisely because it is orchestrated by desire, belief, anticipation, by all those things that can't simply be read off a statistical map or reduced to hard facts. We only have to look at the popularity and prevalence of astrology columns to recognize the tenacity of magical forms within modern secular culture. As Paul Rabinow succinctly stated it, echoing Geertz's words about 'rocks' and 'dreams' mentioned in Chapter One, 'representations are social facts' (Rabinow 1986: 234).

One way of pursuing a realist approach to the study of urban culture is to locate specific texts historically, to bed them down, so to speak, in their relevant contexts. In Chapter Two, the job of historicizing Edgar Allen Poe's short story 'The Man of the Crowd' seemed relatively straightforward: it meant drawing it out, extending it within a particular moment of urban modernity, relating it to forces that were shaping the city at the particular time the text was being written. It also meant looking at the sort of imaginative vehicles that were available for representing the city. That chapter used an abbreviated version of the sort of cultural history most vividly described by Carl Schorske in a classic work of urban cultural history: *Fin-de-Siècle Vienna: Politics and Culture*. For Schorske the cultural historian's job was to locate artefacts 'in a field where two lines intersect':

> One line is vertical, or diachronic, by which he [the cultural historian] establishes the relation of a text or a system of thought to previous expressions in the same branch of activity (painting, politics, etc.). The other is horizontal, or synchronic; by it he assesses the relation of the content of the intellectual object to what is appearing in other branches or aspects of a culture at the same time. The diachronic thread is the warp, the synchronic one is the woof in the fabric of cultural history.
>
> (Schorske 1981: xxi–xxii)

Less concerned with the diachronic thread of literary studies, my reading of Poe's text worked to locate the text in the emergent modernization of London. The expansion of a cultural object along a synchronic axis has been developed particularly by Kristin Ross in her study of the poetry of

Arthur Rimbaud and its relationship to the social geography of Paris at the time of the 1871 Paris Commune. Ross describes her reading as 'centrifugal', as a practice in which the poem 'opens out onto a whole synchronic history, onto the web of social and political discourses and representations that simultaneously place a limitation on and enable meaning to take place' (Ross 1988: 10).

Looking at our contemporary culture, and the film *The Matrix* in particular, this synchronic opening out is not, to my mind, the most productive approach. Often the most vivid aspects of present-day cultural texts are the way they register a number of temporalities simultaneously. While temporal distance (past culture) seems to offer the opportunity for making a text come alive within a particular moment, temporal nearness (recent culture) offers the chance to see how cultural texts articulate a variety of durations from 'the ephemeral, the fugitive, the contingent' (Baudelaire [1863] 1964: 13) elements of our contemporary moment to the more sustained sense of historical continuity (which would include everything from epochs to eternity). The world we live in, after all, is not made in a moment, everywhere we go we are living in a world that Ernst Bloch (1990) described as 'nonsynchronous simultaneity'. An example of non-synchronous simultaneity might simply be a house where the different technologies in operation come from different times even though they are all still functioning (windows from the 1890s, a plumbing system from the 1940s and a newly installed broadband connection). In terms of social relations we live *simultaneously* across various temporalities – from moral codes that have filtered down through 'age-old' religious systems, to more recent 'liquid' aspects of interpersonal life.

Michel Serres, in his conversations with Bruno Latour, provides an example of what he calls 'polychronic' time:

> What things are contemporary? Consider a late-model car. It is a disparate aggregate of scientific and technical solutions dating from different periods. One can date it component by component: this part was invented at the turn of the century, another ten years ago, and Carnot's cycle is almost two hundred years old. Not to mention that the wheel dates back to neolithic times. The ensemble is only contemporary by assemblage, by its design, its finish, sometimes only by the slickness of the advertising surrounding it.
>
> (Serres 1995: 45)

Against the image of a car, the urban environment must seem like a cacophony of different and competing temporalities all impacting on the city at the same time. For Serres:

> Every historical era is likewise multitemporal, simultaneously drawing from the obsolete, the contemporary, and the futuristic. An object, a

circumstance, is thus polychronic, multitemporal, and reveals a time that is gathered together, with multiple pleats.

(Serres 1995: 60)

'Time doesn't flow', writes Serres, 'it percolates' (Serres 1995: 58). Historical and contemporary time is seen as a handkerchief that has been folded, crumpled and torn, where distance and time connect and disconnect in surprising and unstable ways. To view history (which would include our contemporary time) as a crumpled handkerchief works to accommodate a world in which, for Serres, 'we are always simultaneously making gestures that are archaic, modern, and futuristic' (Serres 1995: 60).

The Matrix is a film that visually articulates a number of themes that are associated with an 'information society': the ever-present screens displaying information, a nonphysical world where vast 'worlds of information' can cross the real world in no time at all and so on. But it is also a film that is nostalgic for a time before the machines took over, when food tasted like food, the experiential world was characterized by its physical actuality and choices weren't programmed in advance. Already the film operates with a range of different temporalities. I am going to look at *The Matrix* in relation to two interlinked temporalities. The first of these dates from the mid-twentieth century, when Western cities shifted from being centres of industrial production to becoming increasingly dedicated to service provision. It is, of course, a temporality that we are still living through. The second temporality began to emerge in the late nineteenth century when transport systems and communication networks began to produce a more porous sense of space and transformed our embodied sense of time.

The Body, the Worker and the City

The Matrix provides an initial juxtaposition that links the film to momentous transformations of the modern urban life-world – transformations most prevalent in large cities like Tokyo, New York, Kuala Lumpur and London (for instance). The juxtaposition is between Trinity and Neo, and it is made vivid by their relationship to the built environment and the world of work. Trinity's body is encased in shiny plastic; visual body armour that flaunts her musculature. She is hypermobile; she can move across communication networks, enhance her mobility through an improvised use of buildings and machines (Plate 6.1) and her speed and fighting skills mean that she can overcome most obstacles. She has no job, apart, that is, from ridding the world of the evil rule of machines. In many ways she has all the hallmarks of a comic-book superhero. Neo, to begin with at least, is 'geeky'; he spends too much time in front of a computer, is physically weak and not particularly brave and has a fairly low-status, white-collar job. Neo, then, is not too dissimilar to a myriad of comic-book characters either. And it is Neo's transformation from 'geeky-nerd' to superhero that structures the plot and supplies many of the visual references. These references are the material out of which the film's imaginative life-world is fabricated, and for the most part they are taken from the comic-books and graphic novels that emerged after 1960.

The Matrix's release coincided with a shift in Hollywood superhero films. Throughout most of the 1970s and 80s, it was DC Comics, in the guise of Superman and Batman, that supplied the dominant figures for superhero films.

Both these superheroes were first introduced in their comic-book form in the 1930s, and although Superman was from a distant galaxy and Batman was human, both characters were marked as already socially exceptional (Batman through his extraordinary wealth and Superman because he was from another planet). *The Matrix*'s superhero-like characters are more comparable to the protagonists of Marvel Comics, namely Spider-Man, Daredevil and the Fantastic Four. And it is these comic-book figures that have supplied the narratives of a number of recent films (*Daredevil* was released in 2003, *Spider-Man* in 2002). What distinguishes so-called 'golden-age' comic characters (Superman and Batman) from the 'silver age' of Marvel comic-book characters are the latter's ordinary origins (McCue 1993). Spider-Man was an ordinary, geeky college kid who was bitten by a

Plate 6.1 Trinity jumping across buildings in *The Matrix*

radioactive spider; the Fantastic Four were all fairly ordinary white-collar laboratory workers who again were exposed to radioactive material.

One of the more noticeable features of Marvel Comics is the portrayal of an everyday city of traffic jams and massive office buildings, and Spider-Man, for instance, negotiating it with ease. In an issue of *The Amazing Spider-Man* from May 1963 (Plate 6.2), Spider-Man declares: 'the thing I like best about being Spider-Man is scaling these sheer walls! I don't think I'll ever stop getting a charge out of it' (in Daniels 1991: 250). This silver-age superhero is a fantasy of mobility. Spider-Man's agility is particularly suited to the built-up vertical expansion of Manhattan, as he uses the impediments of high-rise buildings to actually aid his mobility. And Daredevil, although blind, continually takes pleasure in circumventing all those urban elements that impede movement (Plate 6.3). Marvel superheroes are a new species, a species that has adjusted to the modern city and overcome its obstacles. Marvel's 'silver age' begins at the start of the 1960s: *Fantastic Four* is first published in 1961, *Spider-Man* in 1962 and *Daredevil* in 1964. This 'moment' coincides with a range of significant 'moments' in the changing history of work patterns and transformations of the urban environment.

Plate 6.2 Frame from Spider-man comic, May 1963

Plate 6.3 Frame from Daredevil comic, March 1967

Plate 6.3 Frame from Daredevil comic, March 1967

The skyscraper city is the urban form that has systematically articulated an office-based work practice, and offices are the everyday actuality of service industries and information economies. Vertical expansion, in the shape of high-rise office building, has been the dominant feature of many cities since at least the 1950s. New York City can serve as the most vivid example of this. In the late 1950s and early 1960s a number of developments in work patterns and urban living became clearly visible in the city of New York and were the subject of many contemporary commentaries. Although skyscrapers had been a feature of the Manhattan skyline since the early part of the century, it was the period between the Second World War and the mid-1960s that witnessed the most massive explosion of vertical expansion, as Manhattan dedicated itself to office building. Coinciding with the silver age of Marvel comics is an unprecedented expansion of office space: eleven million square feet of office space was built in Manhattan, for instance, between 1960 and 1961 (Wallock 1988: 43).

Coinciding with this vertical expansion is the transformation of New York from a manufacturing centre to a service provider. Along with vertical expansion comes the shutting down of manufacturing industry, the dereliction or abandonment of warehouses and factories. And this also means that jobs are changing: between 1953 and 1955 New York lost 80,000 jobs in manufacturing, and this was just an early indication of a pattern of decline (Wallock 1988: 3). In Sharon Zukin's book *Loft Living*, the transformation of downtown Manhattan is critically narrated as it moves from thriving manufacturing hub, through dereliction and decline and is then remoulded to accommodate art galleries and ultra-chic warehouse lofts (Zukin 1982). But as well as vertical expansion, urban centres witnessed enormous centrifugal (horizontal) expansion. Jean Gottmann, a French geographer writing in the early 1960s, claimed that the northeastern seaboard of the United States was one continuous urbanized megalopolis. From Philadelphia, through New York and New Haven and on to Boston was an expanse of almost continuous urbanization, with a population (in 1960) of 38 million people (Gottmann [1961] 1964: 17–22). This new form of urbanism was recognized by Guy Debord, not as the triumph of the city over the countryside, but as the collapse of their meaningful opposition. The rise of the megalopolis meant the end of any knowable and discrete entity that you could call a city, and replaced it with a viral urbanism:

Economic history, which developed entirely around the city/country opposition, has succeeded to such a point that it has annihilated both terms at once. The contemporary paralysis of total historical development, at the profit of the sole pursuit of the independent movement of the economy, makes of the moment when city and country begin to disappear, not the overcoming of their division, but their simultaneous collapse.

(Debord [1967] 1995: 175)

Urban mobility, urban knowledge and urban agency are faced with an endlessly proliferating environment where differences lie in density rather than categorical distinctions. But if the vertical and horizontal expanse of the city required fantasies of mobility for compensation, changes in work patterns also required fantasies more specific to the muscled body armour of the new superhero.

The year 1956 marked a significant shift in North American work patterns (patterns that were being mirrored in other metropolitan centres): for the first time the United States had more white-collar than blue-collar workers – more people worked in offices than in factories (Plate 6.4). In their 1959 book *Anatomy of a Metropolis*, Edgar Hoover and Raymond Vernon demonstrate how manufacturing was being pushed out of Manhattan as office-based work colonized central metropolitan areas (Hoover and Vernon [1959] 1962: 248). Such changes point to another crucial development: a shift in gender patterns of work. Service provision and information economies may or may not be employers of a majority female workforce but the shift from physical factory work to desk-bound office work can be seen as a form of gender realignment that provoked a host of cultural representations. North American television sitcoms like *Bewitched* (1964–72) centred on the gender struggle between an emasculated and mortal office worker and his supernatural wife. The running joke is her effort in 'remembering' to be a good subservient wife when it is clear that she is by far the more powerful of the two. Office work gradually becomes feminized during the end of the nineteenth century as clerking and secretarial work is transformed from being a male domain to being predominantly female. Figures for North American office-based work in the 1870s, for instance, show only 2 per cent of bookkeepers, cashiers and accountants as women; by 1930 this has become 51.9 per cent. More conclusive, however, is the role of stenographers and typists; in 1870 only 4.5 per cent were women, but by 1930 the figure constituted a massive 95.4 per cent (Davies 1982: 178). As clerical work rose in terms of becoming a majority employment, so did the number of women being employed in these roles. In this context, Marvel's silver-age heroes, drawn from a world of white-collar work, begin to look like a compensatory fantasy of remasculinization: from feminized office-bound weakling to muscle-bound hero.

The domination of the world of work by office-based jobs has generated a range of commentaries. For one thing it severely altered the nature of the class system: no longer was there a clear boundary between the classes of manual and intellectual labour. In many instances male manual workers (especially those whose labour was seen as skilled or dangerous) could earn more money than their male or female office colleagues. Yet because of the connotations of office work, older class identifications (based on economic differences) were refigured as the new 'salaried masses' began to fill the commuter trains into the city (Kracauer [1930] 1998). Many commentaries of the 1950s and 60s wrote about the new office work as

Plate 6.4 Office cubicles in Jacques Tati's *Playtime*, 1967, © Les Films de mon Oncle

producing passivity and structured obedience in the form of the new company man or organization man. William H. Whyte, for instance, in his book *The Organization Man* wrote of a new mass conformity, 'the tyranny of the majority', and saw its most emphatic urban form in the North American suburbs (Whyte [1956] 1960: 361–72). At about the same time Betty Friedan was writing about the women who had chosen or been persuaded to stay home, as wives and mothers, and who experience the suburbs as 'progressive dehumanization' (Friedan [1963] 1992: 245–68).

Throughout the early scenes of *The Matrix*, Anderson/Neo is constantly solicited to remain an 'organization man' and give up his part-time identity as a computer hacker. Keanu Reeves' character is schizophrenically caught between an official office persona (as Thomas Anderson) and an unofficial persona as the computer hacker Neo. Of course, given the genre of the film, any petitioning to join the rank and file of 'little people' is bound to fall on deaf ears. In a scene of wonderful bathos, Thomas

Anderson is being disciplined by his boss at Meta CorTechs, while we see and hear the discordant squeaks of a window-cleaner's squeegee: 'The time has come to make a choice, Mr. Anderson. Either you choose to be at your desk on time from this day forth, or you choose to find yourself another job. Do I make myself clear?' (Wachowski and Wachowski 2001: 287). 'Organization men', are clearly marked out, both as agents policing the 'Matrix' and as bosses and workers. Agent Smith directly addresses Anderson/Neo's social schizophrenia:

> It seems that you have been living two lives. In one life, you are Thomas A. Anderson, program writer for a respectable software company. You have a social security number, you pay your taxes, and you help your landlady carry out her garbage. The other life is lived in computers where you go by the hacker alias Neo, and are guilty of virtually every computer crime we have a law for. One of these lives has a future. One of them does not.
>
> (Wachowski and Wachowski 2001: 20)

Neo is driven by a taste for 'the real' and opts out of respectability in its clerical guise. But this desire for reality is also a desire for a remasculinization in the form of a muscled physique that can only ever be a programmed 'image'. In actuality (on the hovercraft the *Nebuchadnezzar*, for instance) Neo is closer to the machines they are hoping to overcome. When first introduced to the software training programs that are downloaded straight into consciousness, Neo's 'body jumps against the harness as his eyes clamp shut. The monitors kick wildly as his heart pounds, adrenaline surges, and his brain sizzles. An instant later his eyes snap open' (Wachowski and Wachowski 2001: 47). He is immediately asked if he is ready for some more – 'Hell yes!' he replies. Tank (his training instructor and programmer) describes him: 'He's a machine'.

In the Matrix all is digital information, there is no physicality except for the synaptic feedback from the manufactured dream world. When entering the Matrix from outside, as both the agents and the outlaw superheroes do, any body profile can be fabricated. It is, then, unnecessary for the characters to have particular muscle definition when in the Matrix. When Morpheus asks rhetorically 'do you think my being faster than you has anything to do with my muscles in this place?' (Wachowski and Wachowski 2001: 47), the answer, were it necessary, would clearly be 'no'. Yet in Neo's transformation from digital office worker to digital superhero, his body becomes hardened and muscled. The bodies of superheroes are armoured bodies. The writings on the 'armoured' body – from Wilhelm Reich, through to Klaus Theweleit, and on to many accounts of Hollywood action stars (Stallone and Schwarzenegger predominantly) – have understood this armoured body as a psychical defence of a damaged ego. In this way armoured bodies fit in well with a sense of a masculine aggressive defence against encroaching feminization, and so forms a link with our moment of gender realignment.

But we need to be dialectical here and not see this armouring *only* as psychic protectionism: we need to see it also as a less gender-specific fantasy of mobility to compensate for actual urban immobility. In this way we might be able to start to include female armoured bodies in accounts of urban culture, without having to limit ourselves to the language of gender transgression (a language that already assumes masculine priorities). If the film *The Matrix* carries on the tradition of early 1960s comic-book culture, it is because there are good historical reasons for seeing present-day urban culture as an intensification of this moment of urbanism. Today's urban life-world (as well as the cultural representations we are offered) places high value on the toned and muscled body. The environment which creates the omnipresent office block and turns factories into loft apartments (or simply renders them vacant) also generates the now ubiquitous fitness centre. Expensive bars and workout gyms vie for building space (and signal the intensities of gentrification). And as we spend more and more time immobile in front of office computers, beholden to the organization, so too are we encouraged to develop the perfectly fit body.

The promiscuous mix of genre types not only signals what some might see as the knowing postmodernism of the Wachowski brothers' film, but also the logic of compensation that relates to its urban culture. We see Trinity as referencing a barrage of female physical heroes and villains – Cat-Woman in particular. Morpheus dressed in shirt and tie and long shiny leather coat relates to black heroes and villains, most noticeably the figure of Shaft. Neo as hard-boiled, spaghetti western enforcer with dull long dust coat and leather strappings relates to figures played by Clint Eastwood. While these characters expressly link in with gendered and ethnically specific genre figures, they are united in a common currency – all are distinctly antithetical to the organization man or woman. Their acquisition of muscled mobility finds its logic in the generic conventions of a culture haunted by the dual crisis of the city and sexuality. These conventions relate to a historical duration of urban culture where bodies lead sedentary work lives (in front of desks, typewriters and now computer screens) in an environment designed to frustrate bodily (rather than vehicular) mobility, and where gender-shock is a continually destabilizing presence. In this context, the muscled body and the fantasy of mobility are compensations, both to the perceived demasculinization of work culture and the vertical and horizontal expansion of the postindustrial city.

A Culture of Connectivity: From Blood to Nerves

The Matrix is a knowing film that wears its references on its sleeve; the rooftop chase scene that starts the film mimes the beginning of Hitchcock's

Vertigo; the work of Jean Baudrillard on simulation and the simulacra is specifically referenced (Baudrillard [1981] 1994); so too is the monstrous imagination of H. R. Giger, made famous with his visualizations for the film *Alien*, and referenced here in the imagery for the human 'power plant'. The film invites you, or even seduces you, into a world of large symbolic themes and a world of liquid, virtual space. It is a world that offers fantasized images so convincingly realized that they seem to take on their own facticity. Yet there are good reasons to hang back from the seductions on offer and pursue a more realist operation. For one thing its vision of the world is one that provides magical resolutions to what are social and cultural problems. The world on offer is not that different from the 'new cynicism' that Christine Boyer outlines in her book *Cybercities*:

> Here all our bodily senses seem to get transferred to, plugged into, or downloaded into machines, as our body parts become simple emitters and receivers of information stimuli in a sensorial feedback loop that links our senses of sight, touch, smell, and hearing to information flowing through computer data banks and simulation programs. Reality is increasingly immaterial, and our modes of travel become static terminal transmissions. Meanwhile, the contemporary city stands with all of its gaping wounds as crime escalates, megacities erupt, blood continues to spill, disease accelerates, and unemployment and undereducation continue. We experience this global urban disruption instantaneously and continuously with every telecasted news report, yet we remain incapable of immediate action, frozen in front of our computer terminals.
>
> (Boyer 1996: 11)

If we were to scrutinize *The Matrix* for its ideological content, I think it would align all too neatly with Boyer's diagnosis of a technopolitical quietism. Yet it is precisely not an ideology critique that I have been pursuing here. Instead I have been attempting to get cultural objects, including *The Matrix*, to 'testify' to the experiential and tropological dimensions of urban culture. And it is at this level, at the level of analytic realism, that the film offers evidence of a general shift in conceptualizations of the city. This shift, which the film articulates (simultaneously resisting and accepting it), is a shift from the city seen as a cardiovascular body, needing oxygen, healthy blood and so on, to the city seen as a nervous system, requiring faster synapses and more and more information.

At the start of the film Trinity is trying to find a way out of the Matrix via a telephone line that will allow her consciousness to return to her body on the hovercraft the *Nebuchadnezzar*. After the phone box is destroyed and we learn that Trinity has escaped through the telephone line, the camera closes in on the destroyed box and the marooned telephone receiver. The shooting script describes the camera's journey:

We are sucked towards the mouthpiece of the phone, closer and closer, until the smooth gray plastic spreads out like a horizon and the small holes widen until we fall through one
Swallowed by darkness.
The darkness crackles with phosphorescent energy, the word 'searching' blazing in around us as we emerge from a computer screen.
The screen flickers with windowing data as a search engine runs with a steady and relentless rhythm.

(Wachowski and Wachowski 2001: 8)

Telephone wires are points of connectivity and travel. They constitute the city as soft and porous, as transphysical.

The urbanism of *The Matrix* is one of endless connectivity. It relates directly to aspects of our urban actuality. Contemporary urbanism can also be seen as endless connectivity: a connectivity of transport links (railways, expressways and airport terminals making a transglobal transport network) and a connectivity of communication systems so replete as to constitute a virtual world. *The Matrix* consistently juxtaposes two network systems: the now-defunct sewerage system of a derelict city that is used by the *Nebuchadnezzar* as a labyrinthine road system; and the network of the Matrix itself, which generates a virtual worldscape. On the one hand, a system belonging to a cardiovascular and alimentary imaginary, on the other, a world wide web-like system that belongs to a neural imaginary. It is less important, I think, to inquire which system the film supports, than to inquire into the cultural imaginary of the systems themselves.

Writing in 1924 about the city of Naples, Walter Benjamin and Asja Lascis characterize its social architecture as 'porous': 'Building and action interpenetrate in the courtyards, arcades, and stairways. In everything they preserve the scope to become a theatre of new, unforeseen constellations. The stamp of the definitive is avoided' (Benjamin and Lascis [1924] 1985: 169). Benjamin and Lascis are observing an environment that is at once a porous physical space constituted by a porous social practice: 'each private attitude or act is permeated by streams of communal life' (174). Their description of Naples as porous registers the peculiar and particular ways that social practices and architecture coalesce, and the way that outside and inside, public and private, bleed into one another in a specific city in Italy. Yet their figuring of urban space as porous is a suggestive description of a more general condition of urban life.

The city walls (metaphorical and real), the walls of buildings and rooms, the hard surfaces of roads and tracks, the shiny reflectivity of metals and glass, the armour cladding of 'bunker architecture' are continually permeated. Defended and proper space is undone. It is undone most immediately and least noticeably by the myriad forms of connectivity that service the routine existence of urban life. In this room where I write, electricity circulates, distributing light, charging electronic circuits; hot water flows through radiators heated by gas that has been piped in and ignited. Telephone connections bring their digital flows to a terminal and a screen that orchestrates images and words that come from elsewhere and else- when. Spoken and written words flow out (in less quantity) via email and telephone conversation. In other rooms radio and TV receivers (potentially and actually) relay streams of commentary, happenings, imaginings that have been produced in other cities, other countries. Water circulates and is discharged, taking away various waste products. Heat and exhaust seeps out through vents and tiny lesions in the fabric of the building. Unless any of this breaks down it tends to go unnoticed. Such porosity is, globally speaking, a sign of affluence.

In 1965 the architectural critic Reyner Banham could write:

> When your house contains such a complex of piping, flues, ducts, wires, lights, inlets, outlets, ovens, sinks, refuse disposers, hi-fi reverberators, antennae, conduits, freezers, heaters – when it contains so many services that the hardware could stand up by itself without any assistance from the house, why have a house to hold it up?
>
> (Banham [1965] 1981: 56)

Houses, though, have remained and retained their traditional forms in ways that Banham might have assessed as a failure of vision. The endless connections, the webs of communications and the networks of services are, for the most part, kept well hidden. It requires imaginative work to grasp something of the scale of this connectivity. For instance, writing in the introduction to the reissued edition of Harry Granick's 1947 book *Underneath New York*, Robert Sullivan supplied an image of urban connec- tivity that vividly portrays a city's hidden connectivity:

> Imagine grabbing Manhattan by the Empire State Building and pulling the entire island up by its roots. Imagine shaking it. Imagine millions of wires and hundreds of thousands of cables freeing themselves from the great hunks of rock and tons of musty and polluted dirt. Imagine a sewer system and set of water lines three times as long as the Hudson River.
>
> (Sullivan 1991: xi)

Sullivan's image reveals the veiled infrastructure of the city, a structure that is usually only revealed when systems fail, or when unnatural disas- ters shake the very fabric of a city.

Other forms of connectivity are more visible, more concretely realized in the cityscapes of urban modernity. In the nineteenth century, they took forms such as canals, railway tracks and stations, trams, horse-drawn omnibuses and so on. In the twentieth century, underground railways networked large metropolitan centres, and motorized traffic, in the form of automobiles, lorries and buses, became the dominant feature. These physical intracity and intercity connections produced effects, but these effects were uneven and unstable.

Perhaps the most massive change in the nineteenth century was the exponential rise of railway transport in the 1830 and 40s. Writing about railway expansion in England, Asa Briggs records that:

> During the years between 1825 and 1835, fifty-four Railway Acts permitting railway building were passed, resulting by the end of 1838 in 500 miles of track, but it was in 1836 and 1837, when forty-four companies concerned with 1,498 miles of track were sanctioned, that there was the first sense of a railway 'boom'. By 1843 there were 2,036 miles in actual use. And the 1830s boom was to be far eclipsed by the feverish 'railway mania' of 1845–47, when 576 companies and a further 8,731 miles of track were sanctioned.
>
> (Briggs 1985: 210)

This massive expansion of railway networks needs to be understood as an explosion in communication technologies. It allowed bodies and things to circulate in closer proximity than ever before. No longer did the distances between cities seem to impede communication in a fundamental way. But almost simultaneously with railways came another technology that had almost instantaneous effects: telegraphy. Railways and the telegraph came together as the telegraph moved from being a sideshow attraction to being a marketable commodity. In the 1830s and 40s telegraph offices were set up in city railway stations allowing for an intercity communication practice: 'the telegraph will extend from the Paddington terminus to Bristol, and it is contemplated that then, information, of any nature, will be conveyed to Bristol, and an answer received in town in about 20 minutes' (*Inventors Advocate* 1839, quoted in Morus 1996: 361). The telegraph systems presaged a world network of communications, so much so that one writer has called his history of telegraphy *The Victorian Internet* (Standage 1998).

What this historical synchronicity does is reconnect physical mobility with transformations in the world of communication technologies. *The Matrix* can be read as simply trading in the rhetoric of present-day amnesia, whereby the latest technology (here digital simulations) is castigated or congratulated as producing fundamental shifts in our worldscapes (and no doubt this is partly what the film is involved in doing). For the realist critic, though, it is crucial that representational work on communication is seen as part of a larger history of changes in the nature of the city. If the assessment of these changes is to be grounded in social reality (a reality which includes changes in metaphors as much as changes in physical infrastructures), a film like *The Matrix* needs to be seen within a historical period that can accommodate a history of the virtual geography of the city. As Serres noted above, a range of possible historical contexts are always available for cultural objects, yet *The Matrix* seems to encourage a recognition of this by situating itself in a double moment: the year in the Matrix is 1999, the year outside is 2199. Such insistence on the multiplicity of history should allow us to insert cultural objects into a variety of historical durations. So here, the period from the 1950s to the present is crucial for understanding certain aspects of the film (the dream of physical mobility, for instance), while the period from the mid-nineteenth century is crucial for understanding the visualization of a neural, porous, virtual city dominated by information technology. One way of inoculating ourselves against the memory loss of 'gizmo-culture' is to provide a much larger definition of the term 'media'.

Cultural and media studies have tended to look at the city as both a site where media representation takes place (on hoardings, in cinemas and so on), or else as a site that is represented *in* the media. A more extensive figuring of the relationship between cities and media is, however, available within certain strands of media theory. Crucially, what has characterized this strand of inquiry has been a willingness to extend massively the kind of phenomena that can be understood as informational. Writing about the modern city, the media theorist and historian Friedrich Kittler, for instance, in his tellingly named essay 'The City is a Medium', extends the idea of media not just to include a number of service networks within the city, but also to include the city itself:

> What strikes the eye of the passerby as a growth or entropy is technol-ogy, that is, information. Since cities no longer lie within the panopticon of the cathedral or castle and can no longer be enclosed by walls or forti-fications, a network made up of intersecting networks dissects and connects the city – in particular its fringes, peripheries, and tangents. Regardless of whether these networks transmit information (telephone, radio, television) or energy (water supply, electricity, highway), they all represent forms of information. (If only because every modern energy flow requires a parallel control network.)
>
> (Kittler 1996: 718)

Here Kittler suggestively pictures networks such as the sewer system or the road system as informational. One of the reasons for doing this is precisely because such systems are orchestrated and controlled, by traffic police, infrastructure maintenance services and so on.

This extension of media systems is also coupled with an expanded historical field for understanding them. By claiming a 'highway' as a medium, Kittler dispenses with the need to see media forms as represent-ing something else. Instead media is revealed as being characterized by its orchestration of movement. Alongside this, by refusing to see 'media' as something which emerges with the invention of film, for instance, and aligning it to the movement of bodies, information and things, Kittler's approach allows for historical work of a much longer duration: now canals and rivers provide informational systems for communicating both within cities and between cities. This longer durational aspect of media communication was vividly portrayed in the work of the Canadian media theorist Marshal McLuhan:

> It is to the railroad that the American city owes its abstract grid layout, and the nonorganic separation of production, consumption, and residence. It is the motorcar that scrambled the abstract shape of the industrial town, mixing up its separated functions to a degree that has frustrated and baffled both planner and citizen. It remained for the airplane to complete the confusion by amplifying the mobility of the citizen to the point where urban space as such was irrelevant. Metropolitan space is equally irrelevant for the telephone, the telegraph, the radio, and television. What the town planners call 'the human scale' in discussing ideal urban spaces is equally unrelated to these electrical forms. Our electric extensions of ourselves simply by-pass space and time, and create problems of human involvement and organization for which there is no precedent. We may yet yearn for the simple days of the automobile and the superhighway.
>
> (McLuhan [1964] 1994: 104–5)

While McLuhan plays fast and loose with facts (the grid that structures New York, for instance, predates the invention of the railway), he does offer an imaginative challenge to urban historians to think about how technology has impacted on the city.

In her book *Networking: Communicating with Bodies and Machines in the Nineteenth Century*, Laura Otis suggests that: 'If the railways offered nineteenth-century societies a circulatory system, the telegraph offered them nerves' (Otis 2001: 9). As has often been mentioned in this book, the human body has consistently provided a rich source of analogy for thinking about the city. Richard Sennett has demonstrated the importance that the discovery of the blood system had on thinking about the urban environment. William Harvey's publication of his findings in 1628 fundamentally changed the way the body was understood. Prior to this, blood was thought to flow around the body propelled by its own heat, now blood was recognized as being pumped. So rather than movement being a property of the material (blood), it was seen as dependant on mechanical operations (the heart's). This gave a new impetus to urban planners:

> The words 'artery' and 'veins' [were] applied to city streets in the eighteenth century by designers who sought to model traffic systems on the blood system of the body. French urbanists like Christian Patte used the imagery of arteries and veins to justify the principle of one-way streets.
>
> (Sennett 1994: 264)

We have already glimpsed the persistent analogy of city as body in a number of places. Streets pulsing with lifeblood, parks as urban lungs, sewers as the final exit of the alimentary canal and so on.

If we do live in urban environments where circulation has been supplanted by communication, where an imaginary of arteries and veins has been swapped for one of networks and synapses, then we need to think about the consequences of this shift. This is not to suggest a wholehearted paradigm shift; rather it suggests that the 'nervous system' begins to emerge as the most vivid analogy for describing the modern city in an age where communication and information systems seem to take on a funda-mental material reality in the urban environment. There are consequences to this shift that I think are at the basis of how the city is thought of and how it is experienced. The city as analogized by blood flows was open to a discourse of physical and material health. Reform could be directed to opening up places of putrefaction, for instance, to the expulsion of waste and so on. At times such reformers acted like surgeons, prepared to sever what they took to be cancerous limbs. Often enough these reformers brutally disregarded anything that might smack of consultation with the patient. Yet, from the perspective of the neural city, the very idea of plan-ning and reform is beginning to seem like an almost impossible concept, as if it belonged to another age, part of an anachronistic imaginary. If at times a cardiovascular imaginary worked catastrophically against the interests of the poorest members of the city, it did at least offer a perspective on the city where 'cure', and 'reform' could be thought of as procedures for improv-ing the city. The city as nervous system, I want to suggest, doesn't allow for such a position.

In its frenetic portrayal of a virtual urbanism dominated by digital communication, a portrayal enhanced by the juxtaposition of the digital realm with a decaying physical infrastructure, *The Matrix* seems to herald the success of a neural understanding of the city. Yet to describe the present as the loss of one metaphoric system (a cardiovascular metaphor) and its replacement by another (a neural metaphor) is, no doubt, stating the case too starkly. The truth is more uneven, with one system continuing as another emerges, the second slowly taking precedence over the first. It is likely that we are at a point where such overturning is at a crucial stage, and that we are caught between a nostalgia for a previous metaphor (often forgetting the brutality that resulted from it) and the overzealous enthusi-asm for the new tropological regime (which rhetorically veils the multiple temporalities that constitute the city). To analogize the city as an extended nervous system makes vivid something of the growing impact made by transport and communication since the mid-nineteenth century. But it also suggests that rather than suffering from physical problems the city suffers from psychopathology. Nervous systems become dysfunctional, grow paranoid, start having schizophrenic delusions. Dysfunctional cities have fits, become megalomaniacal, homicidal, sociopathic, display passive-aggressive behaviour and so on. Reform is no longer an option: therapy is all that is left.

The Matrix is caught in a plurality of temporalities and the metaphors that go with them. Its vividness lies in its capacity to render a worldscape where transport systems and communication systems have generated a world of unreal immediacy that is haunted by a desire for the real (to be found, for instance, in an old and disused sewerage system). In this worldscape characters are hailed to pledge loyalty to systems that don't return the compliment (see Sennett 1998 for a discussion of how loyalty figures in contemporary work practices in North America). A communications networked world, which has been intensifying since the 1840s, meets the anxieties of new work patterns that have been gradually increasing since the 1950s. If this suggests that *The Matrix* is more about the past than it is about the future, this is the condition for all cultural artefacts. After all, to repeat a point made earlier, the present is largely the continuity of the past into the present. *The Matrix* also works to foreground the extent to which the contemporary urban environment is imagined in terms of a neural metaphorics, one which is seeking to replace older, more fleshy imaginings of the city.

Urban cultural studies, and urban culture more generally, may need to engage not just with the analysis of these competing metaphorics. Its bigger task might be to work in transforming them, and in generating new, more liberatory, tropological possibilities. Michel Serres' plural temporalities, his crumpled handkerchief and percolating polychronic imagination might offer a better, more liberatory metaphorics. Henri Lefebvre's similarly suggestive and interrelated notion of rhythmanalysis might provide a way of orchestrating our varied experiences of the city in less catastrophic ways. There might well be a liberatory supplement for a metaphorics that takes the multitempo rhythmicity of the city as its starting point. Urban cultural studies, as I said at the start, is not urban planning. Yet for all that it might be able to offer something that urban planning seems unable to entertain: a new metaphorics of the city – a metaphorics that is more attentive to the everyday actuality of city life, an everyday which might simultaneously include a blocked drain and the deletion of a barrage of 'spam' emails. It is for this reason that I want to conclude with a chapter on rhythmanalysis.

Chapter Seven
Conclusion – Methodology II: Rhythmanalysis and Urban Culture

Modernism, Modernity and Movement

This book has concentrated on urbanism as an environmental culture that impinges on and generates our various ways of being and becoming. It has taken the theme of movement and mobility as a crucial perspective for studying this culture, and has taken 'rhythmanalysis' as a loose, critical attitude for measuring and registering these ways of being and becoming. Rather than opting to review urbanism in general, I have instead sought to provide various micro-studies that have worked centrifugally outwards from a specific cultural text. This has meant trying to get hold of urban culture *via* textual renderings of city life: worldscapes of urban culture as they have been distilled and secreted within particular formal devices (novels, films, social architectures and so on). But the reading of cultural devices hasn't been the *object* of study: I haven't been claiming to read these texts exhaustively or even scrupulously. Rather than objects of study these devices have provided the means of study. I have been reading *for* the city: with the city as the unmanageable object of attention, an object that can best be accessed via the thickness and force of the descriptions it gives rise to. But although the city is the object of study, this 'object' necessary includes these descriptions as part of its very essence. To live the city is to live a physical geography via a superabundance of imaginary renderings. Our most intimate contact with the city is inseparable from the fears, anxieties, desires, attractions, distractions and propulsions that constitute the lived imaginary of urbanism. The study of cities through specific textual materials is a way of accessing particular kinds of experiences, experiences that are often rendered thickly and forcefully.

To insist once more then: this has not been an exercise in literary studies or film studies, but in cultural studies. And if by culture we mean the shaping and patterning of experience, this necessarily means transforming cultural texts from objects in need of analysis into analytic objects. The reason for starting from short stories, films and novels is because I want to insist on recognizing these items as experimental ethnographic data. In effect I am arguing two things here: firstly, that there is no city that is simply outside the network of texts that circulate and shape our experience of the city; secondly, that cultural texts can't help but reflect and refract their context. This second point might need some clarification. I'm not saying that all texts are equally useful for registering the city (I haven't chosen the texts studied here at random) but all will bear the stigmata of context and all can be opened up to the sort of centrifugal reading that I have been attempting to develop over the preceding chapters. Here I will be looking in more detail at one particular methodological orientation of this work, namely rhythmanalysis.

There is a good reason for assuming that 'rhythm' is going to be a vital aspect of all cities and all texts concerned with figuring the city. After all rhythm is on the side of the dynamic interplay of forces, of which the city gives us the most complex exemplar. Rhythm, in the form of pace, is a crucial ingredient to any text and any experience of the city, no matter how fast or slow that pace is. But while all texts can be made to reveal their rhythmicity (through rhythmanalysis), not all texts are equally concerned with rhythm. There is, however, as I mentioned in Chapter One, a sphere of cultural production that has seen rhythm as a central component of its work and has in various ways instigated a series of rhythmanalyses. Now, while the various works described as 'modernism' often have little in common in terms of either their form or content, they can all, to a greater or lesser degree, be characterized by formal experimentation and a vital engagement with the culture of modernity. So 'modernism' becomes a dialogic term describing a family resemblance that crucially distinguishes it from traditional cultural forms that relate to traditional aspects of life.

Impressionism is probably the first concerted attempt by a group of painters (however loose the affiliations between them were) to register the dynamism of both the city and the countryside. Writing in 1864, the poet, critic and arts administrator Ernest Chesneau described a sketch of a Parisian boulevard by the artist Claude Monet in the following way:

> Never has the prodigious animation of the public thoroughfare, of crowds swarming on the pavement and carriages in the street, of trees swaying in the boulevard in dust and light, never has the fleeting instant of movement been so perfectly captured in its prodigious fluidity as in this extraordinary sketch that M. Monet has listed under the title *Boulevard de Capucines*.
>
> (Chesneau cited in Clay 1978: 269)

Chesneau is, of course, suggesting that the very manner by which Monet depicts the scene, abbreviated rather than detailed picturing, as being appropriate to the hurly-burly of Parisian street life.

But it is Futurism that offers a more insistent rhythm-oriented attempt to register modern urban life. The Futurist painter Umberto Boccioni, for instance, sought to capture the overall sensual cacophony of urban life and the way its varied forces interpenetrated one another. Clearly influenced by the post-Cubist fracturing of space, and an understanding of time that was widely available from the popularization of the philosophy of Henri Bergson, Boccioni's depictions of the city were oriented to the city as a force-field of competing rhythms, durations and densities. Working in the 1910s, in the hastily modernizing city of Naples, Boccioni developed a technical vocabulary that would simulate the chronic dynamism of the city. Elements of the vocabulary (also shared by other Futurists) would include: a directional painting style (brush strokes indicating the direction of the moving object); a perspectival approach that attempts to put the viewer into the space; and an attempt to stretch out the moment of the image by including a number of after images and before images. Dynamism and simultaneity were the crucial themes of Futurism. As Marinetti, the main spokesperson of the group, claimed: 'our bodies penetrate the sofas upon which we sit, and the sofas penetrate our bodies. The motor bus rushes into the houses which it passes, and in their turn the houses throw themselves upon the motor bus and are blended with it' (Marinetti et al. [1910] 1968: 290).

But if Futurism was oriented to the *fastest* and most modern aspects of life, particularly modern forms of transport (cars and planes), it also pictured the city as a dynamically unfinished space. In a number of paintings, for instance Boccioni's *The City Rises* (1910) and *The Noise of the Street Penetrates the House* (1911), Naples seems more unbuilt than built, less governed by industrial transport than by horse-drawn carts and buggies. Boccioni's description of his painting *The Noise of the Street Penetrates the House* (Plate 7.1) characterizes the particular spatial and temporal dimensions of Futurism:

> In painting a person on a balcony, seen from inside the room, we do not limit the scene to what the square frame of the window renders visible; but we try to render the sum total of visual sensations which the person on the balcony has experienced; the sun-bathed throng in the street, the double row of houses which stretch to right and left, the beflowered balconies, etc. This implies the simultaneousness of the ambient, and, therefore, the dislocation and dismemberment of objects, the scattering and fusion of details, freed from accepted logic, and independent from one another.
>
> (Boccioni et al. 1912: 295)

Futurism was an orientation to the city, and it emphasized the fast pace of urban life and the sensual confusion that resulted from it.

Plate 7.1 Umberto Boccioni's *The Noise of the Street Penetrates the House*, 1911, oil on canvas, 100 × 100.6 cm, Sprengel Museum, Hanover. Photograph by Michael Herling

It was in the 1920s, however, that a form of modernist urban rhythm-analysis developed that capitalized on new technological ways of register-ing the city. The film 'symphony' or 'orchestration' became a way of capturing the durational flows of cities, their speeds and forms of congre-gation. Two films stand out: Walter Ruttmann's *Berlin: Symphony of a City* (1927) and Dziga Vertov's *Man with a Movie Camera* (1928). Prior to these two films, however, it is worth mentioning László Moholy-Nagy's filmic storyboard, *Dynamics of the Metropolis: Sketch of a Manuscript for a Film* (1921–2). Moholy-Nagy's 'film' was never made but the storyboard demonstrates the filmic thinking of metropolitan (Berlin) dynamism. The storyboard is made up of directional arrows; photographs of movements (football players, chorus dancers, caged animals and so on) and dynamic structures (chimneys, cranes and so on); and the instructions are taken from musical scores (fortissimo, pianissimo, tempo-o-o). Moholy-Nagy is also interesting because as well as being an artist oriented to filming the rhythms of the city, he also worked as a shop window designer and shop illuminator in London in the 1930s (Passuth 1987: 65).

Ruttmann and Vertov's films have become landmark modernist films, shoring up the intimate connection between modernism, cinema, the city and the accelerating tempo of modern life. These two films both construct a 'day in the life of a city', beginning with a city waking up and ending with festive, illuminated nightlife. It is worth noting that Ruttmann's film begins, not from within the city, but on arrival there. Anton Kaes has suggested that Ruttmann's film (and perhaps by implication many other modernist depictions of the city) takes the position of the migrant experiencing the city for the first time, rather than the position of the citified urban dweller, blasé to the accelerated consciousness of the city:

> The opening sequence of Ruttmann's Berlin film dramatizes the dislocations of millions of people in the decades before and after the turn of the century, who left their homes to come to Berlin. The sequence re-enacts their experience of departure, their disorienting transition from the country to the city, and their arrival in the metropolis.
>
> (Kaes 1998: 184)

Indeed this view from outside, from those new to the city, often gives the modernist representation of the city its particularly frenetic sense of pace and concomitant disorientation. Just to name one example, John Dos Passos's 1925 novel of New York, *Manhattan Transfer*, begins when a group of passengers disembark from the ferry terminals of Manhattan.

Modernist experimentation with rhythm and duration was locked into an assessment of modern urbanism as an insistent acceleration of everyday life. The inheritors of such an assessment are voluminous, and whether they condemn or condone this acceleration strikes me as mattering less than the assessment itself. One particular theorist who vividly exemplifies this modernist orientation is the urban planner and cultural theorist Paul Virilio. Virilio has, since the late 1960s, been grafting together a historical-theoretical approach to what he calls 'accelerated reality' (Virilio 2001: 47). Virilio practises an approach to the world which highlights its machinic components and emphasizes the velocities involved in communication, urbanism and war. Virilio's approach is self-styled and designated as 'dromology' (the study of speed).

Thus modernism is seen here as a particular approach to modernity, an orientation towards the emergent rather than the residual (or the dominant). It is guided, for the most part, by a concentration not on the full panoply of rhythms possible in the city but from a dialogic response to the city of speed (responses which also include the celebration of the purposefully sluggish). Lefebvre's rhythmanalysis has to be distinguished from the dromology of Virilio and the rhythmic orientations of futurists. The migrant rhythmanalysis of Dos Passos or Ruttmann may, however, provide more useful orientations that would warrant further development.

What is Rhythmanalysis?

Éléments de rythmanalyse: Introduction à la connaissance des rythmes was to be Henri Lefebvre's last book. Indeed it was published a year after his death. Like much of Lefebvre's work it is both suggestive and purposefully unsystematic in its approach to its topic. For a committed Marxist philosopher it was unusually experimental and aesthetic in range, and although its critical potential for a reading of capitalist modernity was always evident, rhythmanalysis is not aligned to a political position (it could, for instance, be practised by left-leaning, ecologically minded puritans, or libertine, evangelical right-wingers). Most problematically, but also most provocatively, it was not, for Lefebvre, a form of rigorous 'scientific' analysis, which means that for some schools of thought it will not even count as analytic. The closest analogy to the rhythmanalyst is the poet:

> Does the rhythmanalyst thus come close to the poet? Yes, to a large extent, more so than he does to the psychoanalyst, and still more so than he does to the statistician, who counts *things* and, quite reasonably, describes them in their immobility. Like the poet, the rhythmanalyst performs a verbal action, which has an aesthetic import. The poet concerns himself above all with words, the verbal. Whereas the rhythmanalyst concerns himself with temporalities and their relations within wholes.
>
> (Lefebvre 2004: 23–4)

Describing rhythmanalysis as a form of poetics might not be telling you much about what it actually is, but it does tell you the kinds of things that rhythmanalysis is not. The very fact that it isn't open to statistical measurement, or interpretative decoding, suggests that the object of analysis (the living, breathing world) simply isn't that sort of object. Rhythmanalysis is, for Lefebvre, a form of social and cultural phenomenology. Doing rhythmanalysis is as much about listening as seeing, as much about immersion as gaining epistemological distance. Its analytic potential is not provided by a methodology of distance: 'to capture a rhythm one needs to have been *captured* by it. One has to *let go*, give and abandon oneself to its duration' (Lefebvre 1996: 219).

Lefebvre's work on rhythmanalysis was a continuation of his 'critique of everyday life', a project begun in the 1930s and continuing intermittently for the rest of his life. Rhythmanalysis is the outcome of this critique in as much as it is a particular form of attention directed at what is most pervasive, most alive and most critical in everyday life: 'everywhere where there is interaction between a place, a time and an expenditure of energy, there is rhythm' (Lefebvre 2004: 15). And as always with Lefebvre's writing, rhythmanalysis will work dialectically, which in this case means that it will provide a critical device for bringing into contact a range of dualities, while at the same time superseding their presumed fixities. So rhythmanalysis concentrates on circulation as a way of bridging divisions between production and consumption, its concern for rhythm brings together a spatial and temporal orientation and, perhaps most importantly, rhythm allows for a form of attention that can grasp the contradictions and connections between a body and a machine, an individual and a state.

Firstly, then, rhythmanalysis is concerned with the regulating rhythms of dominating cultural and social forces. The perspicacity of this approach becomes particularly evident when we realize that the terms used to describe unruly and ill-disciplined children are rhythmanalytical phrases. The child who is 'lazy', 'hyperactive' or suffering from 'attention deficit' is the child whose rhythmicity is not fully regulated, whose rhythms haven't adjusted to the dominant rhythms of cultural norms. Lefebvre and Catherine Régulier, his collaborator on the rhythmanalytical project, suggest that 'it takes about ten years to train the body to these rhythms [the dominant rhythms of a regulatory culture], and it is not unusual for children to reject social rhythms' (Lefebvre and Régulier [1985] 2003: 191–2). The term that Lefebvre supplies for describing this rhythmic training is 'dressage':

> To enter into a society, group or nationality is to accept values (that are taught), to learn a trade by following the right channels, but also to bend oneself (to be bent) to its ways. Which means to say: dressage. Humans break themselves in like animals. They learn to hold themselves. Dressage can go a long way: as far as breathing, movements, sex. It bases itself on repetition. One breaks-in another human living being by making them repeat a certain act, a certain gesture or movement.
>
> (Lefebvre 2004: 39)

Dressage is the aspect of social and cultural rhythming that comes closest to the Foucaultian notion of discipline. But while, for Lefebvre, it is socially cohesive, dressage is not simply a form of regulatory domination: after all, potty training allows a child to have some agency over its own body.

Dressage, though, is never a completed ordeal, never an accomplished activity. And this is where Lefebvre is enormously useful in leading social and cultural thought out of the endlessly repetitive dogma of social constructionism. For social constructionists, our social and cultural practices are routinely categorized as the product of historically and socially specific practices. How we act, what we believe and how we live are products of contingent social forces. For some of the strongest advocates of social constructionism, practice and the meaning of practice is reducible to these constructions. For Lefebvre, however, social and cultural practices are the result of a rhythmic assemblage, often enormously dissonant and contradictory, that are formed out of the interaction between dressage, cultural diversity and our material biology and nature. The body, for Lefebvre, is the key site for rhythmanalysis, and this body is always biological and cultural (simultaneously). It can never be a construction (how could it be?), however much it is continually being trained and however much that training is effective in prescribing and proscribing forms of action. The body, then, is the initial site for recognizing the plural rhythms that we live by:

> The living body can and should be seen in terms of the interaction of the organs within it, each one having their rhythms but subject to a spatio-temporal whole. Furthermore, this human body is the locus and seat of interaction between the biological, the physiological (nature) and the social (often called the 'cultural') and each of these areas, each of these dimensions, has its own specificity, and thus its space-time: its rhythm. Hence the inevitable shocks (stresses), disorders and disturbances within this whole, whose stability is never absolutely guaranteed.
>
> (Lefebvre and Régulier [1985] 2003: 196)

This insistence on plural rhythms is crucial to the rhythmanalytical project. It is only when two different rhythms intersect that a rhythm can be recognized at all:

> We know that a rhythm is slow or lively only in relation to other rhythms (often our own: those of our walking, our breathing, our heart). This is the case even though each rhythm has its own specific measure: speed, frequency, consistency. Spontaneously, each of us has our preferences, references, frequencies; each must appreciate rhythms by referring them to oneself, one's heart or breathing, but also to one's hours of work, of rest, of waking and of sleep.
>
> (Lefebvre 2004: 10)

The very possibility of measuring rhythms (in the loose way that Lefebvre seems to envisage) is premised on the differences between two or more rhythms. For Lefebvre, then, rhythmanalysis is always concerned with the interplay of plural rhythms. But we need to return to the critical potential of rhythmanalysis, its concern with the bodily shocks, stresses and strains that might well point in the direction of a specifically urban and industrial rhythmanalysis.

For Lefebvre rhythmanalysis attuned to the rhythmicity of the city will be concerned with two kinds of rhythmicity: on the one hand, the rhythmicity that he calls 'linear' (which are the regulating rhythms of modern social organization), and, on the other, 'cyclical' rhythms (the rhythms of nature and biology). Modernity is, of course, the triumph of a certain rhythmic form that is most straightforwardly signalled by the triumph of the clock:

> From that historic moment, it [clock time] became the time of the every-day, subordinating other aspects of daily life to the spatial organization of work: times for sleep and waking, times for meals and private life, relationships between adults and children, entertainment and leisure, relationships in the home. However, everyday life is shot through and cut across by the larger rhythms of life and the cosmos: days and nights, months and seasons, and more specifically still, biological rhythms. In everyday life, this results in constant interaction between these rhythms and repetitive processes linked with homogenous time.
>
> (Lefebvre and Régulier [1985] 2003: 190)

Urban modernity might signal the triumph of homogeneous time, but it doesn't constitute the wholesale erasure and replacement of other forms of time or rhythm. To put it as starkly as possible: modernization hasn't yet found a way of regulating the seasons, the cycles of the sun or the moon! And it is here in this conflict between cyclical and linear rhythms that the critical power of Lefebvre's work is at its clearest: the very dissonance between different rhythms reminds us of the power of nature and the limits of regulatory modernity, at the same time as it reminds us of the limits of our bodies and the power of modernity.

The conflict here between nature and the culture of modernity is not premised on an *essentialist* notion of the body, but on a *materialist* under-standing of the body and nature. The biological rhythms of the body, for instance, or the durational patterns of night and day, pose a limit to the endless colonization by linear, homogeneous time. Total dressage may well be possible (isn't this what an army is?), but it is only possible if it takes something of its tempo from the rhythms of the body. We might be trained to eat and sleep regularly, but we can't be trained to run at a hundred miles an hour. The rhythms of the body provide a critical and physical commen-tary on the rhythmicity of modernity. This isn't to pit a 'true' biological rhythm against a 'false' machinic one. Instead it begins by recognizing that the body's rhythms are already plural and already cultural and social. 'Polyrhythmia' (the condition of plural rhythms) is the initial starting point. But this polyrhythmic condition can either be 'eurhythmic' (ordered, harmonic and so on) or 'arrhythmic' (discordant, irregular and so on).

Here, though, we must remember that rhythmanalysis is a form of analysis, rather than a formal regime. Eurhythmia is not the adoption of prescribed practices; in the same way that arrhythmia isn't necessarily the result of unregulated rhythms. Overordered rhythms (marching, for instance) can become arrhythmic, just as spontaneous and chaotic rhythms can have a eurhythmic quality. The measure is our own bodies, and rhythmic dissonance becomes the symptom for critically examining urban modernity:

> The notion of rhythm brings with it or requires some complementary considerations: the implied but different notions of polyrhythmia, eurhythmia and arrhythmia. It elevates them to a theoretical level, starting from the lived. Polyrhythmia? It suffices to consult one's body; thus the everyday reveals itself to be a polyrhythmia from the first listening. Eurhythmia? Rhythms unite with one another in the state of health, in normal (which is to say normed!) everydayness; when they are discordant, there is suffering, a pathological state (of which arrhythmia is generally, at the same time, symptom, cause and effect). The discordance of rhythms brings previously eurhythmic organizations toward fatal disorder.
>
> (Lefebvre 2004: 16)

To a degree Lefebvre might simply be talking about a form of adapting to the rhythms of modernity (and adapting those rhythms), a way of recognizing that unless urban and industrial rhythms are in tune with the basic requirements of the human body, then these rhythms will produce illness. He might simply be evoking a form of general ergonomics. Rhythmic dissonance, particularly when it becomes illness, or vividly descriptive of social contradictions, will be a crucial aspect of the rhythmanalytical project. But Lefebvre's notion of the body is not an unchanging fact, nor is it simply a limit structure, it is already cultural and plural, its creatureliness is its adaptability.

This is the other side of rhythmanalysis, the side that recognizes the body as the site of a plurality of biological and cultural forms that are not reducible to the dominant tempos and rhythms of a culture. As far as this goes, the body (and the social body) doesn't simply critique forms of dressage when it gets ill (psychologically or through repetitive strain injuries, for instance), it critiques dressage because it is always capable of evoking other cultural practices, evoking play as well as work, reminding us of our potential creatureliness. Within the study of urban culture, rhythmanalysis is, then, also a measure of other rhythms, festive rhythms practised in the city, and at odds with various forms of dressage:

> The citizen resists the State by a particular use of time. A struggle therefore unfolds for appropriation in which rhythms play a major role. Through them social, therefore, civil time, seeks and manages to shield itself from State, linear, unirhythmical measured and measuring time. Thus the public space, space of representation, 'spontaneously' becomes

[a] place of promenades, encounters, intrigues, diplomacy, trade and negotiations, theatricalizing itself. Time is hence linked to space and to the rhythms of the people who occupy this space.

(Lefebvre and Régulier in Lefebvre 1996: 237)

The body, then, is also a site of cultural practice, and is never simply a privatized space of locked-up and repressed biology: it promenades, it parties.

Rhythmanalysis is thus a description of the contrapuntal rhythms that articulate an experience of the city. All the senses are called upon to provide an analysis of the urban with the aim of 'the least possible separation of the scientific from the poetic' (Lefebvre 1996: 228). Crucially, then, the standoff between a body that maintains its rhythms (the natural attitude) and one that submits to them (the militarized body) is less important that the lived-out contradictions of living within a messy, dynamic and plural set of rhythms.

Why Rhythmanalysis?

This book is not meant as a dogmatic assertion of Lefebvrian rhythmanalysis. In many ways it simply couldn't be, after all Lefebvre's description of rhythmanalysis is observational and concerned with the phenomenological present. I, however, have been concerned with the historical rhythms of urban modernity as they are materialized in cultural texts. Rhythmanalysis is an attitude, an orientation, a proclivity: it is not 'analytic' in any positivistic or scientific sense of the term. It falls on the side of impressionism and description, rather than systematic data collecting. It suggests an approach to texts (some of which are rhythmanalytical texts) that works centrifugally from a close attention to the itineraries of a text to the connections these itineraries make with a larger cultural and historical world. Clearly its benefits can't be judged within the scientific discourse that haunts most discussions of methodology. The question, as I see it, is what can rhythmanalysis supply to the field of urban studies that other orientations either can't or don't? What is it that rhythmanalysis insists on, what issues does it force us to consider? There is a relatively simple answer here: it is an antidote to a number of particularly influential conceptualizations of urban modernity. There are two main conceptualizations that rhythmanalysis is particularly suited to refuting: the first is that the contemporary city is constituted by the wholesale erasure of nature; the second is that urban culture is ineluctably driven by the irresistible speeding-up of daily life. Rhythmanalysis then is pitched against dromological studies of cities, or rather it provides a necessary qualification of those studies, and it is pitched against social constructionists and others who excise any discussion of nature.

Frederic Jameson, in his book *Postmodernism, or, The Cultural Logic of Late Capitalism*, describes postmodernism as the death of nature: 'postmodernism is what you have when the modernization process is complete and nature is gone for good' (Jameson 1991: ix). Of course Jameson is talking about the cultural representations of contemporary life, but the logic suggests that such representation is particularly strong because it actualizes something of the existing state of affairs in metropolitan centres and elsewhere. It would be hard indeed to find a more completely unnatural environment than the metropolitan city, yet there is something too neat about Jameson's conclusion. Postmodernity is a peculiarly open concept, relatively easy to fill with a range of different contents, yet most commentators would agree that it is probably only relevant to the period after the Second World War. Indeed the strongest claims for something like a general change in culture is based on the terrible injuries to moral belief and utopian hope caused by the twin holocausts of the Nazi death camps and the atom bombs dropped on Japan.

My argument here is not with the validity or otherwise of terms like 'postmodern' and 'postmodernity' (just for the record, I'm happy to continue using the term modernity to describe the present); my interest is simply in the death or not of nature. Now one way of responding to Jameson and others' claim that nature dies at some point after 1945 is to say that it wasn't looking too healthy in the 1860s. By this I mean that, within urban centres, there would, by the mid-nineteenth century, be very little that could be called 'natural', if by that we mean such things as areas of ground unaffected by human settlement, for instance. I mention the 1860s partly because there might be good reason for judging something like Haussmannization as the systematic culturing of nature.

During 1867 Paris got ready to host a Universal Exhibition, a chance to show off the prosperity and technical accomplishments of France, at the same time as providing a showcase for the refiguring of Paris, performed with such ferocious precision by Baron Haussmann. Three months prior to the opening of the exhibition:

> The exhibition organisers had decided that the Butte de Chaillot was 'irregular' and wild, and that therefore the view across the river from the exhibition grounds lacked harmony. They ordered the baron to lower the hill by twenty feet or so and make its profile less untidy. It was a large demand to make with so little time left before the emperor was to cut the scarlet ribbon. Haussmann brought in squads of navvies and paid them to work under arc lights through the night; he built a special railway line to cart off the rubble, and used two hundred cars and half a dozen locomotives for the job.
>
> (Clark 1984: 60–1)

The decision to alter the very shape of Paris brings together a number of themes; one is the way that 'image' is not something separate from the physical environment, but is here literally dug into the environment; the other is the way that this is accomplished through the most technologically advanced means (arc lamps and railways).

The usefulness of Lefebvre's approach to rhythmanalysis is that he is prepared to simultaneously recognize the almost total colonizing of social space by the interests of capitalism while also recognizing the persistence of nature. While cities are artificially lit by advertising light (neon and illuminated window displays, for instance) and policing light (street lights and traffic signals), cities are also illuminated by the moon and the sun. Similarly, the architecture and road systems provide a material ground of the city that is entirely fashioned to human needs, yet animals still persist (foxes, for instance, can be more common in cities than in the countryside and seagulls have made the city their home). Flowers, trees, grass, pollen, wind, rain and so on are not empty of culture, but they also point to a rhythmicity that can't be subsumed into a rhythmicity driven by the interests of profit.

This then is the other side to urban modernity, the continual battle to keep nature in check, one that is lost in advance. The city is in the hands of nature in other ways too; cities are constantly in a state of ill-repair, as if the earth is waiting patiently to reclaim its elements – weeds poke through cracks in the pavements, nettles and brambles take over waste ground and ivies colonize old buildings and disused trains (Plate 7.2). Entropy is the condition of the city. Nature in all its forms is present in the city, but one of its forms predominates – its human form. Cities of course seethe with human bodies that are eating, breathing, defecating, dancing, walking, sleeping, working, driving, loving, growing, dying and being born. It is this humanness that is constitutional of the city in insistent and surprising ways. And it is partly the pace set by human bodies that should make us sceptical of any account of the contemporary city that simply sees it as a relentless acceleration. Seen from the perspective of the experiencing urban subject, what might appear as fastest is often experienced as slowest.

We have already seen how modernist artists tended towards an assessment of modernity as a ferocious acceleration of the practices of daily life. That such an assessment carries on into the present is neither difficult to understand nor hard to find examples of. If anything, the assessment of acceleration has itself accelerated. For example, Thomas Hylland Eriksen, in a book titled *Tyranny of the Moment: Fast and Slow Time in the Information Age*, writes about the gradual speeding-up of time, particularly in relation to the use of computer technologies. Eriksen, though, is nostalgic for a time when we took time to complete tasks rather than had our time dictated by the pace capabilities of the latest technology. This is Eriksen's assessment of accelerated culture:

The unhindered and massive flow of information in our time is about to

Plate 7.2 Anonymous photograph of train being taken over by ivy

fill all the gaps, leading as a consequence to a situation where everything threatens to become a hysterical series of saturated moments, without a 'before' and 'after', a 'here' and 'there' to separate them. Indeed, even the 'here and now' is threatened since the next moment comes so quickly that it becomes difficult to live in the present. We live with our gaze firmly fixed on a point about two seconds into the future. The consequences of this extreme hurriedness are overwhelming; both the past and the future as mental categories are threatened by the tyranny of the moment.

(Eriksen 2001: 2–3)

Eriksen gives a vivid prognosis of the way that accelerated information flows will reconfigure our experience of time. What he misses out, though, is the slowness that is often the actual experience of these same technologies, the slowness of downloading dense files on computers that are more than a few years old or that are connected to ordinary telephone lines – the world wide wait, as some would have it.

Rhythmanalysis, because it insists on a dialectical and polyrhythmic attention to urban modernity, won't assess the present and near future only in terms of its speeding-up. It won't ignore it either. Not only does it, through attention to the presence of residual rhythms, suggest that we constantly and tenaciously hold on to rhythms that are closer to the tempos set by our biological and creaturely selves, but it also refuses to simply accept the rhetoric of acceleration as adequate to the experience of modernity. If we think of the example of transport systems within cities, we arrive at a rhythmicity that cannot simply be described in terms of acceleration. Road use and road building, for instance, suggest that speeding-up and slowing-down are constitutionally related. Some of the most persuasive arguments against building new roads today suggest that they actually increase rather than decrease the amount of congestion by encouraging road use, which then requires further road building, which encourages more road use and so on. Anyone who tries to make their way across cities during rush hour will know that the sense of being able to rush is precisely what is least available. Is the term 'rush hour' used ironically, or is it evidence of a more unshakeable belief that speed dominates city life, an attempt to disavow a more intimate relationship between stagnation and rapid movement?

Modern city planners have strived to facilitate free movement within cities, and they have had to do this in a response to the almost constant sense that the city was either perched on the precipice of paralysis or had actually fallen into the grip of gridlock. James Winter, in his book *London's Teeming Streets: 1830–1914*, provides evidence of how urban modernity has been experienced in terms of blockage and immobility, and how the modernizing impulse has always had to work to alleviate a state of near-stasis, rather than simply to instigate faster and faster networks of movement (see Winter 1993: 16–33). Winter's work not only points to the *longue durée* of the dialectic between circulation and entropic stagnation, he also shows how modernization is always the *failure* to unblock the city (Plates 7.3 and 7.4). Caught between the dream of the city in full flow and the fear, as well as the actuality, of the city as stagnation, urban modernity needs to be seen in such a way that its multiple rhythms can be differentiated. Rhythmanalysis is well placed to describe the complex and contradictory rhythms of urban mobility, to register the sense of frustration as buses are simply brought to a standstill on a Friday afternoon, or whole transport systems are closed down due to their decrepit state.

Rhythmanalysis is about experience as well as structure, and in this it can often be invaluable in pinpointing some of the rhythmic contradictions of urban modernity. I can, for instance, fly from one city to another at speeds that make motorway travel appear ludicrously slow. But my experience and perception of speed is not necessarily determined by this knowledge. Waiting for two or more hours in an airport, to be followed by a seven-hour flight of cramped immobility, air travel might well be

Plate 7.3 Gustave Doré 'traffic jam'

Plate 7.4 Los Angeles traffic jam

experienced as sedentary travel, where time is elongated by the lack of any physicality of movement. The assembly line, that characteristically modern formation and exemplar of fast and efficient production, might evidence a speeding-up of throughput, but seen from the shop floor it often affects a more exhaustingly lethargic experience. For those who submit to the relentlessness of the machine, the experience is often one of slowing-down, time stretching out, a torturous boredom as the line sluggishly and insistently moves; fast enough to stop you doing anything else, slow enough to leave you constantly waiting.

Rhythmanalysis, then, is an essential ingredient for studying urban culture for two negative reasons (it prevents wholesale acceptance of the rhetoric of limitless acceleration and the death of nature) and for a whole host of positive ones. Rhythmanalysis is dedicated to the living, breathing, dynamic existence of cities, and it achieves this because it is in essence dialectical – it simultaneously speaks of structures and experience, the planned and the unplanned, production and consumption, entropy and emergence. Rhythmanalysis is oriented to the specific and to its connectivity with the totality – it is never simply particular, but finds the totality through the particular. Its concentration on the body grounds it in an active and already rhythmic assemblage that provides a complex perspective on the larger rhythms of the city. In this, rhythmanalysis is well aware that bodies and their rhythms are different, even though aspects of them provide a shared corporeal perspective. In this no singular viewpoint can hope to exhaust the possible readings of urban rhythmicity: a body is always a body that has been marked by culture, whether it is the body of a stranger to the city or a taxi driver, a policewoman or a migrant, a para or a Muslim schoolgirl. As far as this goes, rhythmanalysis is always a situated knowledge (see Haraway 1991), a knowledge that doesn't speak for the universal subject, but for the subject grounded by a geography and a history. But rhythmanalysis would seek to follow Barthes' advice 'to multiply the readings of the city' (Barthes [1967] 1988: 201), to pluralize the situations of knowledge, and it can do this by attention to the traces of it that can be found in a host of textual registerings.

Rhythmanalysis's greatest contribution might well be its systematic challenge to the representational bias of social constructionist thinking. As far as this goes, it is always situated in the experiential world even when that world is only accessible through texts. By placing the body as the experiential locus of urbanism, it encourages us to think beyond the restrictions of social constructionism and take some real account of the pressures and limits (the determining agency) of the body. Its insistence that the body can assess rhythms is also an encouragement to think about how cities might be changed. In this it would refuse some of the nostalgia of recent demands to produce slow cities. Present-day urban planning, which seems to posit an athletic disposition that few can access, has disabled human bodies. We need rhythmanalyses by and for children, rhythmanalyses by and for wheelchair users, postal deliverers and bicycle couriers, tourists and asylum seekers, the homeless and jobless. This means thinking outside and against the tyranny of the healthy body paradigm, or the exemplary 'average person', and thinking instead of a range of possible bodies. What would be the eurhythmic condition for young children and their carers, or those whose senses are impaired?

A Future for Rhythmanalysis

This book has tried to inhabit the spirit of rhythmanalysis and orient it towards historical and contemporary texts. A rhythmanalytical orientation has meant that certain aspects of urban culture have necessarily been foregrounded. It has constantly been necessary to insist that plurality provides the only *essence* to the urban life-world of modernity, even when (maybe especially when) there are dominating forces striving to regulate and homogenize urban life. In the chapter on Edgar Allen Poe's short story and in parts of the chapter on detective fiction, this has meant that the uneven development of capitalist urbanism has provided the critical form for looking at how the city exacerbates spatial divisions (between gentrified and abandoned space, for instance), while simultaneously attempting to hide this process. In the chapter on shopping, it has meant both looking at the varied rhythms of the most exorbitant forms of spectacular consumption, while also recognizing that more residual forms of recycling – the selling of second-hand clothes and furniture and produce that is past its best – continue and actually increase during the rise of the department store. In the chapter on colonial and neocolonial urbanism, it has meant that the varied spatial practices of colonizer and colonized are seen as both dialogic and internally varied. Just as there is no single colonial tempo, so there is no single colonized response. A stress on plurality has meant that the city has to be continually recognized as a space of movement and migration.

Rhythmanalysis has also meant stressing the experiential aspect of urban life. But rhythmanalysis also challenges us to refuse the tendency towards solipsism and subjectivism that can be the result of privileging experience. The urban imaginary is endlessly rhythmic and animates our emotional responses to the city, and makes us, in the most intimate of ways, *collective* subjects. By stressing emotional affect – desire and anxiety, for instance – I have sought to provide a more general economy of urban experience and its rhythmic coordinates. In stressing the urban imaginary, I have been claiming that rhythmanalysis needs to attend to the living, material fantasy of urban life, which finds some of its most condensed articulations in films, novels and urban forms. Throughout the book I have been working to show how an urban imaginary tells us something about the livedness of urbanism, even if any one experience might never coalesce precisely with the contours of its world-view. To put it more concretely:

none of us may hold the views of a Gustave LeBon, yet how we experience crowd behaviour in cities, whether we fear crowds or actively and passionately participate in them, often bears an emotional relationship to the crowd energies described by LeBon ([1895] 1995). This is another way of saying that tropes, metaphorics, are a living, experiential aspect of urban life.

Rhythmanalysis has been employed in this book partly as an analytic orientation and partly because it is, I think, able to provide a new metaphorics of urban life. In the chapter on *The Matrix*, and elsewhere in the book, we saw how various body as city metaphors were continually employed for understanding and experiencing the city. It is because the cardiovascular metaphors and the neural metaphors are inadequate to describe city life in all its collective heterogeneity that I have been keen to demonstrate the descriptive vitality of rhythmanalysis and rhythm-analytical texts. Rhythmanalysis, I have been arguing, allows for a greater adequacy of description for everyday urban culture. And it is the power of description, the production of a material imaginary that has always been the substantive subject of this book.

Rhythmanalysis, however, is never limited to work that calls itself by that name. Most rhythmanalytical-type projects will never mention this term. There is a mass of recent work that is attentive to the experiential pace and movement of modern life while simultaneously stressing the mythic/metaphoric dimensions of the urban. I'm thinking, for example, of Iain Sinclair's recent *London Orbital*, which is Sinclair's account of walking around the M25 (London's 125-mile ring road). Sinclair's tale evidences a historical density to the landscape from a perspective that purposefully refuses the tempo of the motorway system (Sinclair 2003). Another example might be Setha Low's evocative and detailed ethnohistory of two plazas in San José, Costa Rica, which weaves together oral accounts of plaza life with investigations into the history of the plazas (Low 2000). Another example might be François Maspero's journey into the suburbs of Paris, as he stops off at every stop on the metro heading out towards Roissy. Maspero reveals an unevenly developed landscape (housing projects, hostels, abandoned canals and so on) animated by the endlessly varied practices of those who live in these suburbs (Maspero 1994).

Less recent examples might include Chris Marker's 1982 film *Sunless*, with its concentration on the everyday practices of the Japanese, framed by a series of letters written by an anonymous film maker. The concentration on body gestures, the foregrounding of the perceiving subject, and the interest in memory, metaphor and the politics of everyday life might well provide a distinctive constellation for a rhythmanalytic approach (see Kear 1999, for a commentary on the film). John Berger and Jean Mohr's account (written and photographic) of the migrant lives of Turkish workers in Germany and Switzerland, is, I think, inspirational in suggesting the possibilities of a very loose rhythmanalytic approach that contrasts the everyday practices of 'guest workers' as they move from rural Turkey to relentlessly industrial urban enclaves in Stuttgart and Geneva (Berger and Mohr 1975).

Already I think we can see a future for rhythmanalysis and what that future might look like. There is something distinctive about these projects, something that might well constitute a direction for further studies. What we are witnessing is the reanimation of a form of travel literature and travel film that weaves across many different registers to provide a montaged account of urban life. In Berger and Mohr's project, for instance, economic theory is accompanied by poetry, which is set alongside photographs of hostel accommodation and personal accounts of the 'guest workers'. This multilayered approach provides a form that can articulate the varied kinds of accounts of the different rhythms of migration: global economic networks; emotional dislocations; and the movements of train journeys, letters home and so on. There is a blurring of genres in all this work that brings together history and ethnography, poetic description and brute facts.

We can also see that rhythmanalysis undoes a common-sense geography of the city. Instead of concentrating on the symbolic centres of cities, there is a concerted effort to explore their peripheries or treat their peripheries as new centres of urban life. Transport systems and terminals reposition the city in particular ways. To make them the focus of urban studies shifts the focus of attention onto the movement in and out of the city as well as onto movement within the city. It also privileges different sorts of urban experiences: those of the tourist, for instance, the asylum seeker or the commuter. The architectural critic Deyan Sudjic, in his book *The 100 Mile City*, takes up something of the themes of endless urbanism that geographers like Jean Gottmann were suggesting in the 1960s. But Sudjic's account of sprawling urbanism works to rethink what we might mean by centre and periphery and what we might mean by terms like a 'civic public space'. For Sudjic, present-day urban thought requires finding the city's centre in places that are usually understood as being on the outskirts. This is Sudjic describing London's Heathrow airport in the early 1990s:

> It is a place which attracts tourists and plane spotters, job hunters and salesmen, criminals, retailers and caterers. Businessmen come here for conferences. Punjabi women from nearby Southall find work as cleaners and kitchen staff. Entrepreneurs, fresh from their business school MBA courses, come to put their marketing theories into practice with new ideas for retail franchise chains. Its immigration halls have become the setting for political demonstrations: Tamil refugees have stripped naked here rather than quietly submit to deportation. Libyans have bombed the baggage hall and, along with those at Gatwick, the airport's approach roads are the only place in mainland Britain on which the Army regularly deploys armoured vehicles. The Wapping paparazzi keep the place permanently staked out on watch for passing celebrities.

Clearly this is as highly charged a part of the public realm as Trafalgar Square. By most reasonable definitions it is as urban an environment as you can get, a forum as well as a gateway.

(Sudjic 1992: 145)

Sudjic's description of Heathrow is a possible beginning for a contemporary rhythmanalytic urbanism. It makes the airport a space of conflict, contradiction and connectivity. Seen from various perspectives at the same time, it is a space of leisure and work, control and protest, ordinariness and celebration. Airports are extraordinarily ordinary, and ordinarily extraordinary. Intense emotions are witnessed there, as children leave home, people are forced to migrate, but also emotions of coming home, or the high spirits of holidaymakers. Airports let you know who you are on a global scale. Are you going to have the full body search, are your papers in order, is your 'country of origin' one that is regarded favourably by the country of destination?

The challenge for rhythmanalysis at its most general is not to remain closeted as just another academic enthusiasm or fad. For it to succeed as a project, it will have to fire people's imagination at the level of the more general intellectual culture. Rhythmanalysis, if it is going to provide an alternative *materialist metaphorics*, one that is sensitive to difference but doesn't surrender a sense of collective responsibility, will have to operate creatively and passionately. It will have to show that description can have the power to change perception – and to do this it will have to produce truly popular and persuasive descriptions.

Bibliography

Abelson, Elaine S. (1989) *When Ladies Go A-Thieving: Middle-Class Shoplifters in the Victorian Department Store*, New York and Oxford: Oxford University Press.

Adburgham, Alison (1975) *Liberty's: A Biography of a Shop*, London: George Allen & Unwin.

—— (1979) *Shopping in Style: London from the Restoration to Edwardian Elegance*, London: Thames & Hudson.

Alloula, Malek (1986) *The Colonial Harem*, translated by Myrna Godzich and Wlad Godzich, Minneapolis: University of Minnesota Press.

Althusser, Louis (1971) 'Ideology and Ideological State Apparatuses (Notes towards an Investigation)', in *Lenin and Philosophy and Other Essays*, translated by Ben Brewster, New York and London: Monthly Review Press, pp. 127–86.

Arnold, Dana (2000) *Re-presenting the Metropolis: Architecture, Urban Experience and Social Life in London 1800–1840*, Aldershot: Ashgate.

Asendorf, Christoph (1993) *Batteries of Life: On the History of Things and Their Perception in Modernity*, translated by Don Reneau, Berkeley, Los Angeles, and London: University of California Press.

Banham, Reyner ([1965] 1981) 'A Home is not a House', in *Design by Choice*, London: Academy Editions, pp. 56–60.

Barthes, Roland ([1967] 1988) 'Semiology and Urbanism', translated by Richard Howard, in *The Semiotic Challenge*, New York: Hill & Wang, pp. 191–201.

—— ([1968] 1986) 'The Reality Effect', translated by Richard Howard in *The Rustle of Language*, Oxford: Blackwell, pp. 141–8.

Baudelaire, Charles ([1863] 1964) 'The Painter of Modern Life', in *The Painter of Modern Life and Other Essays*, translated by Jonathan Mayne, London: Phaidon Press, pp. 1–40.

Baudrillard, Jean ([1968] 1996) *The System of Objects*, translated by James Benedict, London: Verso.

—— ([1981] 1994) *Simulacra and Simulation*, translated by Sheila Faria Glaser, Ann Arbor: University of Michigan Press.

Benjamin, Walter ([1935] 1999) 'Paris, the Capital of the Nineteenth Century' [or Arcades exposé of 1935], in *The Arcades Project*, translated by Howard Eiland and Kevin McLaughlin, Cambridge, MA and London: Harvard University Press, pp. 3–13.

—— ([1938] 1983) 'The Paris of the Second Empire in Baudelaire' in *Charles Baudelaire: A Lyric Poet in the Era of High Capitalism*, translated by Harry Zohn, London: Verso, pp. 11–101.

—— ([1939] 1983) 'Some Motifs in Baudelaire', in *Charles Baudelaire: A Lyric Poet in the Era of High Capitalism*, translated by Harry Zohn, London: Verso, pp. 109–54.

—— (1985) *One Way Street and Other Writings*, London: Verso.

Benjamin, Walter and Asja Lacis ([1924] 1985) 'Naples', in *One Way Street and Other Writing*, translated by Edmund Jephcott and Kingsley Shorter, London: Verso, pp. 167–76.

Bennett, Tony (1990) *Outside Literature*, London and New York: Routledge.

Berger, John and Jean Mohr (1975) *A Seventh Man*, Harmondsworth: Penguin.

Bignardi, Irene (2000) 'The Making of *The Battle of Algiers*', *Cineaste*, **25**(2): 14–22.

Bloch, Ernst (1990) *Heritage of Our Time*, translated by Neville and Stephen Plaice, Berkeley: University of California Press.

Boccioni, Umberto Carlo D. Carria, Luigi Russolo et al. ([1912] 1968) 'The Exhibitors to the Public', in *Theories of Modern Art: A Source Book by Artists and Critics*, edited by Herschel B. Chipp, Berkeley: University of California Press, pp. 294–8.

Boyer, Christine (1996) *Cybercities: Visual Perception in the Age of Electronic Communication*, New York: Princeton Architectural Press.

Brand, Dana (1991) *The Spectator and the City in Nineteenth-century American Literature*, Cambridge: Cambridge University Press.

Briggs, Asa (1985) *A Social History of England*, Harmondsworth: Penguin.

Çelik, Zeynep (1996) 'Gendered Spaces in Colonial Algiers', in Diana Agrest, Patricia Conway and Leslie Kanes Weisman (eds) *The Sex of Architecture*, New York: Harry N. Abrams, pp. 127–40.

—— (1997) *Urban Forms and Colonial Confrontations: Algiers under French Rule*, Berkeley, Los Angeles and London: University of California Press.

—— (1999) 'Colonial/Postcolonial Intersections: *Lieux de mémoire* in Algiers' in *Third Text*, **49**: 63–72.

—— (2000) 'Colonialism, Orientalism and the Canon', in Iain Borden and Jane Rendell, *InterSections: Architectural Histories and Critical Theories*, London: Routledge, pp. 161–9.

Chandler, Raymond ([1943] 1977) *The High Window*, Harmondsworth: Penguin.

—— (1950) *The Simple Art of Murder*, London: Hamish Hamilton.

—— (1993) *Three Novels*, Harmondsworth: Penguin.

Clark, T. J. (1984) *The Painting of Modern Life: Paris in the Art of Manet and his Followers*, London and New York: Thames & Hudson.

Clay, Jean (1978) *Modern Art 1890–1918*, Secaucus: Wellfleet Press.

Cornwell, Patricia (1991) *Body of Evidence*, London: Warner Books.

Cresswell, Tim (1996) *In Place/Out of Place: Geography, Ideology and Transgression*, Minneapolis: University of Minnesota Press.

—— (2001) 'The Production of Mobilities', *new formations*, **43**: 11–25.

Daniels, Les (1991) *Marvel: Five Fabulous Decades of the World's Greatest Comics*, London: Virgin Books.

Davies, Margery W. (1982) *Woman's Place is at the Typewriter: Office Work and Office Workers 1870–1930*, Philadelphia: Temple University Press.

Deaver, Jeffery (1997) *The Bone Collector*, London: Hodder & Stoughton.

—— (1998) *The Coffin Dancer*, London: Hodder & Stoughton.

—— (2000) *The Empty Chair*, London: Hodder & Stoughton.

—— (2002) *The Stone Monkey*, London: Hodder & Stoughton.

—— (2003) *The Vanished Man*, London: Hodder & Stoughton.

De Certeau, Michel (1984) *The Practice of Everyday Life*, Berkeley, Los Angeles and London: University of California Press.

Debord, Guy ([1967] 1995) *The Society of the Spectacle*, translated by Donald Nicholson-Smith, New York: Zone Books.

DeRoo, Rebecca J. (1998) 'Colonial Collecting: Women and Algerian, *Cartes Postales'*, *Parallax*, **4**(2): 145–57.

Deutsche, Rosalyn (1996) *Evictions: Art and Spatial Politics*, Cambridge, MA: MIT Press.

Dickens, Charles ([1839] 1995) *Sketches by Boz*, Harmondsworth: Penguin.

Djebar, Assia ([1980] 1999) *Women of Algiers in their Apartment*, translated by Marjolijn de Jager, Charlottesville and London: University Press of Virginia.

Döblin, Alfred ([1929] 1996) *Berlin Alexanderplatz: The Story of Franz Biberkopf*, London: Continuum.

Dos Passos, John ([1925] 1987) *Manhattan Transfer*, Harmondsworth: Penguin.

Doy, Gen (2002) *Drapery: Classicism and Barbarism in Visual Culture*, London and New York: I B Tauris.

Edwards, Steve (2001) 'The Accumulation of Knowledge or, William Whewell's Eye' in Louise Purbrick (ed.) *The Great Exhibition of 1851: New Interdisciplinary Essays*, Manchester: Manchester University Press, pp. 26–52.

Eisenstein, Sergei ([1923] 1977) 'Montage of Attractions' [edited] in *The Film Sense*, translated and edited by Jay Leyda, London: Faber, pp. 181–3.

Engels, Friedrich ([1845] 1987) *The Condition of the Working Class in England*, Harmondsworth: Penguin.

Eriksen, Thomas Hylland (2001) *Tyranny of the Moment: Fast and Slow Time in the Information Age*, London: Pluto.

Evenson, Norma (1989) *The Indian Metropolis: A View Toward the West*, New Haven and London: Yale University Press.

Fanon, Frantz ([1959] 1980) *A Dying Colonialism*, translated by Haakon Chevalier, London: Writers and Readers.

Foucault, Michel (1984) 'Space, Knowledge, and Power' (interview with Paul Rabinow), in *Foucault Reader: An Introduction to Foucault's Thought*, Harmondsworth: Penguin, pp. 239–56.

Freud, Sigmund ([1900] 1976) *The Interpretation of Dreams*, translated by James Strachey, Harmondsworth: Penguin.

—— ([1919] 1985) 'The "Uncanny" ' in *Art and Literature*: volume 14, *The Pelican Freud Library*, Harmondsworth: Penguin, pp. 339–76.

Frieberg, Anne (1993) *Window Shopping: Cinema and the Postmodern*, Berkeley, Los Angeles and Oxford: University of California Press.

Friedan, Betty ([1963] 1992) *The Feminine Mystique*, Harmondsworth: Penguin.

Frisby, David (1988) *Fragments of Modernity: Theories of Modernity in the Work of Simmel, Kracauer and Benjamin*, Cambridge: Polity.

—— (2001) *Cityscapes of Modernity: Critical Explorations*, Cambridge: Polity.

Frisby, David and Mike Featherstone (eds) (1997) *Simmel on Culture*, London: Sage.

Geertz, Clifford (1973) *The Interpretation of Cultures: Selected Essays*, London: Fontana Press.

Geist, Johann Friedrich (1983) *Arcades: The History of a Building Type*, translated by Jane O. Newman and John H. Smith, Cambridge, MA: MIT Press.

Gottmann, Jean ([1961] 1964) *Megalopolis: The Urbanized Northeastern Seaboard of the United States*, Cambridge, MA and London: MIT Press.

Grafton, Sue (1994) *K is for Killer*, London: Pan Books.

Greene, Graham (1988) *The Third Man*, London: Faber and Faber.

Greenhalgh, Paul (1988) *Ephemeral Vistas*: The Expositions Universelles, *Great Exhibitions and World's Fairs 1851–1939*, Manchester: Manchester University Press.

Gronberg, Tag (1998) *Designs on Modernity: Exhibiting the City in 1920s Paris*, Manchester: Manchester University Press.

Gunning, Tom ([1986] 2000) 'The Cinema of Attraction: Early Film, Its Spectator and the Avant-Garde', in Robert Stam and Toby Miller (eds) *Film and Theory: An Anthology*, Oxford: Blackwell, pp. 229–35.

Hammett, Dashiell (1982) *The Four Great Novels*, London: Picador.

Haraway, Donna J. (1991) 'Situated Knowledges: The Science Question in Feminism and the Privilege of Partial Perspective', in *Simians, Cyborgs, and Women: The Reinvention of Nature*, London: Free Association Books, pp. 183–201.

Hargreaves, Alec (1995) 'Perceptions of Place among Writers of Algerian Immigrant Origin in France', in Russell King, John Connell and Paul White (eds) *Writing Across Worlds: Literature and Migration*, London: Routledge, pp. 89–100.

Harootunian, Harry (2000) *History's Disquiet: Modernity, Cultural Practice, and the Question of Everyday Life*, New York: Columbia University Press.

Highmore, Ben (2002) "*Street Life in London*: Towards a Rhythmanalysis of London in the Late Nineteenth Century', *new formations*, **47**: 171–93.

Himes, Chester ([1957] 1985) *A Rage in Harlem*, London: Allison & Busby.

Hobhouse, Hermione (1975) *A History of Regent Street*, London: Queen Anne Press.

Hoffmann, E. T. A. ([1822] 1992) 'The Cousin's Corner Window', in *The Gold Pot and Other Tales*, translated by Ritchie Robertson, Oxford and New York: Oxford University Press, pp. 377–401.

Hoover, Edgar M. and Raymond Vernon ([1959] 1962) *Anatomy of a Metropolis: The Changing Distribution of People and Jobs Within the New York Metropolitan Region*, Garden City: Anchor Books.

Horne, Alistair (1977) *A Savage War of Peace: Algeria 1954–1962*, London: Macmillan.

Jackson, Peter (1992) *Maps of Meaning: An Introduction to Cultural Geography*, London and New York: Routledge.

Jacobs, Jane (1961) *The Death and Life of Great American Cities*, Harmondsworth: Penguin.

Jameson, Fredric (1970) 'On Raymond Chandler', *Southern Review*, **6**(3): 624–650.

—— (1991) *Postmodernism, or, The Cultural Logic of Late Capitalism*, London and New York: Verso.

Joyce, James ([1922] 1971) *Ulysses*, Harmondsworth: Penguin.

Kaes, Anton (1998) 'Leaving Home: Film, Migration, and the Urban Experience', *New German Critique*, **74**: 179–92.

Kear, Jon (1999) *Sunless – Sans Soleil*, Trowbridge: Flicks Books.

King, Anthony D. (1976) *Colonial Urban Development: Culture, Social Power and Environment*, London: Routledge.

King, Russell, Paul White and John Connell (eds) (1995) *Writing Across Worlds: Literature and Migration*, London: Routledge.

Kittler, Friedrich (1996) 'The City is a Medium', *New Literary History*, **27**: 717–29.

—— (1997) *Literature Media: Information Systems*, Amsterdam: Overseas Publishers Association/G+B Arts International.

Kluge, Alexander (1981) 'On Film and the Public Sphere', *New German Critique*, **24/25**: 206–20.

Knabb, Ken (1981) *Situationist International Anthology*, Berkeley: Bureau of Public Secrets.

Kracauer, Siegfried ([1930] 1998) *The Salaried Masses: Duty and Distraction in Weimar Germany*, translated by Quintin Hoare, London: Verso.

—— ([1937] 1972) *Orpheus in Paris: Offenbach and the Paris of his Time*, translated by Gwenda Davis and Eric Mosbacher, New York: Vienna House.

—— (1995) *The Mass Ornament: Weimar Essays*, translated by Thomas Y. Levin, Cambridge, MA: Harvard University Press.

Kuhn, Annette (ed.) (1999) *Alien Zone 2: The Spaces of Science Fiction*, London: Verso.

LeBon, Gustave ([1895] 1995) *The Crowd*, New Brunswick and London: Transaction.

Lefebvre, Henri ([1962] 1995) 'Notes on the New Town', in *Introduction to Modernity*, translated by John Moore, London and New York: Verso.

—— ([1974] 1991) *The Production of Space*, translated by Donald Nicholson-Smith, Oxford: Blackwell.

—— (1992) *Éléments de rythmanalyse: Introduction à la connaissance des rythmes*, Paris: Éditions Syllepse.

—— (1996) *Writing on Cities*, translated and edited by Eleonore Kofman and Elizabeth Lebas, Oxford: Blackwell.

—— (2004) *Rhythmanalysis: Space, Time and Everyday Life*, translated by Stuart Elden and Gerald Moore, London and New York: Continuum.

Lefebvre, Henri and Catherine Régulier ([1985] 2003) 'The Rhythmanalytical Project', in *Henri Lefebvre: Key Writings*, edited by Stuart Elden, Elizabeth Lebas and Eleonore Kofman, New York and London: Continuum, pp. 190–8.

Lemann, Nicholas (1991) *The Promised Land: The Great Black Migration and How it Changed America*, London: Macmillan.

Light, Alison (1991) *Forever England: Femininity, Literature and Conservatism Between the Wars*, London and New York: Routledge.

Low, Setha M. (2000) *On the Plaza: The Politics of Public Space and Culture*, Austin: University of Texas Press.

Macey, David (2000) *Frantz Fanon: A Life*, London: Granta Books.

Malinowski, Bronislaw (1922) *Argonauts of the Western Pacific*, London: Routledge.

Marcus, Steven (1973) 'Reading the Illegible', in H. J. Dyos and M. Wolff (eds) *The Victorian City: Images and Realities*, London: Routledge & Kegan Paul, pp. 257–76.

Marinetti, F. T. et al. ([1910] 1968) 'Futurist Painting: Technical Manifesto', in *Theories of Modern Art: A Source Book by Artists and Critics*, edited by Herschel B. Chipp, Berkeley: University of California Press, pp. 289–93.

Marx, Karl ([1852] 1968) *The Eighteenth Brumaire of Louis Bonaparte*, in *Marx/Engels: Selected Works in One Volume*, London: Lawrence & Wishart, pp. 96–179.

Maspero, François (1994) *Roissy Express: A Journey Through the Paris Suburbs*, translated by Paul Jones, London and New York: Verso.

McClintock, Anne (1994) 'The Angel of Progress: Pitfalls of the Term 'Postcolonialism', in Francis Barker, Peter Hulme and Margaret Iversen (eds) *Colonial Discourse/Postcolonial Theory*, Manchester: Manchester University Press, pp. 253–66.

McCue, Greg S. with Clive Bloom (1993) *Dark Knights: The New Comics in Context*, London: Pluto.

McLuhan, Marshall ([1964] 1994) *Understanding Media: The Extensions of Man*, Cambridge: MIT Press.

Merrifield, Andy (2002) *Metromarxism: A Marxist Tale of the City*, New York and London: Routledge.

Metcalf, Thomas R. (1989) *An Imperial Vision: Indian Architecture and Britain's Raj*, Berkeley: University of California Press.

Miller, Michael B. (1981) *The Bon Marché: Bourgeois Culture and the Department Store, 1869–1920*, Princeton: Princeton University Press.

Mills, C. Wright ([1959] 1963) 'The Cultural Apparatus', in *Power, Politics and People: The Collected Essays of C. Wright Mills*, Oxford: Oxford University Press, pp. 405–22.

Morus, Iwan Rhys (1996) 'The Electric Ariel: Telegraphy and Commercial Culture in Early Victorian England', *Victorian Studies*, 3(3): 339–78.

Mosley, Walter (1994) *Black Betty*, London: Serpent's Tail.

—— (1995) *The Walter Mosley Omnibus (Devil in a Blue Dress [1990], A Red Death [1991], White Butterfly [1992])*, London: Picador.

—— (1996) *A Little Yellow Dog*, London: Serpent's Tail.

—— (1997) *Gone Fishin'*, London: Serpent's Tail.

—— (2002) *Bad Boy Brawly Brown*, London: Serpent's Tail.

—— (2003) *Six Easy Pieces*, London: Serpent's Tail.

Munt, Sally R. (1994) *Murder by the Book: Feminism and the Crime Novel*, London: Routledge.

Musil, Robert ([1930] 1995) *The Man Without Qualities*: volume 1, translated by Eithne Wilkins and Ernst Kaiser, London: Minerva.

Nava, Mica (1996) 'Modernity's Disavowal: Women, the City and the Department Store', in Mica Nava and Alan O'Shea (eds) *Modern Times: Reflections on a Century of English Modernity*, London and New York: Routledge, pp. 38–76.

Nead, Lynda (1997) 'Mapping the Self: Gender, Space and Modernity in Mid-Victorian London', in Roy Porter (ed.) *Rewriting the Self: Histories from the Renaissance to the Present*, London: Routledge, pp. 167–85.

—— (2000) *Victorian Babylon: People, Streets and Images in Nineteenth-century London*, New Haven and London: Yale University Press.

Ogborn, Miles (1998) *Spaces of Modernity: London's Geographies 1680–1780*, London: Guilford Press.

Otis, Laura (2001) *Networking: Communicating with Bodies and Machines in the Nineteenth Century*, Ann Arbor: University of Michigan Press.

Ou-fan Lee, Leo (1999) 'Shanghai Modern: Reflections on Urban Culture in China in the 1930s', *Public Culture*, 11(1): 75–107.

Paretsky, Sara ([1982] 1993) *Indemnity Only*, Harmondsworth: Penguin.

—— ([1984] 1993) *Deadlock*, Harmondsworth: Penguin.

—— ([1986] 1993) *Killing Orders*, Harmondsworth: Penguin.

—— (1987) *Bitter Medicine*, Harmondsworth: Penguin.

—— ([1988] 1990) *Toxic Shock* [*Blood Shot* in UK] Harmondsworth: Penguin.

—— (1999) *Hard Times*, New York: Dell.

—— (2002) *Total Recall*, Harmondsworth: Penguin.

Passuth, Krisztina (1987) *Moholy-Nagy*, London and New York: Thames & Hudson.

Plain, Gill (2001) *Twentieth Century Crime Fiction: Gender, Sexuality and the Body*, Edinburgh: Edinburgh University Press.

Poe, Edgar Allan ([1836] 1986) 'Watkins Tottle', in *The Fall of the House of Usher and Other Writings*, Harmondsworth: Penguin, pp. 411–13.

—— ([1840] 1986) 'The Man of the Crowd', in *The Fall of the House of Usher and Other Writings*, Harmondsworth: Penguin, pp. 179–88.

Porter, Dennis (1990) 'The Language of Detection', in Tony Bennett (ed.) *Popular Fiction: Technology, Ideology, Production, Reading*, London: Routledge, pp. 81–93.

Porter, Roy (1996) *London: A Social History*, Harmondsworth, Penguin.

Prochaska, David (1990) *Making Algeria French: Colonialism in Bône, 1870–1920*, Cambridge: Cambridge University Press.

Rabinow, Paul (1986) 'Representations are Social Facts: Modernity and Post-Modernity in Anthropology', in James Clifford and George Marcus (eds) *Writing Culture: The Poetics and Politics of Ethnography*, Berkeley: University of California Press, pp. 234–61.

—— (1995) *French Modern: Norms and Forms of the Social Environment*, Chicago: University of Chicago Press.

Rabinovitz, Lauren (1998) *For the Love of Pleasure: Women, Movies, and Culture in Turn-of-the Century Chicago*, New Brunswick: Rutgers University Press.

Rappaport, Erika Diane (2000) *Shopping for Pleasure: Women in the Making of London's West End*, Princeton, NJ: Princeton University Press.

Rendell, Jane (1996) 'Subjective Space: A Feminist Architectural History of the Burlington Arcade', in Katerina Rüedi, Sarah Wigglesworth and Duncan McCorquodale (eds) *Desiring Practices: Architecture, Gender and the Interdisciplinary*, London: Black Dog, pp. 216–33.

—— (1999) 'Thresholds, Passages and Surfaces: Touching, Passing and Seeing in the Burlington Arcade', *de-, dis-, ex-*. **3**: 168–91.

—— (2002) *The Pursuit of Pleasure: Gender, Space and Architecture in Regency London*, London: Athlone Press.

Rice, Shelley (1997) *Parisian Views*, Cambridge, MA: MIT Press.

Richards, Thomas (1990) *The Commodity Culture of Victorian England: Advertising and Spectacle 1851–1914*, Stanford, CA: Stanford University Press.

Rosaldo, Renato (1993) *Culture and Truth: The Remaking of Social Analysis*, Boston: Beacon Press.

Ross, Kristin (1988) *The Emergence of Social Space: Rimbaud and the Paris Commune*, Basingstoke: Macmillan.

—— (1992) 'Watching the Detectives', in Francis Barker, Peter Hulme and Margaret Iverson (eds) *Postmodernism and the Re-reading of Modernity*, Manchester: Manchester University Press.

—— (1995) *Fast Cars, Clean Bodies: Decolonization and the Reordering of French Culture*, Cambridge, MA: MIT Press.

Said, Edward (2000) 'The Dictatorship of Truth: An Interview with Gillo Pontecorvo', *Cineaste*, **25**(2): 24–5.

Schivelbusch, Wolfgang (1986) *The Railway Journey: The Industrialization of Time and Space in the Nineteenth Century*, Leamington Spa: Berg.

—— (1995) *Disenchanted Night: The Industrialization of Light in the Nineteenth Century*: Berkeley, Los Angeles, and London: University of California Press.

Schlör, Joachim (1998) *Nights in the Big City: Paris, Berlin, London 1840–1930*, London: Reaktion Books.

Schneer, Jonathan (1999) *London 1900: The Imperial Metropolis*, New Haven and London: Yale University Press.

Schorske, Carl E. (1981) *Fin-de-Siècle Vienna: Politics and Culture*, Cambridge: Cambridge University Press.

Schwartz, Vanessa R. (1998) *Spectacular Realities: Early Mass Culture in Fin-de-Siècle Paris*, Berkeley, Los Angeles and London: University of California Press.

Sekula, Allan (1986) 'The Body and the Archive', *October*, **39**: 3–64.

Sennett, Richard (1986) *The Fall of Public Man*, London and Boston: Faber and Faber.

—— (1990) *The Conscience of the Eye: The Design and Social Life of Cities*, London and Boston: Faber and Faber.

—— (1994) *Flesh and Stone: The Body and the City in Western Civilization*, London and Boston: Faber and Faber.

—— (1998) *The Corrosion of Character: The Personal Consequences of Work in the New Capitalism*, New York: W.W. Norton.

Serres, Michel with Bruno Latour (1995) *Conversations on Science, Culture, and Time*, translated by Roxanne Lapidus, Ann Arbor: University of Michigan Press.

Showalter, Elaine (1992) *Sexual Anarchy: Gender and Culture at the Fin de Siècle*, London: Virago.

Simmel, Georg ([1903] 1971) 'The Metropolis and Mental Life', in *On Individuality and Social Forms*, Chicago and London: University of Chicago Press, pp. 324–39.

Sinclair, Iain (2002) *London Orbital: A Walk Round the M25*, Harmondsworth: Penguin.

Smith, Neil (1984) *Uneven Development: Nature, Capital and the Production of Space*, Oxford: Blackwell.

—— (1996) *The New Urban Frontier: Gentrification and the Revanchist City*, New York and London: Routledge.

Sobchack, Vivian (1993) *Screening Space: The American Science Fiction Film*, New York: Ungar.

—— (1999) 'Cities on the Edge of Time: The Urban Science-Fiction Film', in Annette Kuhn (ed.) *Alien Zone II: The Spaces of Science Fiction Cinema*, London: Verso, pp. 123–43.

Soitos, Stephen F. (1996) *The Blues Detective: A Study of African American Detective Fiction*, Amherst: University of Massachusetts Press.

Soja, Edward W. (1996) *Third Space: Journeys to Los Angeles and Other Real-and-Imagined Places*, Oxford: Blackwell.

—— (2000) *Postmetropolis: Critical Studies of Cities and Regions*, Oxford: Blackwell.

Solinas, PierNico (ed.) (1973) *Gillo Pontecorvo's The Battle of Algiers*, New York: Charles Scribner's Sons.

Staiger, Janet (1999) 'Future Noir: Contemporary Representations of Visionary Cities', in Annette Kuhn (ed.) *Alien Zone II: The Spaces of Science Fiction Cinema*, London: Verso, pp. 97–122.

Stallybrass, Peter and White, Allon (1986) *The Politics and Poetics of Transgression*, Ithaca: Cornell University Press.

Stam, Robert (1975) *The Battle of Algiers: Three Women, Three Bombs*, Mount Vernon: Macmillan Films, Inc.

Standage, Tom (1998) *The Victorian Internet: The Remarkable Story of the Telegraph and the Nineteenth Century's Online Pioneers*, London: Weidenfield & Nicolson.

Stern, Robert A. M., Thomas Mellins and David Fishman (1995) *New York 1960: Architecture and Urbanism Between the Second World War and the Bicentennial*, New York: Monacelli Press.

Stevenson, Robert Louis ([1886] 1992) 'The Strange Case of Dr Jekyll and Mr Hyde', in *The Strange Case of Dr Jekyll and Mr Hyde and Other Stories*, London: Everyman, pp. 99–156.

Sudjic, Deyan (1992) *The 100 Mile City*, London: Andre Deutsch.

Sullivan, Michael (1997) *The Meeting of Eastern and Western Art*, Berkeley, Los Angeles and London: University of California Press.

Sullivan, Robert E. Jr (1991) 'Introduction', in Harry Granick, *Underneath New York*, New York: Fordham University Press, pp. xi–xxviii.

Theweleit, Klaus (1989) *Male Fantasies: Male Bodies – Psychoanalyzing the White Terror*, Minneapolis: University of Minnesota Press.

Thomson, John and Adolphe Smith ([1877] 1994) *Street Life in London* [renamed *Victorian London Street Life in Historic Photographs*], New York: Dover.

Tylor, E. B. (1871) *Primitive Culture*, two volumes, London: John Murray.

Vidler, Anthony (2000) 'Agoraphobia: Psychopathologies of Urban Space', in *Warped Space: Art, Architecture, and Anxiety in Modern Culture*, Cambridge, MA and London: MIT Press, pp. 25–50.

Virilio, Paul ([1977] 1986) *Speed and Politics: An Essay on Dromology*, translated by Mark Polizzotti, New York: Semiotext(e).

—— ([1984] 1991) *The Lost Dimension*, translated by Daniel Moshenberg, New York: Semiotext(e).

—— (2001) 'After Architecture: A Conversation [with Sylvère Lotringer]', *Grey Room*, **3**: 32–53.

Wachowski, Larry and Andy Wachowski (2001) *The Matrix: The Shooting Script*, New York: Newmarket Press.

Walker, Lynne (1995) 'Vistas of Pleasure: Women Consumers and Urban Space in the West End of London, 1850–1900', in Clarissa Campbell Orr (ed.) *Women in the Victorian Art World*, Manchester: Manchester University Press, pp. 70–85.

Walkowitz, Judith R. (1992) *City of Dreadful Delight: Narratives of Sexual Danger in Late-Victorian London*, Chicago: University of Chicago Press.

Wallock, Leonard (1988) 'New York City: Capital of the Twentieth Century', in Leonard Wallock (ed.) *New York: Cultural Capital of the World 1940–1965*, New York: Rizzoli, pp. 17–50.

Ward, Janet (2001) *Weimar Surfaces: Urban Visual Culture in 1920s Germany*, Berkeley, Los Angeles and London: University of California Press.

Whyte, William H. ([1956] 1960) *The Organization Man*, Harmondsworth: Penguin.

Wichmann, Siegfried (1981) *Japonisme: The Japanese Influence on Western Art Since 1858*, London: Thames & Hudson.

Wigley, Mark (2001) 'Network Fever', *Grey Room*, **4**: 82–122.

Willett, Ralph (1996) *The Naked City: Urban Crime Fiction in the USA*, Manchester: Manchester University Press.

Williams, Raymond ([1973] 1993) *The Country and the City*, London: Hogarth Press.

—— (1977) *Marxism and Literature*, Oxford: Oxford University Press.

Williams, Rosalind (1982) *Dream Worlds: Mass Consumption in Late Nineteenth-Century France*, Berkeley, Los Angeles and Oxford: University of California Press.

Wilson, Elizabeth (1991) *The Sphinx in the City: Urban Life, the Control of Disorder, and Women*, London: Virago.

—— (2001) *The Contradictions of Culture: Cities, Culture, Women*, London, Thousand Oaks and New Delhi: Sage.

Winter, James (1993) *London's Teeming Streets 1830–1914*, London and New York: Routledge.

Wollen, Peter (1992) 'Delirious Projections', *Sight and Sound*, **2**(5): 24–7.

—— (1999) 'The Vienna Project' *Sight and Sound*, **9**(7): 16–19.

Wright, Gwendolyn (1991) *The Politics of Design in French Colonial Urbanism*, Chicago and London: University of Chicago Press.

Zola, Émile ([1883] 1992) *The Ladies Paradise*, Berkeley, Los Angeles and Oxford: University of California Press.

Zukin, Sharon (1982) *Loft Living: Culture and Capital in Urban Change*, Baltimore: Johns Hopkins University Press.

Index

eurhythmia 148–9
European city, Algiers 74–5, 76–9,
    83–4
everyday life
    acceleration of 150, 152–7
    critique of 145–6
excitement 30
exhibitions, international 13
exoticness 63
experience, and representation 86–7
exploitation 105–6

Fanon, F. 82–3
Fantastic Four 123–4, 126
fantasy films 118–19
    see also Matrix, The
feminism 59–60
Ferris wheel 1–3
figuration 5–6, 22
films
    *The Battle of Algiers see Battle of
        Algiers, The*
    fantasy 118–19
    The Matrix see Matrix, The
    modernist 143–4
    The Third Man 1–5, 8
first person narration 97–8
fitness centres 131
flânerie 40–1, 61
FLN (Algerian National Liberation
    Front) 70–4, 83–4, 86
force of culture 21
forensic expert fiction 107–12
Foucault, M. 85–6
France 76
    Algerian migrants in 88–9, 89–90
    banning of *hijab* 89
    Paris *see* Paris
Freud, S. 4, 42
    'The "Uncanny"' 43–4
Frieberg, A. 46
Friedan, B. 129
Frisby, D. 31, 92, 95, 97
Futurism 142–3

Galeries Lafayette, Paris 48
Gatian de Clérambault, G. 55
Geertz, C. 17, 19
gender
    bow/bay windows in London 45
    gendering of the Casbah 80–1, 85
    patterns of work 128

performativity and detective fiction
    106
genre fiction 94, 113–14
    see also comic-books; detective
    fiction
genre figures 131
gentrification 65, 104–5
Giger, H. R. 132
gin shops 37–8
glass 46
Godin, J.-B. 85
Gottmann, J. 127
Grafton, S. 102
Great Exhibition of the Industry of all
    Nations 1851 13
Greene, G. 2, 4
    see also Third Man, The
Greenhalgh, P. 13
gridlock 154, 155, 156
Gronberg, T. 46
guest workers 159–60
gumshoe culture 92–5
Gunning, T. 49

haggling 58
haik (Muslim veil) 81–3
hailing, ideological 50–1
Hammett, D. 92
hard-boiled detective fiction 92–3,
    95–9
    see also detective fiction
Hargreaves, A. 88–90
Harlem, New York 97
Harvey, W. 137
Haussmann, Baron 32–3, 69, 151–2
Heathrow airport 160–1
hijab (Muslim headscarf) 89
Himes, C. 96–7
Hiroshige, A. 14
historicity 119–22
history 4–5
Hitchcock, A. 131–2
Hobhouse, H. 65
Hoffmann, E. T. A. 39–40
Hokusai, K. 14
home 101–2
homosexuality 42–3
Hoover, E. 128
Horne, A. 80
housing density 75

ideology 50–1

poverty 30–1, 33–5, 37–9
Powell, D. 96
practical and symbolic activity 86–7
private and public space *see* public and
    private space
prostitutes/prostitution 59, 63
psychoanalysis xii
psychological simulation 111
public and private space
    Algiers 80
    impact of department stores 57–64

Rabinow, P. 120
racialization 27–8
racism 12–13, 15
railways 134–5, 137
Rawlins, Easy (Mosley's detective) 93,
    99–103
reading 94
realism 21–3
    detective fiction 112–13
    and historicity in *The Matrix*
    119–22
reality, intractability of imaginary and
    5–6
reality effects 106
Reed, C. 1
    see also Third Man, The
refashioning, spatial 57–64
references 131–2
Regent Street, London 36–7, 65
regulation 6–7
Régulier, C. 146, 147, 148
Rendell, J. 45, 61–3
representation 18–20
    experience and 86–7
reshaping 57–64
resistance 70–4, 75, 79–80, 82–3, 85, 90
Rhyme, Lincoln (Deaver's protagonist)
    93, 107–12
rhythm xiii
rhythmanalysis 24–5, 31–2, 140–61
    consumption and shopping 64–9
    future for 158–61
    modernism, modernity and 140–5
    movement and 8–12, 140–5
    nature of 145–50
    rationale 150–8
rhythmic dissonance 149
Rimbaud, A. 120–1
road building and road use 154
rocks, and dreams 17

'rookeries' 30–1, 33–5, 37–9
'ropers' 95
Rosaldo, R. 21
Ross, K. 120–1
ruins 1–4
Ruttmann, W. 143, 144

San José, Costa Rica 159
Schivelbusch, W. 11, 32, 46, 47
Schneer, J. 63–4
Schorske, C. 120
second-hand shops 66, 67, 68
second-hand worlds 5
second-orderness 18–20
Sennett, R. 4, 57–8, 137
Serres, M. 121–2, 135–6, 139
Seven Dials, London 34, 35
sewers 1–4, 33
sexuality 44
    homosexuality 42–3
    and knowledge 110–11
    women, shoplifting and 54–5
'shadows' 95
Shanghai 15–16
shantytowns (*bidonvilles*) 75, 89–90
Shepherd, T. H. 37
shoplifting 54–6
shopping 23, 45–69
    choreographed 45–53
    refashioning the city 57–64
shopping malls 59, 67–8
Showalter, E. 42–3
Simmel, G. 11
Sinclair, I. 159
situated knowledge 157
Sketches by Boz (Dickens) 37–8
skyscrapers 127
slums 30–1, 33–5, 37–9
small retailers 65–8
Sobchack, V. 118
social constructionism 146–7, 157–8
social distance 39
social practices 85–6
Soja, E. 87
Solinas, F. 71–2, 74, 83
Solinas, P. 70, 74, 80
spatial politics 74–80
spatial refashioning 57–64
Spider-Man 123–4
St Giles, London 33–5
Stallybrass, P. 41–2
Stam, R. 75–6